D0916982

RELATIONSCAPES

Technologies of Lived Abstraction
Brian Massumi and Erin Manning, editors

Relationscapes: Movement, Art, Philosophy, Erin Manning, 2009

RELATIONSCAPES

Movement, Art, Philosophy

Erin Manning

The MIT Press
Cambridge, Massachusetts
London, England

For information about special quantity discounts, please email special_sales@mitpress.mit.edu

This book was set in Syntax and Minion by Graphic Composition, Inc.
Printed and bound in the United States of America.

Library of Congress Cataloging-in-Publication Data

Manning, Erin.
Relationscapes : movement, art, philosophy / Erin Manning.
p. cm. — (Technologies of lived abstraction)
Includes bibliographical references and index.
ISBN 978-0-262-13490-3 (hard cover : alk. paper) 1. Movement (Philosophy) 2. Technology I. Title.
B105.M65M36 2009
128'.6—dc22

2008031040

10 9 8 7 6 5 4 3 2 1

For Brian

The self is only a threshold, a door, a becoming between two multiplicities.
—Gilles Deleuze and Felix Guattari, *A Thousand Plateaus*

Contents

Series Foreword

"What moves as a body, returns as the movement of thought."

Of subjectivity (in its nascent state)
Of the social (in its mutant state)
Of the environment (at the point it can be reinvented)

"A process set up anywhere reverberates everywhere."

The Technologies of Lived Abstraction book series is dedicated to work of transdisciplinary reach inquiring critically but especially creatively into processes of subjective, social, and ethical-political emergence in the world today. Thought and body, abstract and concrete, local and global, individual and collective: the works presented are not content to rest with the habitual divisions. They explore how these facets come formatively, reverberatively together, if only to form the movement by which they come again to differ.

Possible paradigms are many: autonomization, relation; emergence, complexity, process; individuation, (auto)poiesis; direct perception, embodied perception, perception-as-action; speculative pragmatism, speculative realism, radical empiricism; mediation, virtualization; ecology of practices, media ecology; technicity; micropolitics, biopolitics, ontopower. Yet there will be a common aim: to catch new thought and action dawning, at a creative crossing. Technologies of

Lived Abstraction orients to the creativity at this crossing, in virtue of which life everywhere can be considered germinally aesthetic, and the aesthetic anywhere already political.

"Concepts must be experienced. They are lived."

Prelude: What Moves as a Body Returns as a Movement of Thought

Do not count upon thought to ensure the relative necessity of what it thinks. Rather, count upon the contingency of an encounter with that which forces thought to rise up and educate the absolute necessity of an act of thought or a passion to think.
—Gilles Deleuze, *Difference and Repetition*

Something in the world forces us to think. This something is not an object of recognition, but a fundamental *encounter*.
—Gilles Deleuze, *Difference and Repetition*[1]

In 2005, with members of the Sense Lab[2] and the Workshop in Radical Empiricism,[3] Brian Massumi and I started thinking about how we might envision a collaborative event that would create a movement of thought. For over a year, we considered what constitutes an event and how techniques of creation create concepts-in-the-making. In May 2006, the Sense Lab hosted "Dancing the Virtual," the first of four events scheduled to take place over a four-year period under the larger rubric of Technologies of Lived Abstraction.[4]

"Dancing the Virtual" was conceived as a challenge to the often upheld dichotomy between creation and thought/research. The specific aim of "Dancing the Virtual" was to produce a platform for speculative pragmatism where what begins technically as a movement is *immediately* a movement of thought. In the active passage between movement and movements of thought, the participants of "Dancing the Virtual" collaboratively began to build a repertoire of new techniques for experimentation that performatively bridge the gap between thinking/speaking and doing/creating. Not only did this facilitate creation and communication across fields of inquiry during the event itself, it also provoked a continued exploration among many participants of ways to orchestrate future participatory events that challenge the active/passive model of speaker/listener or artist/spectator. For the events in the Technologies of Lived Abstraction series, new forms of collaboration are conceived not simply as locales for experimentation but as matrices of cultural becoming. We want experimentation to function as much at the collective level as at the conceptual level.

In August 2007, we hosted our second event, "Housing the Body—Dressing the Environment." The force of thinking still emanating from "Dancing the Virtual" had by then created its own momentum: the participants from "Dancing the Virtual" were active collaborators in the fashioning of this second event.

For "Housing the Body—Dressing the Environment," we attempted to shape the intensity of our collaboration by sending an open call for "platforms for relation," relational techniques proposed and carried out by teams of participants who had either already participated in "Dancing the Virtual" or who would become new members of the series of events. "Housing the Body—Dressing the Environment" built on the concerns outlined for "Dancing the Virtual." It was dedicated specifically to a collective exploration of the dynamic cross-genesis of the body and its constructed environment, where the environment is taken to include not only the architectural surround but also technological and cultural extensions of it. From selected platforms, we developed skeletal structures for relational improvisation through sound, skin, textiles, movement, architecture, and new media. These platforms were conceived as pragmatic points of departure for thinking/doing throughout the event. The way they took form throughout "Housing the Body—Dressing the Environment" made apparent the force of well-designed creative techniques to further the thinking of doing and the doing of thought.

For Henri Bergson, as for theorists of "embodied cognition," the relation between perception in all its modes is one of reciprocal reach-and-return. This cross-genesis of action and perception opens onto thought. Every perception is already a thinking in action. Every act is a thought in germ. The premise of all Sense Lab events in the Technologies of Lived Abstraction series is that there is a generative nexus between action, perception, and conception that can be modulated from the environmental side. In constructing our environment we not only house the body, we build modes of embodied experience and thought.

This is a micropolitics in the making that in turn fashions us: we refit the body for new forms of life, cross-dressing its self-expressive potentials.

Relationscapes: Movement, Art, Philosophy was conceived amid the movements of thought generated by the Technologies of Lived Abstraction series. Like the events, it is a book that is immediately collaborative.[5] I wrote it with the force of movement moving. Every aspect of the Sense Lab's events-in-the-making folded into the writing, provoking exploration into how thought works, where creation begins, what constitutes novelty, what a politics of movement might do, and how thinking through movement can alter the force of thought.

Sincere thanks are due to all those who have fueled our initiative to create movements of thought. Here in Montreal, I am indebted to those who make the Sense Lab the singular node it is. For your generosity, humor, and brilliance, thank you Brian. For your passionate dedication to thought-in-the-making, Nadine Asswad, Antoine Blanchet, Tagny Duff, Nasrin Himada, Valérie Lefebvre, Paul Mélançon, Céline Pereira, Chiara Paganini, Stamatia Portanova, Felix Rebolledo, Troy Rhoades, Bianca Scliar-Mancini, Alanna Thain, and Jon Yu deserve a special mention. Thanks also to all who participated in the first two events of the Technologies of Lived Abstraction event series and to those who are involved in designing the two final events, "The Society of Molecules" and "Generating the Impossible." We couldn't experiment without you!

Much of our thinking happens across various kinds of divides. I want to thank those who make these divides fluid, fielding difference with curiosity.

For your close reading of the manuscript in various stages, and your regenerating enthusiasm about all things processual, thank you Ken Dean, Sher Doruff, Brian Massumi, Steven Muecke, Andrew Murphie, Luciana Parisi, Philipa Rothfield, Steven Shaviro, Philip Thurtle.

For making thinking and doing coincide politically, artistically, and philosophically, a warm thanks also to Michelle Barker, Lone Bertelson, Jean-Claude Bustros, William Connolly, Luc Courchesne, Joao Da Silva, Scott de la Hunta, Toni Dove, Pia Ednie-Brown, Nora Heilmann, José Gil, Heidi Gilpin, Michael Goddard, Steve Goodman, Catherine Herrmann, Yvan Joly, Thomas Lamarre, Bruno Latour, Andre Lepecki, Derek McCormack, Anna Munster, Sally-Jane Norman, Christopher Salter, Monique Savoie, Michael Shapiro, Christine Shaw, Isabelle Stengers, Sha Xin Wei.

For your generous openness toward improvisation and relation in dance, thank you Mireille Painchaud.

For believing in the Technologies of Lived Abstraction book series and for your ongoing encouragement, thank you Doug Sery.

For inviting thought, thank you to my family: Ben Jones, Margaret McCullough, Eric Manning, Pascale Manning, Yves Manning, and Jesse Massumi.

Thank you also to all the students in my classes who allow me to experiment with ideas in the making, and who take the risk of learning collaboratively. Relationscapes often start in the classroom.

Relationscapes was written with the generous assistance of a Canadian Social Sciences and Humanities Research Council Grant.

Introduction: Events of Relation—Concepts in the Making

Concepts are events in the making. An event in the making is a thought on the cusp of articulation—a prearticulated thought in motion. How thoughts in motion become articulations is the subject of *Relationscapes: Movement, Art, Philosophy*. Throughout, my concern is to address the malleability of concepts that move, the expressivity of thoughts as they become feelings, the ontogenetic potential of ideas as they become articulations. This complex passage from thought to feeling to concepts-in-prearticulation to events-in-the-making foregrounds how thinking is more than the discrete final form it takes in language. To come to language is more than to finalize form. To come to language is to feel the form-taking of concepts as they prearticulate thoughts / feelings.

Many concepts are at work in *Relationscapes*. This proliferation of concepts builds on the necessity for language to create new parameters for thought in the passage from feeling to articulation. To create concepts is to move with language's prearticulations. In this mode of thinking / feeling, language does not yet know what it means. It has not yet defined where it can go. Language is creatively mired within the affective tonalities of how it can be heard, lived, written, imagined.

To arrive at language in the making, *Relationscapes* begins with the concept not of prearticulation but of preacceleration. The reason for this is that to think language before it takes form we must first understand how to conceive of taking form itself. Taking form, I suggest, is key to a developing vocabulary of movement that foregrounds incipience rather than displacement. What I mean by this is that movement need not be thought, in the first instance, as a quantitative displacement from a to b. Following Bergson, *Relationscapes* places the emphasis on the immanence of movement moving: how movement can be felt before it actualizes. Preacceleration refers to the virtual force of movement's taking form. It is the feeling of movement's in-gathering, a welling that propels the directionality of how movement moves. In dance, this is felt as the virtual momentum of a movement's taking form before we actually move. Important: the pulsion toward directionality activates the force of a movement in its incipiency. It does not necessarily foretell where a movement will go.

Incipient movement preaccelerates a body toward its becoming. The body becomes through forces of recombination that compose its potential directionalities. When I take a step, how the step moves me is key to where I can go. Gravity acts on the step such that the time span of the step's creativity is relatively short-lived. Nonetheless, there is an incipient potentiality even here, where the step can move eventfully in a withness of movement moving that exceeds the predomination of the ground: the step *can* become a spiral. Preaccelerated, what is felt is neither stepness nor spiralness. What is felt is incipient potential to move-with the intensity of extension. Moving-with the intensity of extension means that movement gathers first in the potential of its incipiency, not in the extensity of its displacement. By the time movement displaces, few options for surprise remain: gravity's pull over the movement's directionality has taken over.

The dynamic form of a movement is its incipient potential. Bodies are dynamic expressions of movement in its incipiency. They have not yet converged into final form. Throughout *Relationscapes*, I refer to bodies as pure plastic rhythm. I propose that we move toward a notion of a becoming-body that is a sensing body in movement,[6] a body that resists predefinition in terms of subjectivity or identity, a body that is involved in a reciprocal reaching-toward that in-gathers the world even as it worlds.

These bodies-in-the-making are propositions for thought in motion. Thought here is not strictly of the mind but of the body-becoming. Thought is never opposed to movement: thought moves a body. This movement-with is durational in the first instance. Duration is the plane of experience on which expressive finality has not yet taken hold. As thought shifts toward expression, it moves through concepts in prearticulation. How thought becomes concept is parallel to how duration becomes experiential space-time.

Albert North Whitehead's concept of actual occasions is central to understanding the spacedness and timedness of events throughout *Relationscapes*. As Gilles Deleuze and Felix Guattari emphasize by dating each of the plateaus in *A Thousand Plateaus*, events take form in the concreteness of time and space. This does not mean that time and space precede them. Quite the contrary: events *create* time and space. Whitehead demonstrates this by foregrounding the eventness of perception. For him, events of perception are always called forth through prehensions, which are the pulling out of expression from the durational plane of experience.[7] When a becoming-event is pulled out, the activity of perception is experienced as such. This initial prehension creates the parameters for the taking-form of space-time in the context of a discrete experience.

The prehension "chair," for instance, brings with it the capacity to experience sitability as a key modality of chair-expression. We feel the sitting as part of how "chair" is prehended: the event-in-the-making becomes one of sitability. This actual occasion of chairness culminates in what Whitehead calls the subjective form of the experience: in this case, chair-as-sitability. What is prehended is not chair per se but the relation between body and chair, between movement and concept with the chair-as-object just one pole in the actual occasion. Once the actual occasion takes form (as a movement of thought, or as an actual experience of sitability), it perishes, its culmination marking the opening for future relational experiences colored by sitability. Chair has given way to sitability on a dated and timed relational nexus of experience. The event exists as such in a concrete (and perished) experience of space-time, even as chairness continues to collaborate in future events.[8]

Actual occasions are monadic in the sense that they are contemporarily independent. An event is always singular, completely absorbed by its particular iteration. Events are never relational in their actualization: they relate across the nexus of experience in their incipiency—their pastness—or in their perishing—their future-pastness. Whitehead warns that without this monadic quality to events, there would be no elbow room in the universe. Within a vocabulary of movement, this can be explained by foregrounding the difference between preacceleration and displacement. In the preacceleration of a step, anything is possible. But as the step begins to actualize, there is no longer much potential for divergence: the foot will land where it lands. Incipiency opens up experience to the unknowable, follow-through toward concrescence closes experience on itself. Of course, this closing-in is always a reopening toward the next incipient action.

Whether incipient movement or thought prearticulated, novelty is situated within process. When movement converges into its taking-form, or when thought converges into words, very little potential for creative expression remains. This is not to suggest that language cannot express creatively. It means that to remain post-iteratively creative, language must continue to express itself in a realm where thought remains prearticulated, where concepts continue to evolve. We must conceive of language as the eternal return of expression in the making.

Thought is ontogenetic: it propels more thought. *Relationscapes* takes this idea to the limit, proposing various engagements with movements of thought, from Leni Riefenstahl's complex movement-images to Umberto Boccioni's atmospheric body, from Dorothy Napangardi's dance with the ground to Clifford Possum Tjapaltjarri's maps and Emily Kame Kngwarreye's own relationscapes. With the concept of individuation—which also becomes infra-individuation—*Relationscapes* attempts to create a vocabulary for how movement becomes thought and vice-versa. In this eternal return of movement-becoming-thought and thought-becoming-movement, what emerges is the uncanny realization that movement tells stories quite differently than does a more linear and stable historicization.

This is particularly resonant in the animate form of Étienne-Jules Marey's cinematic experiments, which seek to locate durational movement's imperceptibility within a positivist framework *and* develop a vocabulary for movement that exceeds representation within a stable matrix of calculable coordinates. Although never explicitly outlined in chapter 5, I would argue that had Marey's experiments with movement been foregrounded within the history of cinema, cinema's early emphasis on theories of semiosis might have been derouted into a more developed exploration of how cinema moves. This might have redirected the study of cinema from its early academic embededness within formalist thought toward early twentieth-century expressions of movement such as the invention of modern dance, Futurism's concern with ontogenesis, Bergson's theory of duration. The effect of this convergence of cinema and movement would have been a foregrounding less of narrative strategies within the cinematic than experimentation with how images provoke durational flows that are themselves mobile even before passing through a projector.

Seen through the specter of movement, the history of cinema converges around concepts of force rather than ideas of representation. This is a key difference between Marey and Eadweard Muybridge, one rarely exploited in theories of cinema: Marey's practice invests in the exploration of movement's durational force, whereas Muybridge's work focuses on movement's poses. Throughout *Relationscapes*, I explore durational force through the Deleuzian idea of series. This allows me—via Riefenstahl's work in particular—to foreground how movement does not work primarily across immobile cuts. Riefenstahl's extraordinary images make incipient movement felt, her "stills" mobile. Within her work we experience not images as contained by frames but a proliferation of relational series that move conjunctively across shots and frames. This serial aspect of her shots can be experienced without any effort by capturing images from her films: I encourage you to try this at home. Whereas with most filmmakers it is a challenge to find a striking image when capturing the movement into a still, with Riefenstahl each capture is evocative, foregrounding never a body as such, but how a body moves and becomes-body. What we are left with, always, is immanent movement, still-moving.

The elasticity of movement as developed in chapter 2 makes a case for bodies always reconverging around the elasticity of their becoming. Riefenstahl's work makes this elasticity felt both within and across the frame, opening thought toward the articulation of how movement can also be felt within stillness (within a "still"). Working from a perspective of incipient movement, I explore how force takes form through an elastic movement that is curved through inflection. Inflection is a mathematical concept that demonstrates how lines are moved by nodal points that not only change the line's direction but also alter the parameters for its mapping. Inflection makes apparent how even a "still" can move as it curves with the force of preacceleration: movement's elasticity is felt in its curving-through a nodal shift that redirects its force. This nodal shift is movement's elastic point.

Thought also moves through the elasticity of the almost. The elastic point is the creativity of movement in the making. It is the ontogenetic force through which becoming-form is felt. Movement folds around this elastic point such that what is felt is not the point per se but the elasticity of its becoming. This is a topological sensation—which is a paradox in itself: a topology of experience is a force-form before it is a feeling. Still, when we feel this sensation of ontogenetic force-taking-form, we do tend to smile, laugh, or at least feel surprised by the event as it expresses us.

There is a rhythm to all of this. To posit rhythm as extra or external to experience is to misunderstand how rhythms make up events. Rhythm gives affective tonality to experience, making experience this and not that. Rhythm techniques are not solely dedicated to sound: there is rhythm in inflection, in Kngwarreye's brushstrokes, in William Forsythe's movement improvisations, in Marey's chronophotographies.

Rhythm comes to the fore through techniques for invention. Gilbert Simondon (1995) defines techniques as modalities for the creation of machinic resonances that defy a machine's strict organization. He suggests that a technical system is one where the whole cannot be subsumed to its parts, where what converges is more than the sum of its coordinates. Techniques are imbued with rhythm, they move-with the machine's own forces of recombination. To understand the relay between technique and machine, it is useful to be acquainted with Guattari's concept of the machinic. For Guattari, the machinic expresses forces of creativity: "A machinic assemblage [is] an assemblage of possible fields, of virtual as much as constituted elements, without any notion of generic or species' relation" (1995, 35). Machines demand life: they process always in the realm of the more-than, constantly recombining. Pure plastic rhythm is a machinic way of redefining what a body is, and even more so, what a body can do.

Techniques for invention cannot be captured. When they are, they become redundant: you cannot recompose with something that has already been spoken for. Techniques for invention must remain on the plane of composition. This means that *Relationscapes* is not a how-to book on movement. It does not provide a theory of movement that can be mapped onto all forms of movement. Each preacceleration must be experienced in its complexity, concepts must be found to invent with it, and tendencies for its actualization have to be diagrammed. When these diagrams are made, they cannot read as maps. They must remain intensities-in-the-making, force fields for future thought. This is what Francis Bacon means when he evokes the concept (Deleuze 2003). He is not talking about a map but about a field that resonates beyond the image-content of a painting. The diagram is the feeling for the painting that moves with its force for expression.

In chapter 6, I extrapolate from this notion of the diagram toward the concept of the biogram, as proposed by Brian Massumi in "Strange Horizon."[9] I define the biogram as that which propels a becoming-body. This force of becoming is a reconvergence of affective tonalities that transpire into a form that is itself continually mutating. Whereas a diagram makes felt the force of a painting, the biogram propels a moving-with of the ontogenetic body.

Ontogenesis is a reminder not to get stuck in ontologies of being. Ontologies must remain thresholds—from being to becoming, from force to form to force. Identities do take form, but these are always brief individuations. To still becoming into a lingering identity is to try to stop movement. What must be sought is neither a total becoming nor a fixed identity: the dynamic equilibrium between identity and individuation is metastable. This means that it converges on many planes at once, more stable on some, more active on others. To locate identity as the point of departure of a body is to deny the complexity of the concurrent planes of thought, expression, conceptualization, articulation.

Simondon's concept of the associated milieu is a provocative way of conceptualizing how different planes converge around a concept. *Relationscapes* resides in the associated milieu of conceptual metastability. All concepts mobilized for *Relationscapes* emerged through the process of writing. Never was writing an add-on to this process: writing developed through the activity of thinking-with that movements of thought propel. As with prehensions that invent the subject of perception through their activity of pulling forth, writing wrote me into the process of inventing-with relationscapes.

Incipient Action: The Dance of the Not-Yet 1

Relational Movement

There are always at least two bodies. These two stand close, facing one another, reaching-toward an embrace that will signal an acceleration of the movement that has always already begun. The movement within becomes a movement without, not internal-external, but folding and bridging in an intensity of preacceleration. This means you are never stopped. To move is to engage the potential inherent in the preacceleration that embodies you. Preaccelerated because there can be no beginning or end to movement. Movement is one with the world, not body/world, but body-worlding. We move not to populate space, not to extend it or to embody it, but to create it. Our preacceleration already colors space, vibrates it. Movement quantifies it, qualitatively. Space is duration with a difference. The difference is my body-worlding, always more than one. Our embrace quickens the molecules that compose us. An adaptation occurs—we begin to recompose. Volumes, always more than one, emerge from surfaces, recombining with lines, folding, bridging, knotting. This coming-together proposes a combination of form-forces where preacceleration potentially finds passage. The passage flows not in a preinscribed direction: this is an intensive flow. Preacceleration: a movement of the not-yet that composes the more-than-one that is my body. Call it incipient action.

Two bodies: compositions—actual, virtual, organic, prosthetic. As we move with them, remember: there are always at least two, even when you perceive one, connected. Connection, not the locus of all beginnings, but the invisible-but-palpable link between bodies. To move together, the connection must be alive. As they move, they reconnect. Call it a relational shape-shifting. Potential physical points of contact: chest, arm, stomach, shoulder, breast. William Forsythe calls this *cz*, the connection between two limbs where "the pressure of one limb on the other gives the alterations in the skeletal mechanic" (2003, 65). In relational movement[10] we will not always have the same contact, but contact will remain. This contact will be the impetus for creating movement. Remember: we also shape-shift at a distance.

We take a step. My step leads me forward, but before I can step I must call on you to move almost before my own displacement. It is this almost-before I must communicate. This silent question takes the form of an opening. Technically: the energy that is preaccelerating through my body convenes in a direction that can be harnessed. The direction becomes a potential movement that repositions an almost-shifting body in a towardness that has not yet actually moved. The towardness draws you in. What they see: we move forward together—I step forward, she steps back. It looks seamless. Result: they think this must be choreographed.

"I consider choreography to be a secondary result of dancing" (Forsythe 2003, 24). The appearance of choreography signals a reaction to a movement that seems to have been known in advance. Yet nothing here is known in advance. What moves is a feeling more than a direction. The feeling can be harnessed into a repetition—a choreography of sorts. But what emerges in the first instance is an openness toward moving, a movement moving.

The concept of preacceleration is a way of thinking the incipiency of movement, the ways in which movement is always on the verge of expression. Bodies invent motion incessantly, creating habits to satisfy the carrying out of these inventions. These habits tell us how to keep our balance as we take one step after another, how to reach the floor with our toes as we crawl out of bed in the morning, how to find the bathroom at night without running into the walls. Proprioception provides us with clues that precede our cognitive understanding of where we are going.[11] Preacceleration: we are going, always already.

The dancer's body—in the case of relational movement, the two of us moving together—provides a glimpse into the ways in which movement creates the potential for unthinking dichotomies that populate our worlds: abstract-concrete, organic-prosthetic, alive-dead, mind-body, actual-virtual, man-woman. It's not that movement directly undermines these dialectical concepts. It's that movement allows us to approach them from another perspective: a shifting one. When we are no longer still, the world lives differently.

We can think of movement in at least two ways:

1. I enter a room and see that room as preexisting me. I walk across the room, drawing an imaginary line that cuts the space.
2. My movement creates the space I will come to understand as "the room." The room is defined as my body + the environment, where the environment is an atmospheric body. Without that particular moving body that particular environment does not exist.

In Umberto Boccioni's terms, the first way of thinking movement might be termed "relative movement" and the second "absolute movement." In the first instance, we participate in a hylomorphic quandary where form preexists matter.[12] The matter—my body—enters into the form—the room. Both body and room are pregiven in this instance. The room defines the limits of my body's potential. In the second instance of "absolute movement," individuation occurs in intimate connection between the moving body and its atmospheric potential.

The room becomes *configuring* as the body *recomposes*. There is no "body itself" here because the body is always more than "itself," always reaching toward that which it is not yet. The not-yet takes form through the intensities of preacceleration that compel recompositions at the level of both strata, the body and the room. What this means is that both body and space are experienced as alive with potential movement. The body-room series takes on an infinite variety of potential velocities. These velocities take form at certain intervals, remaining virtual at others. The body-room stratum is therefore neither object nor form, but infinite potential for recombination. When an event takes form within this malleable stratum, there is a configuration. Displacement is one such event. When a displacement actually occurs—directing the force of preacceleration that holds the series in anticipation—a shift takes place that alters the coordinates of space-time, beginning the process anew, bringing new configurations to the machinic phylum body-room.[13]

The body-room series opens the way for thinking the "pure plastic rhythm" of bodies. For Boccioni, "pure plastic rhythm" is not "the construction of bodies, but the construction of the *action* of bodies" (1964, 48). In his work, Boccioni is concerned with sculpting the body, not as an immobile body that is modeled *as though* it were in motion, but *as* a body in movement. To sculpt movement is to prolong a spiral potential that is already inherent to matter. This prolongation of the spiral is what Boccioni calls dynamism, or *dynamic form*. Pure plastic rhythm is dynamic form in potentia. In a Spinozean gesture, Boccioni seeks to create a movement that is preaccelerated, a movement that never stops, yet has not come to full expression through displacement. That a body moves without displacing itself means that rest becomes an instance of absolute movement. Rest becomes an activity of rhythm. Boccioni calls this *continuity in space*. Continuity in space does not imply a static concept of space with a moving body transposed into its interior. For Boccioni, space moves. What Boccioni (with the other Futurists) seeks is a simultaneity of form and content where the virtual (preacceleration) is felt as creating a simultaneity of body and environment. Preacceleration forces movement to take form: "By its centrifugal direction, the form-force is the potential of the living form" (Boccioni 1964, 48). Force taking form.

Boccioni does not seek a *representation* of movement. He *creates* movement. To create movement is not to sculpt movement's illusion. It is to make movement felt in the recreation of new body-world series. This sculptural ambition is political. Through it, the political achieves a thickness, a volume. The immobile silhouette of the stable subject is usurped by a recomposing body that "seeks complete fusion of environment and object by means of the interpenetration of planes" (Boccioni 1964, 49). Gesture becomes dynamic: there are not two legs moving, but twenty. It's all about rhythm: "Rhythm appears, not only dependent on the velocity, fastness, and linear measurement of an extensive movement, but also on the intensive capacity of the body, on its passage between direct potential states and its affective relations to the states of other bodies" (Portanova 2005, 34).

Duration is key. The two dancers have now taken a step forward. Their embrace connects them. It is not the touch "as such" that holds them to one another, but the movement-toward that is the continuous repetition of the touch.[14] This inframodal experience of touching awakens their bodies to all kinds of perceptions, alerting the dancers to the continuous recompositions of the space-times that world them.[15] Inframodal vitality propels the dancers to become more-than, to embody more than the strict envelopes of their individual bodies. The dancers begin to feel the dance take over. They feel the openings before they recognize them as such, openings for movement that reach toward a dance of the not-yet. What takes place in this not-yet? Facing forward on the crowded dance floor, I feel the urgent presence of bodies moving behind me. Even if they seem still, they press against my back, creating space in front of me. The music lends urgency to the moment. The music begins to move us. I lead an interval. This interval is not mine alone to lead. She invites me to instantiate it, feeding it with her own intensive preacceleration. Inframodally, we shape-shift this interval. As it takes form, the intensity of moving together translates into a step, this time to the front and around. She moves around me, urging my moving body-form to propel her shifting axis into a turn as I step back, repositioning my axis in direct relation to hers. The interval moves with the music, with the shifting axes, moving us, creating a shared body. We move the relation.

The interval is duration expressed in movement. It is not something I create alone, or something I can re-create by myself. It exists in the between of movement. It accompanies my movement, yet is never passive. It activates the next incipient movement. The interval is the metastable quality through which the relation is felt. Many potential intensities populate it. It expresses itself as the shifting axis that connects us. Proposition: the interval creates the potential for movement that is expressed by at least two bodies.

Intensive Magnitudes

Duration is a way of thinking space-time qualitatively without subsuming it to a certain measuring out of space. Duration is the rendering of what Bergson calls intensive magnitudes: "Pure duration might well be nothing but a succession of qualitative changes, which melt into and permeate one another, without precise outlines, without any tendency to externalize themselves in relation to one another, without any affiliation with number; it would be pure heterogeneity" (2002, 61). When space-time is no longer *entered* but instead *created*, it becomes possible to think the body-world as that which is generated by the potential inherent in the preacceleration of movement. Movement takes time. But movement also makes time. Forsythe suggests that the velocity of the movements he proposes to his dancers could not be choreographed without first slowing them down. To choreograph is to hold incipiency to measure.

Movement provokes duration even as duration provokes movement. Measurable quantity is anathema to duration. This is why the displacement itself—the movement from a to b—is not what is essential about movement. Movement is the qualitative multiplicity that folds, bends, extends the body-becoming toward a potential future that will always remain not-yet. This body-becoming (connecting, always) becomes-toward, always with. I move not you but the interval out of which our movement emerges. We move time relationally as we create space: we move space as we create time.

The displacement is not the event. The event is the composition of space-time that qualitatively alters the topological dimensions of our sensing bodies in movement. In Bergson's words: "We attribute to the motion the divisibility of the space which it traverses, forgetting that it is quite possible to divide an object, but not an act: and on the other hand we accustom ourselves to projecting this act itself into space, to applying it to the whole of the line which the moving body traverses, in a word, to solidifying" (2002, 65). In preacceleration there is never simply one movement: different rhythms, different durations coexist. The displacement is how the decision to move one way or another takes form. Movement is a process of individuation where matter and form remain in flux, virtually shape-shifting into malleable environments. These environments—alive in the interval—are always singular, but never one.

The time of the interval is incipiency. This is a future-past that is prolonged at the interface of the becoming-actual of the virtual. Just because you cannot see the interval does not mean it's not real. The interval's concreteness is what allows me to feel the movement in the before or the even-as of my body's displacement. I can't think fast enough to catch the interval in the making. The interval is the production of movement before we know it as such. It is the residual we tap into in a quick change of direction that causes her leg to fly into the air, magically circling her already recomposing body. The interval is salient throughout, but I cannot name it or locate it exactly. I feel it only momentarily in the instant where I catch a glimpse of her eyes wide with wonder asking herself, "How did I *do* that?"

William Forsythe's technologies of improvisation are a rich lexicon for the interval. Forsythe explores movement as both extensive and intensive space. His interest in what a body can do takes the movement-space of the body and extends it as far as the body can reach. He pushes the limit of extension, exploring how space is created through the infinite lines of flight of expansive bodies.[16] In a space-time of continuous reorientation, not only do bodies metamorphose, but so does the space created by the incessant reorientation of the malleable coordinates of stagecraft. Space and body are in continuous shifting dialogue.

The relational body is populated by virtual intervals. Yet these shifting intervals are also always in a potential state of disappearance. They are like spirals of preacceleration poised to be tapped. Movement revels in the potential of the interval precisely because it contains the magic of forgetting that assures that every movement will begin anew, despite and because of the endless potential of its preaccelerated state. For preacceleration cannot be known as such. It is felt in its effects. It colors the way the movement becomes. But it can't be repeated in exactly the same way. Preacceleration is the expression of movement's capacity for invention.

Preacceleration does not predict one displacement over another. It holds in abeyance openings, out of which shapes emerge, but control is not of the essence. Movement always begins with a certain degree of open improvisation mixed with a certain degree of habit. Every step we take when we walk is a replaying of a habit. This habit is a tendency to move to a certain rhythm, to take a certain size step, to bend at the hip or at the knee. These habits hold our walk to a practiced repetition: a choreography of sorts. Yet each of these habits takes its shape from a preacceleration that proposes openings toward different shades of movement. These shades of movement are likely more visible in the walk of the dancer than in everyday movement, but even the everyday walk is an improvisation before it is a choreography.

When we are speaking of movement, we must remember: the virtual and the actual are aspects of the same event (there is no actual without the virtual, and vice versa). What takes form as we move is the actualization of virtual potential rich in each displacement. The eventness of movement is a virtually concretized differentiation of matter-form that creates a dynamics that is of the order of speed itself. "You can . . . move with tremendous acceleration provided you know where you leave the movement—not where you put the movement, but where you leave it. You try to divest your body of movement, as opposed to thinking that you are producing movement" (Forsythe 1995, 1). Speed is preacceleration virtually prolonged, always already evading actualization. Absolute speed: magnitude of acceleration, qualitative transformation. When speed actualizes (quantifies), it slows down. Divesting movement of displacement, preacceleration becomes palpable. Evaporation, exfoliation, dissolution. "Movement is a factor of the fact that you are actually evaporating" (Forsythe 1995, 1).

We never evaporate alone. To posit this is to succumb to what Whitehead calls "the fallacy of misplaced concreteness" (1938, 18). The concrete must remain potentially virtual: its process of relationality must never be completed. The interval is a way of conceptualizing the concreteness of movement where the concrete remains relational and the movement remains virtual.

Anexact yet Rigorous

Although the interval cannot be directly perceived, it can be prehended. For Whitehead (1929/1978), the actuality created by a prehension is called an actual occasion. In the case of the two dancers, the actual occasion will not be the fact of the displacement as such but the act of it. How the movement is prehended is a unique experience. The singularity of prehension serves to remind us that there is not one common interval but an infinity of relational intervals that together create space-time as we experience it. Like prehensions, actual entities are multiple, operating on a nexus. Each series—of a walk, of a dance—is composed of a nexus of differentiated prehensions recomposed into actual occasions. Each of these actual occasions operates in a specific space-time on a nexus that shape-shifts in the recomposing space-time of sensing bodies in movement. The interval operates in the multidimensionality of the nexus, becoming with a region of vague and material essences. These essences, defined by Edmund Husserl as "anexact yet rigorous," are neither metric nor fixed. The interval that is prehended remains incorporeal, yet inextricably connected to the corporeal, resulting in what Deleuze and Guattari call "an ambulant coupling, events-affects, which constitutes the vague corporeal essence and is distinct from the secondary linkage, 'fixed essence-properties of the thing deriving from the essence'" (1987, 409).

The interval belongs to a certain qualifying vocabulary such as that expressed through Whitehead's "eternal objects." The interval is not a *thing* but a *quality* of light, speed, closeness, purpleness. In Whiteheadian terms, this means that the interval preexists all actual occasions, composing them but not perishing along with them (when they have become "satisfied"). While a prehension may create an actual occasion that in time will have served its purpose and disappear, the interval that incites that actual event to shape-shift will remain potentially active for the next preacceleration. The interval is eternal.[17]

If we had to locate creativity, the interval could serve as its nexus. I cannot show you how to move my movement, but I can show you how to potentialize the interval to help extend your movement to its qualitative limit. This is what Forsythe means when he says that he must work *with* the dancers to help them find *their* movement. To find movement is to work with preacceleration. This just-before is also a way to think duration rather than succumbing to linear time. It is not that I will know the movement in a potential future, but that I will invent the now in a time-slip I will come to know as the just-before. This just-before will never be about an individual movement, but about the relation between preacceleration and motion, between an infinity of intervals apprehended in the not-yet of our quantitative displacement. "When you're actually dancing, it is seldom that the principles occur in isolation" (Forsythe 2003, 18).

Novelty is produced by the body-becoming. Novelty is dynamic, active through the plasticity of its rhythms, emergent always in excess of its form. "You make a voluntary decision, and you let yourself move into space and then gravity and velocity and several other factors are going to affect that decision and force you into another one" (Forsythe 2003a, 24). The interval cannot be shaped as such. It creates a folding into which bodies capitulate, an opening into which we surge. Bodies become many-timed, many-spaced: "Then your body would take over and dance at that point where you had no more idea. I see that as an idealized form of dancing: just not knowing and letting the body dance you around" (Forsythe 2003, 26).

Whitehead writes: "Every actual entity is what it is, and is with its definite status in the universe, determined by its internal relations [its interval] to other actual entities. Change is the description of the adventure of eternal objects in the evolving universe of actual things" (1938, 59). The dance floor moves the dancers. The ground shifts, and through its shifting, bodies recompose. The actual occasions created through the relational event of movement taking shape form a nexus of degrees of relevance, where every actual occasion is in some way present in every other actual occasion. This despite the fact that each interval is singular, coloring the particular actual occasion with a qualifier that distinguishes it from the plethora of other actual occasions. We may thus prehend the whole (the nexus—the dance as such) or a singularity (one particular movement). When the singularity surprises us the interval will come to light: a moment of magic! Total exfoliation: laughter. We feel the interval's eternality: there will always have been more than one. The eternality of the interval carries an infinity of potential preaccelerations, an infinite subrealm of experience and expression. When movement makes us laugh (or cry), this laughter captures a singular interval, activating its relevance above the nexus. We feel the movement moving us.

The Many Become One

"At any given moment you have to be able to say: What is the potential of this configuration of my body?" (Forsythe in Mei 2003, 1). The potential of a movement is its ability to dynamically extend the many from the one. "The novel entity is at once the togetherness of the 'many' which it finds, and also it is one among the disjunctive 'many' which it leaves; it is a novel entity, disjunctive among the many entities which it synthesizes. The many become one, and are increased by one" (Whitehead 1929/1978, 21). The potential of a configuration is its evanescence: the ways it will have become. This evanescence can be heard in Whitehead's concept of concrescence, which is the way he combines togetherness and the production of novelty. The potential of a configuration must always be the production of novelty. This production will always be based on a togetherness where the interval will guide and extend/extrude the process. This togetherness is the relationality out of which all consequent (and simultaneous) intervals are produced. Concrescence is, literally, growing together.

"You don't start dancing. You dance."[18] We dance our way to concrescence. Concrescence can be a political moment: the interval we are dancing is always more than the qualified "we." This "we" transfers any thought of subjectivity beyond the individual not simply to individuation but also to infra-individuation, to a thought of the collective that does not emerge from a group of individuals but precedes the very concept of individuality. To locate the many in the one and add one is to suggest that every movement is first and foremost collective: collective and singular. It is collective in the sense that it is relational, that it has a profound effect on the composition of its intensive extensions. These intensities become movements of thought, where thought is never distinct from the movement itself. Movements of thought are potential articulations of the political. Such articulations propose that we are never alone in the world: movements of thought are worldings that recombine the potential for collective thought.

Felix Guattari proposes a composed matrix of subjectivity that resists a return to the realm of the unconscious to enhance its recombinations. Guattari's concept of subjectivity depends on an active and dynamic recombination of the virtual and the actual. Subjectivity is no longer exclusively located in a body: it is a collective moving-through. Remapped onto the vocabulary of the interval, we might see subjectivity as a provocation that effects the recomposing of bodies-in-the-making, creating not fixed subjects but infra-individuations.

Guattari sees this process of subjectivization as parallel to worlding, continuously reactualized through events of the present passing. This productive consciousness depends on machines of combination such as the series individual-group-machine-world. This series is always already collective in the sense of its operating at vectors of relation and exchange. Subjectivity as Guattari proposes is a kind of heteropoiesis, a self-production in which the myriad components (prosthetic-organic) participate in the production and transformation of one another. Subjectivity "makes itself collective" (Guattari 1995, 22). This does not mean that subjectivity as inherently collective is already political[19] or social, but that the collectivity that is an emergent sensing body in movement is invariably an emergent articulation of the political.

Collective must be understood here in terms of the nexus of actual occasions prehended through the eventness of the interval. Collectivity deploys itself in excess of any individual (one or many) to an idea of the infra-individuating recombination that is never one or many but always at the threshold from one to the other. To develop a thought of relation that refrains from positing the individual as the starting point allows us to multiply the interval. Despite the fact that prehension restricts us to an actual occasion that is monadic in its completion, it provides the potential for Guattari's notion of subjectivity: prehension produces the potential for a nexus through which the collective as singularity can be thought.

The Refrain

Creating an actual occasion harnesses an event, foreclosing momentarily the potential for recombination. There will of course be simultaneous recombinations at the level of the nexus, but a singular actual occasion—like Gottfried Leibniz's monads—will always remain what it is in this instance. When this instance has outgrown its potential, the actual occasion will perish, leaving an opening for a repopulation of the recomposing nexus. Only the interval will survive this perishing. Although the interval as such can never be grasped or contained, it "ingresses" into new actual occasions, magnifying the potential within them. This shape-shifting of the interval is a rhythm that returns as a refrain, emphasizing that which populates the in-between. There is no empty space: space is the interval that creates refrains, rhythmically altering body-worlds.

The refrain is used here to convey time-slips within territorializations. To territorialize is always to stop movement, to begin the analysis from a stopping, and then to make the body move. To think movement through the refrain allows us to locate the interval as an absolute tempo whereby "time ceases to be exterior in order to become an intensive nucleus [*foyer*] of temporalization" (Guattari 1995, 16). Rhythm is experiential duration that dislodges any concept of universal time. "From this perspective, universal time appears to be no more than a hypothetical projection, a time of generalized equivalence, a 'flattened' capitalist time; what is important are these partial modules of temporalization, operating in diverse domains (biological, ethological, socio-cultural, machinic, cosmic . . .), and out of which complex refrains constitute highly relative existential synchronies" (Guattari 1995, 16). Incorporeal becomings are made up of rhythmic intervals, rhythms that are detected as they are produced only to find themselves always already there.

Time is not endured. It is activated. To dance is not to make steps. "This dance can only be made from the inside."[20] The interval is prehended not in the displacement as such but in the event of being-connected: the interval is a connection machine. The interval reminds us that the body-world (in recombination) is a technology.[21] It is a technology insofar as it is capable of accessing the connection machine, of creating the movements of thought that extend the interval across space-time. It is a technology insofar as it is a "Body without Organs" (BwO)—a body always qualitatively more-than the organization of its biological composition (Deleuze and Guattari 1987). The interval is a technology of the body-becoming: organic insofar as it qualitatively alters the molecular and molar composites that make up our experience of space-time, prosthetic in the sense that the body is populated by senses that extend the regions of the body beyond its organic envelope to "technologically" connect it to its process of worlding. In this process of worlding, what *exactly* is prosthetic and what is biological is contestable: processes of relay are always at once machinic and biological, organic, and technological.[22] Ontogenetic bodies as pure plastic rhythm are always recomposing, proposing relations between series. Movement is a technology of the becoming-body.

The Virtual

The interval is virtual, incorporeal. Yet it has substance: it is palpable. For Spinoza, substance is not prior to its attributes, nor does cause precede effects. As Deleuze writes, "Substance is 'its' infinite diversity itself; it is realized in this diversity and is nothing other than the process of production without beginning or end (beyond teleology, without goals or direction) of itself through the infinity of its attributes" (1997, xvii). The substance of the interval is its capacity to retain qualities even after its perishing within an actual occasion. This quality of movement *is* not: it *acts*. As pure duration, the interval creates a schism in linear time, preserving the future in the present. The time-slip of the interval is the future anterior: the will-not-yet-have-happened. The interval never marks a passage: it creates the potential for a passage that will have come to be. This duration is defined less by succession than by coexistence, virtually.

Repetition is at the heart of the interval. The structure of repetition-in-duration is not one of resemblance but of difference. This repetition takes place within the virtual potential that is translated into an actual movement. The interval provokes the movement but does not actually move. The body moves. Repetition is the recomposing of the moving-with that is the relational body. This movement-with can be a spiral of preacceleration that incites a displacement, or it can be a movement of thought. It is always repetition with a difference. When this difference takes form, it becomes an actuality, an event in and of itself. This becoming-event creates a memory that feeds into future movement. Moving is repeating the future: dancing the not-yet. "What is recollected . . . is repeated backwards, whereas repetition is recollected forwards" (Kierkegaard 1983, 131).

Preacceleration is tapped into by the interval, actualized not in the displacement as such but in the potential of its actualization. Preacceleration is like the breath that releases speech, the gathering-toward that leaps our bodies into a future unknowable. It goes something like this: preacceleration—relation—interval—intensification—actualization—extension—displacement—preacceleration. Simultaneity of experience creates sensing bodies in movement creates shifting space-times of experience. "Space . . . is not matter or extension but the schema of matter, that is, the representation of the limit where the movement of expansion (*détente*) would come to an end as the external envelope of all possible extensions" (Deleuze 1991a, 87). Bodies are never independent of the extensions of space and the matter of time: bodies are durational. The interval makes this duration manifest, virtually.

Curve the Motion!

Tango is a walking dance. In a liquid embrace we move together, counterclockwise around a crowded dance floor. Floorcraft is key to the experience of the movement we seek. If the room moves with us, we feel as though we are dancing not with one other person, but with a hundred people. In this case, we experience a simultaneity of intervals: many rhythms and durations, one cadence. Repetition is another word for magic. One foot in front of another what we repeat is not the walk as such but the creation of intervals to the refrain of a simultaneous becoming. I move to move with you to move with them to move you moving me. Bodies recompose along new vectors, and the organs disperse. The connected intervals affectively transform our collective relation: the music moves with us, our collective steps sounding like a beating of a marked continuity. Boccioni's continuity in space. And yet these movements are improvised. Continuity in space becomes continuous discontinuity. The interval is always more than one, beyond the actual occasion.

To repeat is to act, to live the interval. Repetition is forgetting (in the Nietzschean sense): preacceleration not to find a previously lost displacement but to encounter the potential of what is not-yet. On the dance floor I lose my place when I repeat to remember. The music dulls, the interval dissolves, and I am no longer dancing with you. Now everything has become a question of displacement: the flow of dance falls apart. Important: we cannot dance together alone. Repetition must remember relation while it actively forgets past combinations. Relation must be reinvented. To dance relationally is not to *represent* movement but to *create* it.

To create movement for the sake of movement, Merce Cunningham adopts randomness as a choreographic method and decomposes sequences of movement by multiplying traditional articulations (Gil 2002, 118). Randomness becomes a way of awakening the interval, thereby shifting the focus from the body as subject to the production of movement itself. This production of movement potentially becomes a recomposition of the body not as subject but as collective infra-individuation. The goal is to "break the patterns of personal remembered physical coordinations" (Cunningham 1951, 59). Movement is no longer asked to express something outside it: movement becomes its own artwork (*oeuvre*).

When the body becomes a mobile form-force rather than a stable axis, anything is possible. Cunningham, and later Forsythe, seek not to capture the form-force of the body but to prolong the interval that emanates from this form-force to disarticulate what we too often have come to define as movement. The goal is not to displace but to create, to qualitatively change the composition (of the bodies, of space-time). This recombination is an active process that configures an event. Multiplicities are created that take the form of re-potentialized limbs reaching-toward what would seem to be the body's outside, but will become the re-centering of that body's reconfiguring. In Forsythe's vocabulary: transport the line, curve the motion, reorient and follow until your movement reaches a point where it can no longer develop. Capture the intensity! Redirect it, or let it go. Field residual movement. Prolong it! Extrude it! Fold it! Feel how it populates the interval. Use torsion to reclaim this residual movement, create a multiplicity. Play with what's left over, share it.

Mobile axes are the specialty of the interval that can morph and recompose at will. The stable axis of Cartesian geometry never creates movement: it produces displacement. To create movement necessitates a metastable sense of balance, the extrusion of a line into a plane: energetic recomposition. To the forming-matter/mattering-form that is the embodiment of pure plastic rhythm, the interval adds the potential for energetic materiality-in-movement. The preaccelerated state of matter projects not a displacement but a topological form-taking that in-forms the body more than it displaces it.

Think of displacement not as a movement through space but as a process of in-formation whereby space becomes what it is not-yet. Forming to deform, the body composes to recompose. To move is to exfoliate. Intensive affects are added to matter-form such that the envelope we thought we could decipher is no longer what is tangible. The effects of the virtual are felt. Relationally, we move through these effects, experiencing the texture of the interval. When the relational movement flows, it is because we surrender to the interval: the interval in-forms our movement. We re-form: we create a collective body.

A Politics of Movement

When articulation becomes collective, a politics is made palpable whereby what is produced is the potential for divergent series of movements. This is a virtual politics, a politics of the not-yet. In-forming analogously to the interval, these politics of touch are substantial but ungraspable. These are not politics we can choreograph but politics in the making. These are politics not of the body, but of the many becoming one, increased by one. The body-in-deformation is a multiplying sensing body in movement: many potential bodies exist in a singular body. These are politics of that many-bodied state of transition that is the collective.

When thinking a politics of movement, it is important to remember that repetition involves the intangible moment of transition between the virtual and the actual where preacceleration is in-formed by its potential becoming. This duration is always on the cusp of taking form: there is no "afterwards." When movement has ensued in displacement, acceleration is re-intensified into preacceleration, and the interval is active once more, ready to in-form the next infra-individuation. In this regard, there is always simultaneity of movement, always an overlapping of actual, actualizing, virtual, and virtualizing movements. Divergent series—nexuses of actual occasions—converge.

Concrescence—growing together—signals the potential of such politics: the world as dancing room.

Simultaneous movement implies a transgression of duration: movement not only creating space-time but recomposing the virtual. Preacceleration—intensive movement—keeps the virtual active, poised: a political preemption of the not-yet? All gestures extend beyond what we can perceive into the non-existence of their virtuality. These residues of movement are not lost or stored. They are active: actively virtual. "Organic, yes, but out of the multiplicity of organic virtual bodies that constitute one same body there merges an impossible body, a sort of monstrous body: this is the virtual body. This body prolongs gesture into virtuality, since what follows from gesture can no longer be perceived by an empirical, actual body" (Gil 2002, 123). Politics as radical empiricism.[23] As we move our body, we move not only with the force-form that seems palpable—the interval we create—but also with the multiplicity of virtual bodies that recompose along the plane of immanence of our sensing bodies in movement. "The unit of virtual movement (or the virtual unity of movement) creates a space where 'everything fits,' a space of coexistence and of consistency of heterogeneous series" (Gil 2002, 123).

What Gil calls the plane of immanence is the interval. It populates the dance and makes tangible, through dance, how movement operates. It underscores the fact that movement is never displacement. Movement is incipient action: a dance of the not-yet. "To dance is to create immanence through movement: this is why there is no meaning outside of the plane nor outside of the actions of the dancer. . . . The meaning of movement is the very movement of meaning" (Gil 2002, 125).

To move the interval rather than "the body" is to create space-time for politics, to open the concept of the empirical to movement, to begin to express the inframodality of the sensing body in movement. The plane of immanence is fragile, yet persistent. We can try to do away with the interval, but it always returns. Political philosophy has not made space for the interval within the vocabulary of the rational modern subject, yet the interval has nonetheless leaked into the complex iterations of pure plastic rhythm's political becomings. In dance, the interval has never absented itself, but has recently become more visible, more palpable, through movement's enhancement with new digital technologies. Urgently: let us move the relation. But let us not devise for it a presence that denies its virtuality, the micropolitical potential of its in-betweenness.

2 The Elasticity of the Almost

Movement is not explained by sensation, but by the elasticity of sensation, its *vis elastica*.
—Gilles Deleuze, *Logique de la sensation*

Relational Movement

Walking is the constraint. When you walk, you keep one foot on the ground, always. Two feet off the ground and you're jumping. With one foot on the ground, you can move in three directions: forward, backward, sideways. If you move sideways in the "wrong" direction, you move across. That's walking: one foot at a time.

Now take a sidewalk and add walking: you are moving quickly, trying to get through the crowd to catch the bus. You have two blocks to navigate, and the crowd makes it difficult. You weave through the people, taking bigger and smaller steps, looking for holes and then filling them, inhabiting them momentarily before they close. Hopefully no child, friend, or lover is lagging behind: sidewalk holes are rarely big enough for two people. And yet walking "alone" does not exist. Walking in/with the world: the only kind of walking.

From walking to relational movement is no big leap: it's already what you do. Except you may not have noticed, you may not yet have perfected your technique, because you were too busy trying to "get through" the crowd. The most straightforward way to conceive relational movement is side by side, or face to face. Think walking with a lover, or dancing tango. Walking relationally means: when you walk into the hole, you walk-with. Walking-with is more than taking a step, it is creating a movement.

Creating a movement is initiating a dance. This dance demands grace, a grace that is not a succumbing to an outside, but a feeling of the inside, inside-out. "Grace is like the paradigm of intensity that escapes all quantitative reduction of movement" (Bergson 1959/1970, 12–13). Grace is never felt solely through a step. Grace is the becoming-dance of the step, when walking flows in the between of directions where holes become emergent openings rather than missed opportunities.

Relational movement means moving the relation. Moving the person will never result in grace. Intensity of movement can only be felt when the in-between—the interval—created by the movement-with takes hold. This interval is ephemeral, impossible to grasp as such, yet essential to the intensive passage from a step to a graceful movement.

The Dance

I begin by taking her in my arms. We embrace, her left arm around my neck and over my left shoulder, right hand in my left hand, her cheek barely grazing mine. Our upper bodies are connected with a sense of horizontal intensity, not a pressure, not a weight, but a texture of commitment. This first embrace signals to both us that we are open to invitation, and that we will move to the constraint of the walk's structural parameters.

We walk. I am leading. But that does not mean I am deciding. Leading is more like initiating an opening, entering the gap, then following her response. How I follow, with what intensity we create the space, will influence how our bodies move together. I am not moving her, nor is she simply responding to me: we are beginning to move relationally, creating an interval that we move together. The more we connect to this becoming-movement, the more palpable the interval becomes. We begin to feel the relation.

Having both danced for many years, we embody dance, a pastness of movement that allows dance-already-danced to move through us. This is not a learning by heart. It is not a choreography. It is improvising with the already-felt. It is associated to a deep feeling of becoming-ground that we nurture as we continue to learn how to walk. Walking together feels like moving space-time. Our walk is not the walk of the toddler, where each step fulfills itself in a fall, the fall almost part of the experience of getting ahead. Ours is a walk where the interval takes on consistency. The falling-to-walk of the frustrated toddler is transformed into a sustained reaching-toward. This reaching-toward is a walking that feels like a horizontal force rather than a taking of steps, where a change of direction signals not an immanent fall but the potential to invent.

In an intimate embrace, our relational walk moves counterclockwise around the dance floor, our bodies beginning to take on the rhythm of the intervals our movement is creating. These intervals—fed by the preacceleration that is the feeling of movement-to-come—are the virtual nodes through which each initiated movement becomes the invitation of a step. In the interval, the direction we've chosen gains a texture that encourages the step to fold through movement moving. The complexity of relation translates displacements into open prearticulations. We preaccelerate to prearticulate. Displacement is hardly felt as such. When our bodies begin to fold around the interval, we know we are creating a dance.

Relational movement is always improvisational. For sustained improvisation, constraint is essential. Without the rules of walking, we could invent infinitely, but this infinity would likely be chaotic. In the chaos, the tightness of relational movement's interval would likely be dispersed. What the constraint of the walk allows is a particular texture of a shared interval. Without the interval, the very real possibility emerges that we would walk on each other's feet and lose the connection. To displace another body rather than moving the relation is to move-to rather than with. The essence of relational movement is the creation of a virtual node, an in-between that propels the dance, that in-forms the grace that is not strictly of the body but of the movement itself.

As I walk with her, the constraint of the walk holds me to a certain pattern. We create out of this pattern, asking of the interval that it fold the movement toward displacements-to-come. This folding is the transduction of a step into the reaching-toward of a directionality out of which another relational movement will be produced.

She feels the preacceleration of my movement even before I move, responding by taking a step back around me, across the front of my body. As she steps across, the velocity of a spiral feeds the becoming-movement such that we participate in a centrifugal force. With her body in my arms, moving across yet still in front, I take a small step forward, which completes the incipient spiral. This spiral is intensive—it does not move away, it moves-with. Moving-with, our bodies spin together, turning on a shared axis that emerges out of the movement itself. Grace in the making.

The language of tango—out of which this particular version of relational movement finds its consistency—identifies this centrifugal spiraling as a colgada—a hanging spiral—the interval wider at the top while our feet stay together, our centers still facing one another. Intervals are not stable. Relational movement insists on morphogenesis. I may lead you into a colgada, a hanging-out, which creates a triangular interval, closed where our feet touch, opening upward and out, or, as we hang outward together in a colgada, we may reverse it into a leaning-in, a triangular form that opens downward into an intensive ground—a volcada, centripetal.

Either way, what occurs is a qualitative reshaping of a force. Taking form through the preacceleration of the movement, and sustained by the movement itself, the interval folds into an intensive expansion, or an expansive intensity, languidly "holding" the movement. This holding is not structural: it is elastic. It is almost the next movement, almost the next axis, almost the next equilibrium, but not quite yet. This elasticity of the almost is the intensive extension of the movement, a moment when anything can happen, when our bodies are poised in a togetherness beginning to take shape. The next movement has not yet come, the past movement is passing. No step has been taken, and yet in this elastic the microperception of every possible step can almost be felt.

Folding

It is a question of the curve. In Leibniz, the curvature of the universe expresses itself in three fundamental notions: the fluidity of matter, the elasticity of bodies, elasticity as mechanism. Matter springs into curvature. Matter does not in and of itself curve: it curves because force acts upon it. We would not curve to fill the hole if there were no one in our way. "But the universe is compressed by an active force that gives matter a curvilinear or vortical movement, following a curve without tangent" (Deleuze 1988a, 8). Beyond the tangent that expresses a straight line, there is a curve replete with microtornados that produce microperceptual intervals. A curve within a curve within a curve.

As we move together, this curving can be felt. But only when we move the relation. When I begin by moving her, what I feel is resistance. I pull, push, trip. The movement becomes a series of steps we fall into, always a little early or a little late, our balance in disequilibrium, our mood darkening. Moving the relation moves not a person but the elasticity of relation. We move-with the togetherness of a curving that fields metastable equilibriums. This does not mean that we never lose our balance. It means that balance can no longer be thought as something to be lost or gained: there is no stable axis around which I lead her for us to "lose." We curve together, creating a folding interval out of which pure plastic rhythms begin to take form.

Folding undoes the finality of form. Form becomes a folding-into, a force-toward that is a threshold, a becoming-spiral, a becoming-turn, a becoming-triangle. These are forms-in-the-making, resonant only in relation to the movements they give rise to. Emergent forms are more than steps. They are porous steps—porous because unidentifiable as such ("What was that!" she will ask as the movement completes itself), yet felt. You will know that something happened, that your body became something, but the "what" of the step will rarely reveal itself as such.

It is not simply the speed of the movement that keeps form from holding to a step. It is incipient movement's wave, of which the elastic is the emergent force. As the wave forms, we feel an interval creating itself. Through the interval, we feel the elasticity, the becoming-form of a relational movement. This is a microperception, active only in transition, at the cusp of the actual. As the elasticity compresses, the impetus for becoming-form is infinite. But if we lose it by allowing its intensity to disperse, or if we want to hold onto it for too long, the elastic point of the movement will evaporate and only the step will be felt.

The labyrinths of folds virtually active in the interval are becoming-bodies of movement. They are not steps, nor can they be translated as such. They are potential directions, potential elasticities, potential preaccelerations. Separating them out is impossible. Their indivisibility is what gives the interval its intensity. Intensive movement is always populated by such microperceptions. When we move the relation, we are creating and harnessing microperceptions that express themselves (virtually) in every movement. It is not that they preexist the movement, or that they can be called forth as such. They are the potential that is felt in the incipiency of the action, the potential that transduces matter into form. Mattering-form is movement not as identifiable figuration but as intensive figure.[24] Figure as force taking form, as movement-with that shapes bodies-in-the-making.

An intensive figure does not represent. It durationally evokes. It provokes and propels. A figure is active transience from one form to another, a molecular, mattering-form that transduces. Referring to Cézanne's theory that the figure produces sensation, Deleuze writes: "The figure is the sensible form related to a sensation; it acts immediately on the nervous system, which is of the flesh" (2003, 31). Sensation is what is produced, but not a sensation of, a sensing-with and toward. Moving relationally we sense not the step per se (though we do step it, otherwise we would not walk)—we sense the intensity of an opening, the gathering up of forces toward the creation of space-times of experience into which we move. As the movement begins to fold into another movement, we feel its elasticity, opening the movement's shape to its inevitable deformation.

Deformation—topological becoming—gives relational movement its rhythm. The sensation of moving the relation is rhythmic, a topological transformation that folds to infinity. The sensation is multiple, but not multiplied. It works on many levels at once—macro- and microperceptual—operating on planes rather than in divided sequences. These planes of sensation are amorphous—they never produce a recognized feeling that can be repeated in the same way. They are felt not in their form but in their effects. Sensation is accumulated, it morphs and coagulates and disperses, always operative between levels. Sensation is in and of movement.

The in and of movement folds. Elastic, we feel the becoming-form of movement's shape. In the amodal tactility of elasticity, force is stored and then released. Elasticity acts on the movement. The release liberates the figure, not a figure that was there all along, but a figure that is virtually creating itself in the interval. Almost-virtual.

The folds of potential movement ingress into the dance. A folding-unfolding as much as an involution-evolution propulses the movement. This movement-with is alive in the associated milieu that is the interval, productive, brimming with sensation. Rhythm, the regenerative force of the associated milieu, is the transducer of sensation, the élan vital that provokes projections of sense into becoming-movement. Without rhythm, becoming-movement tends to divide and become diffuse. For relational movement, intensive rhythmic movement is key—diffusion guarantees confusion. This does not mean that we move *to* a rhythm. It means we move rhythm—that the very becoming of the movement is rhythmic.

Rhythm takes two. Moving the relation is a rhythmic encounter with a shifting interval. Rhythm moves us before we know where we are going, even when we momentarily lose our connection. A typical situation: I change my mind suddenly and move not where the pulse of preacceleration was moving the relation but where I suddenly decide I want to go. What happens: she hesitantly move not into the space I physically open, but into the opening I preaccelerated toward before leading the direction I now expect her to follow. She moves where the movement was moving us—where I thought about going—rather than where I went. Although I never actually moved where the relation was moving, she felt a kind of doubled force of movement moving and responded to its first tendency: the direction I thought I had not led. She moved into my hesitation. Of course, this is part of moving together. At best, my response will be to follow her lead, moving-with the force of the initial preacceleration into the experiential space-time I didn't think I had opened up. Rhythms are never predictable.

What we want to avoid is a falling-into. We want to nurture the elasticity of movement moving, and for that reason, we want to be in sync with the force of our relation as it develops. If we lose this intensity of force taking form, what we have first and foremost is a step.

Relational movement produces a curve or curvature. The elasticity is felt more than seen. It is an intensive curve that was never led as such, because created relationally. The law of curvature is the law of folds, and folds have a tendency to refold, to pleat, to crease, to wrinkle. As the fold compresses, what results is not necessarily a smaller movement but a more intensively compact one. This compactness produces a force that opens the movement to its taking-form. The curve does not result from the movement. The curve *is* the movement, a contraction into an elasticity that moves the relation. The body-elastic is pure plastic rhythm, the body of the between where the movement is on the verge, quasi-actual, almost virtual, hanging, pulsing, spiraling.

Inflection

The elasticity of the almost is part of the curve. It is the curve's point of inflection. "Inflection is . . . the elastic point" (Deleuze 1988a, 20). Inflection is the genetic element of the active line. It is not a hard point, nor is it a point directed from outside the movement. The elastic point is of the movement. It is that which culls from the movement's potential its becoming-form. This singularity carries the curve, is the event of the curve. This singularity is what expresses the virtual fullness of the interval, its plenitude. This plenitude is the worlding of the movement. That interval is worlding does not mean that it contains the world, but that it potentially expresses the infradimensional, which is the worlding of pure plastic rhythm.

Inflection gives expression to this worlding, and in the elasticity of its activity, it makes palpable the tangibility of sensation. As the movement perishes, preaccelerating toward the next movement, the interval fills up with the potential still languishing in the pastness of the last movement. It is not that the new movement contains the specificity of the past movement—its steps. What the new movement contains are all of the micromovements, the potential elasticities of the past movement. Movemented tendencies. Virtual events.

Inflection is inseparable from infinite variation. There is no elastic point that resides on the curve in the same way each time. The curve creates an elastic point as much as the elastic point becomes the curve. The elastic point is a traveling node along a fluctuating line that has no beginning nor end, "enveloping a world infinitely spongy and cavernous, constituting more than a line and less than a surface" (Deleuze 1988a, 23). This is not a measurable point—its elasticity makes it infinitely malleable. It is a folding point, a curvilinear detour that moves not from point to point but in an infinite circumvolution that becomes the movement itself. The interval created by relational movement is the plane of consistency of this circumvolution, elasticity the plane of composition.

The elastic point inflects the curve with an almost. This almost is the slight delay, almost imperceptible, that occurs at the interstice of the actual re-becoming virtual. The vortical force of the elasticity shapes the movement such that it becomes fully actual at the same time as it recomposes through microperceptual intensities virtually active in the interval. The elasticity of the almost is a rare instance of an almost-actualization of the microperceptual within the actual. In the elastic moment, the movement becomes more-than, enveloping in its folds all of the potential of its pastness and its futurity. This elastic becoming-actual is thus also a becoming-virtual, an inflection on the curvature of pure experience that demands that its effects be felt. In the elasticity of the almost, what is felt is the rhythmic sensation of the fullness of movement, movement beyond its actualization.

The elastic point is preemptive. It anticipates curvature. In the becoming-curve of movement, elasticity is always operative, but not always felt as such. Often, this elasticity is curtailed—for example, when a change of direction is fallen into, rather than moved into. But when it is felt, it is experienced as though after its occurrence, an "after" that is copresent with its actualization but feels differed because elastics take time. Elasticity is the durational element in the becoming-curve of movement.

In relational movement, elasticity always produces spirals. Whether these spirals are extensive movements or whether they remain intensive, force is centrifugally recombined with movement moving. The interval becomes intensively relayed with the force of the spiral, creating a turbulence that moves the relation. This can be a quiet, even serene turbulence, a graceful intensity, or it can be a wild, excessive turbulence. Either way, it envelops the contours of the steps, creating a spur, a trace of the line of flight that characterizes the displacement of the moving relation.

The elasticity of the almost shifts the associated milieu of the interval toward a field of curvature. The movement curves and the two bodies moving feel the approach as a joining of the forces of movement. The effect opens the dance to an actualization that is not a displacement per se but a virtual intensity becoming actual. We become spiral. Intensive connection. To remain in the elasticity for as long as possible is the goal—but remaining on the edge of virtuality is a challenging task. Sometimes we linger.

Lingering Events

"The world is the infinite curve that touches in an infinity of points an infinity of curves, a curve with a single variable, the convergent series of all series" (Deleuze 1988a, 34). The elastic point is eventful. It makes felt the lingering of actuality as it begins to fold back into the virtual, preaccelerating into the next becoming-movement. This lingering is part of the walk, part of its constraint—back, front, side. The infinite potential in three directions makes itself felt in the elasticity of the almost, but is as present in all of movement's stages. To improvise is to be able to pull incipient movement out of the directions, to create the elastic out of the line (that itself becomes elastic), to redirect force, and move with it. To create an event.

For an event to occur, experience has to be pulled out of the indeterminate, activated from the virtuality of the not-yet. This provocation is the event of the occasion's taking form. As we move together, an opening to the side may announce itself. This prehension is not simply a cue, it is a detail of activity that produces a tendency for a relational encounter. This relational encounter precedes cognitive understanding. Prearticulation fuels preacceleration, inciting a reaching-toward, not into a space predetermined, but toward a curving of space-time. Curving space-time moves the relation, activating a becoming-body. Movement's intensive unfolding creates an embodiment of pure plastic rhythm. The fulfillment of the occasion is not the step but the recombination of forces out of which future movements will take form.

Every new interval is the virtual node of that actual occasion. As the elasticity of the curvature makes itself felt, we feel the completion of what Whitehead calls the subjective form of the event.[25] The actualization of the subjective form marks the almost-perishing of that actual occasion because it satisfies the event. Satisfaction occurs when the event has fulfilled itself and is ready to be backgrounded into the nexus of perished actual occasions.

The event is as much vibration as action. It never fully actualizes, since the actual is always replete with the virtual. The fullness of virtuality within the movement gives it complexity. Without this, the movement would simply be a displacement, a falling into step. The event of movement moving is a quasi-virtual experience: actual because all steps actually take place, virtual because all the microperceptions of pastness and futurity are enveloped in the becoming-movement.

The elasticity of the almost is textured, its texture that of unbounded creativity. The movement's elastic point produces conjunction, but not conjunction in a one-to-one relation. What is produced is the conjunction of the one-many, of the infinity of potential series coming together. This coming-together is a concrescence. It is a growing together activated through the elastic point, not a coming together of two subjectivities or two movements, but the germ of pure experience—novelty in the making—expressing itself. "No things are 'together' except in experience; and no things *are,* in any sense of 'are,' except as components in experience or as immediacies of process which are occasions in self-creation" (Whitehead 1933, 236).

The elasticity of the almost brings together formed experience and pure experience,[26] creating a doubled event that is always either on the verge of actualization or revirtualization, at once actual and virtual. The elastic point is pure experience in relational movement. It is an actualized event in the dance, as well as an opening to a virtual suspension. As we stretch the movement (and the movement stretches us), we know that its perishing is near, and yet we flirt with this nearness. At the elastic point we find we can linger, but on its edges the spiral perishes, and we risk falling. Lingering is the pure experience of experimenting with the almost.

Perishing

Perishing is inevitable. Events are only events because they perish. It is their perishing that culminates their potential. The perishing is not the end: it propels the preacceleration of a new occasion of experience. Once the subjective form composes itself, the experience has been constituted, and the event is nearing its completion. It has done its work. To feel the elasticity is always to know we are on the edge. When the elastic contracts, we feel at once the perishing of the event and the propulsion of the next preacceleration. This is because the elastic force is as present in its stretching as in its contraction, always stimulating the intensive spiral of a new becoming-movement.

Perished actual occasions populate the nexus out of which experience is made. There is no movement that is not nested within another movement with which it is in continuity. As events become and perish, they create openings for new events. Every opening in relational movement marks the potential for an infinity of approaches. "When they perish, occasions pass from the immediacy of being into the non-being of immediacy" (Whitehead 1933, 237). Events do not perish into nothingness. Like memories, they can be reactivated. To reactivate an event is not to recreate the same movement again but to invent a new movement that calls forth a certain array of recognizable elastic points. This new movement will be virtually populated with the pastness that constitutes the experience of moving *in that way*. In relational movement, once I know that it is possible for my body to move a certain way, it is much more likely I will experiment with that way of moving. Whitehead calls these "non-beings of immediacy" that populate this feeling of knowing in relational movement *stubborn facts*. They are stubborn because we are never completely free of them. They tense up our shoulders, lock our knees. But they also teach us techniques that open up possibilities for movement that in turn become emergent potentialities, proposing entries into otherwise impossibly small holes, inviting us to move-with in ways which even yesterday we wouldn't have imagined possible.

Concern

The different planes that compose a given movement are like modes. The movement composes itself through each of these modes in its own singular way. When a mode fulfills its process, another mode takes over. In relational movement, modes would include preacceleration, intervals, spirals. The planes of movement are felt in the shifting of preacceleration toward the creation of an interval (moving the relation) through the propelling of a spiral, curving into the elastic point toward the becoming-form of the almost, leading back into preacceleration. Although there is a certain linearity in these modes, it would be a mistake to think of them divisively. Each of these modes produces the opening for the next mode, and together they constitute an event. This event produces an affective tone that gives rise to the consistency of that particular movement-experience. This affective tone is the concern—in Whiteheadian terms—for the event itself. Leader and follower are no longer individuals expressing their roles in a movement of steps: they are co-constituted by the very experience they are relationally creating. Concern is not concern for but concern with.

The event created by relational movement is not only concerned with two dancers. An occasion of experience always carries the many in the one. The modes of functioning that make the experience palpable jointly constitute its process of becoming. These modes can never be separated out from the worlding of the event: each event contains the world within it. This means that each movement-event is invested with all of the currents of worldness that have made that singular movement possible. Worldness is the future-past (the intensive background) out of which all movements-with compose. The relationality of relational movement moves the world as much as the world moves through it.

Relations are inseparable from affective tone, or concern. And affective tone is inseparable from the modes that relations create and through which relations move. The becoming-body of dance is the composition of a relation. How this becoming-body does what it can do is its concern. The body in this case is not the individual but the mattering-form that emerges through inflection's elastic point. In its taking form this becoming-body is always relational, produced in the between of the mobile relation. It is pure plastic rhythm, an intensive body.

Modes affect us. In the mode of the interval, for instance, as she and I move together, we may feel the rhythm change, propulsed by a syncopation of the music that takes hold of the in-gathering of the movement and expresses it as tight or bumpy, taking us suddenly out of a flowing interval and into a new preaccelerated movement, the elasticity of the almost not quite experienced. More than a shift in our steps, what we experience is an altered affective tone. This colors the rest of the dance. Another instance: someone nudges us from behind, infringing on the precarious metastability of our becoming-relation, creating a sudden displacement that takes over the relation, bringing on frustration and inner tension. Or, as we create an opening toward an extensive movement backward (for her) where her almost-step will transduce into a linear kick, I note with alarm that she is about to kick the wall, leading me to introduce a quick change in direction that shifts our linear energy toward an intensive curving, bringing the elastic point to the movement earlier than anticipated, curving her leg in a tight *boleo* that wraps around a shifting spiral axis we could not have foreseen. The surprise makes us smile. Improvisation makes room for all of these contingencies. Relation cannot be foretold: it must be experienced. This experience is affective. Its modes will always change, perishing when no longer relevant, opening the way for new modes that continuously affect our becoming-dance.

Becoming Elastic

The relation is always already elastic. Even a simple walk can feel elastic when the movement carries us, when the goal is not the first thing on our mind. The elasticity of the relation is perceptible in its affective margin, in the emergence of the unknowable where what is felt stretches and contracts into a propulsion of experience toward the unfathomable. Every event is in some sense imbued with such virtual curvature. What relational movement can do is make this elasticity felt, actualize it in an almost-form that takes shape in its incipient deformation.

Relational movement depends on a fluid assemblage that operates always in the between of constraint and improvisation. Each mode acts both as constraint and opening. "We do not even know of what affections we are capable, nor to the extent of our power," writes Spinoza. "How could we know this in advance?" (qtd. in Deleuze 1990a, 226). Concern is movement's capacity to propel experience to its transmutational potential. Modes emerge and shift according to the requirements of the relation, altering the relation and opening it to new modes. Modes in this sense can be thought of as techniques of relation. These techniques of relation are operational in the sense that they open the way for relation to be experienced. "While a mode exists, its very essence is open to variation, according to the affections that belong to it at a given moment" (Deleuze 1990a, 225–226).

Techniques of relation produce events. Every event is relational. Events create relation as much as relation creates events. We cannot know in advance what an event can do, any more than we can know what a body can do. Spinoza's question will remain unanswered: to know of what a body is capable would be to divest a body of its elasticity. The essence of a technique of relation is not its content per se but its capacity to become more-than and to create more-than. "A conatus is indeed a mode's essence (or degree of power) once the mode has begun to exist. A mode comes to exist when its extensive parts are extrinsically determined to enter into the relation that characterizes the mode; then, and only then, is its essence itself determined as a conatus" (Deleuze 1990a, 230). Conatus is an affirmative existence, a way of creating a more-than that is not added to the mode but is part of its technique. To create more-than is to move beyond what it seemed a body could do: to transduce a body toward pure plastic rhythm. This striving is not goal-directed. It is a reaching-toward the capacity to inhabit the almost-virtual of the more-than of experience. This more-than will always be the production of a new actual occasion, the creation of a pure experience out of which a world will emerge. Moving the relation is a striving toward the ineffable experience of the elasticity of the almost.

Interlude: A Mover's Guide to Standing Still

"It is more difficult to stand than to move" (Feldenkrais 1981, 44). Standing still is a metastable activity: the stillness demands precise adaptation to the micro-movements of a shifting equilibrium. To stand still you have to move.

Everyone sways. You may think you're standing still, but actually you're drifting, shifting slightly to the left, your ankle twitching as your weight moves to the ball of your foot, your knee bending slightly as you take in a breath. As Bruce Schechter noted after trying to measure the stillness of people standing: "It doesn't matter whether you are feeble or fit, the fact is you have never stood stock still in your life" (2001, n.p.). Standing still requires constant correction. These are not conscious corrections. They are virtual micromovements that move through the feeling of standing still. When these micromovements are felt as such, they take over the event of standing, and you experience co-contraction: you lose your balance.

Stillness is always on its way to movement. When you stand still, you don't feel the "how" of movement stilling unless you're asked to feel the stillness. Then you find you can't stop thinking about how you're moving. You feel your wobbly ankle, your thoughts moving, your nose itching, your back aching. All you really want to do is move through the movement. Not that surprising, then, that when J. J. Collins and C. J. de Luca asked participants to stand still, they found that the foot's center of pressure "wriggl[ed] around like a demented eel" (qtd. in Schechter 2001, n.p.).

Standing still is often associated to posture. "Stand still!" sounds to me like "Stand up straight!" Yet, like "stillness," posture is elusive. Posture is less a stopping of movement than a passing-through. If standing still is a shifting between thousands of micromovements in the making, posture is how its incipient action is felt.

Moshe Feldenkrais defines posture as "dynamic equilibrium." He suggests that posture is how we move *through*. Posture is how we carry our movement stilling. This movement stilling is allied to the movements of experiential space-time. We move with the reaching-toward of experience as it moves us.

Posture is not a stopping. It is a stilling of the between of the body's reconfigurations in extensive and intensive space-time. "Between one displacement and the next there is always a moment when the body is, practically speaking, not changing position significantly" (Feldenkrais 1981, 47). Every shift depends on a moving-through. Posture is the quality of the moving-through. It is not a position, not something to aim for or to attain: it is a movement with movement reconfiguring. For Feldenkrais, the relative immobility of the betweenness of posture is not something associated only with humans. All animals have this quality as part of their movement reconfigurations. Feldenkrais calls it "the special characteristic of a given body" (1981, 47).

Asking you to stand still is like asking you to become aware of your special characteristic. Why does it feel so punitive? Perhaps because we think we should not move. Because we believe we should have the capacity to stop. But we can't. And so we move, and we try to hide that moving by ignoring the movement moving. But the more we ignore the movement within stillness, the more we lose our balance. To be balanced is in fact to move with micromovements moving. In Feldenkrais's terms, it is to become aware of how our special characteristic moves-with our body moving. "All species of animals have a characteristic form of posture, which usually we think of as standing, although dynamically this is the configuration of the body from which any act is made" (Feldenkrais 1981, 48). Dynamically speaking, we can still standing. As long as we keep moving through posture. Moving through movement stilling means dancing posture's small dance.[27]

A posture is a quality of movement stilling that infects moving. The strange thing about posture is that you can only alter it from within a movement moving. If you try to stop the movement, you don't get a single posture, you get a multitude of micropostures that move in tandem with the rejigging of micromovements. Stopping is virtually impossible.

Posture is less a stance than a tendency of momentariness. It is a metastable stilling that leads toward a spinal spiral around which all movement turns. You never reach it once and for all. Posture is a dynamic that is co-constitutive of the body's tendencies for reconfiguration. That's why there is no ideal posture: if the tendency of your intensive movement is a fidget or a squirm, the quality of your posture will itself be a squirm in the making. Neither can a posture be an end-point. Beware of those who tell you to improve your posture. They're probably the same ones who told you to stand still.

Posture is the intensive magnitude of a movement-forming. It is not the incipiency of a movement as much as the passing-through toward that incipiency. It is the zero-point of absolute movement, the quasi chaos on the cusp of an incipient change in direction.

When we move, we move around the posture's quasi-chaotic center. It is quasi-chaotic because it contains in their incipiency all of the tendencies for reconfiguration of a movement moving. The most frequent movement for which a standing body prepares itself is a movement around. This turning around the spinal axis will generally revolve around a whole body moving. If the head turns, the shoulders will follow, and then the hips, the knees, the feet. This seemingly organic movement can take many surprising forms. Anywhere along the way, the incipient nextness can be dislodged, and the movement's equilibrium can be altered. "The preliminary ingredient movements do not usually evoke the final act" (Feldenkrais 1981, 93). The quasi chaos of the movement's immanent centering is itself a change of equilibrium, an individuating of the becoming-body of the movement.

Part of what keeps movement out of equilibrium is the way it worlds. Every movement is not simply of the body but moves-with the associated milieu of the body-world nexus that enfolds it. Reaching-toward can be a trip as much as it can be a touch. "It is not always at all easy to decide whether a particular movement has originated as an immediate response to a provocation from the environment, or if we ourselves have initiated the stream of motor activity" (Feldenkrais 1981, 139).

Standing still makes felt the incipient force of micromovements reconfiguring the body's stilling. Since we're not so busy getting somewhere, we can feel our movement moving still. The feeling of losing our balance is amplified by the quietening of the reconfiguration. This is not yet consciousness of a movement. What we experience are virtual forces recombining, microperceptions shifting. Consciousness comes after the fact, when we realize we've lost our balance. A shift in space-time makes us aware of the displacement. We know what we've felt when we are no longer in the feeling.

If we were conscious of the quality of our movement—our posture—passing through every reconfiguration of the body moving, we wouldn't move much. We would be too busy tweaking our movement as it was happening. In fact, we would be trying to stop-start the movement, getting in the way of the reconfigurations of the pure plastic rhythm of movement moving. It would be like trying to get at the force of movement to alter its trajectory by holding it back.

Moving with movement requires an altered idea of consciousness. This consciousness is not of the body but with the body moving. This is what Feldenkrais and Paxton call "awareness," a feeling-with of the body moving. This feeling-with is a virtual dance. It is too quick for conscious thought, and yet it composes with it as a layering of felt experience in the making. As José Gil writes: "The immanence of body awareness emerges on the surface of consciousness and henceforth constitutes its essential element" (2006, n.p.).

We are aware of the quality of our movement without being conscious of it. You might ask: what about pain? Aren't we conscious of pain when it "gets in the way" of our movement moving? Pain produces a shift in awareness that makes us conscious of how we can't move, but this consciousness is not of the movement per se. It is consciousness of how movement hurts. This awareness interrupts the intensive magnitude of a durational attitude. Pain shifts the texture of a movement. It makes the quality of the movement felt: a particular intensity in the durational attitude of the movement has differentiated itself. We feel the safe parameters of movement moving and resist those that cause a resurgence of pain. The negative of the movement has made the movement's edge appear for consciousness. As Whitehead writes: "The negative perception is the triumph of consciousness" (1929/1978, 161).

For Whitehead, consciousness is always felt after the fact. Consciousness is a recollection of a movement having moved. We cannot be conscious of posture as such because it is a durational attitude of a becoming-movement. It is the breath of movement's in-gathering. The quality of posture is expressed virtually in the displacement that follows. Posture is the threshold, the incipient grace, the texture that contributes to having known what it felt like to move. It has a consistency, which explains why other people can recognize postural tendencies when they watch you move. But you cannot know it as such because how you move movement is not something you are conscious of.

To be conscious of movement is to have known that movement moved you. Movement felt is available to consciousness only in terms of how it was left behind as a trace for the next movement moving. We are conscious of our lower back pain, not in terms of how we pass through posture, but in terms of how that pain incites us to invent new ways of moving. We are conscious of how that pain keeps us from moving solely out of habit.

"Consciousness flickers, and even at its brightest, there is a small focal region of clear illumination, and a large penumbral region of experience which tells of intense experience in dim apprehension" (Whitehead 1929/1978, 267). To have known what it felt like to feel pain is not the same as to have known how it altered our movement moving. The recombinations are infinite. We now move with new composite tendencies that realign the taking form of the moving body. Consciousness is of the pain, and of the lack of pain. Consciousness is how the irradiation of experience gathers itself into a final form. This final form is not the experience as a whole. It is what Whitehead calls the *acme of emphasis.*

Standing still foregrounds the quality of the activity of relation of micromovements necessary in the stilling of the body's temptation to lose its balance. Losing balance is the quickest way to get moving. Find the balance moving, and move with the imbalance as it corrects itself. Feel the quality of the movement, its tendencies, its potential directionalities. Create an instable body, an elastic stance. Be aware of movement coursing through the stillness. Feel the dynamism of the force of movement beginning to take form. Call this incipient action.

3 Taking the Next Step

Walking is all about taking the next step. Walking is never one-off: the momentum of the last step feeds the advance into the next one. To take the next step is to step with the feeling of walking. To step with the feeling of how we are already moving is to move-with the immanent activation of the senses spacing. This means that we walk with, as well as within, the environment perceived relationally.

To take the next step is to move-with the interval produced by preacceleration, to feel-with the shape-shifting of smells encroaching, to hear-with the wall's approach. This feeling-with is proprioceptive, immediately linked to our sense of balance, to our ability to space space. We don't need to put our hands on the walls to feel them, or to touch the ground to know where it is. Touch crossed with vision and sound fields the environment, opening it to the relational multiplicity of movement, sensation, and space-time co-mingling. Even walking alone is replete with relation: we move-with the feeling of the ground as it expands toward the pelvis, giving into the weight of gravity's pull, participating kinesthetically in the shifting dynamics of one leg grounding at a time. We move-with the edge of a room approaching or the horizon line receding. To take the next step is to move-with the world.

But what if we cannot *begin* to move? This is the case with the post-encephalitic patients Oliver Sacks describes in his book *Awakenings*. These patients are characterized by their incapacity to activate displacement without assistance.[28] In the worst stages of their disease, these patients seem catatonic, completely incapable of making contact with the outside world.

Take the case of Hester Y. At the age of thirty, Hester began to feel the effects of post-encephalitis lethargica syndrome. At first, Hester experienced a simple loss of flow: "She would be walking or talking with a normal pattern and flow, and then *suddenly*, without warning, would come to a stop—in mid-stride, mid-gesture, or the middle of a word; after a few seconds she would resume speech and movement, apparently unaware that any interruption had occurred" (Sacks 1990, 95). Because of the progressive nature of the disease, soon Hester could no longer auto-resume the flow. Then for decades Hester was immobilized with a blank and vacuous expression on her face.

What Oliver Sacks found when he started to work with Hester and others suffering from post-encephalitic syndrome at Mount Carmel hospital in 1965 was that these patients could in fact move. They just couldn't do it by themselves. To move, they had to be activated. One of Sack's hypotheses was that he was dealing with an acute kind of Parkinsonism, whereby the usual symptomatic "shaking" was translated into immobility. It was as though the shaking had become so severe as to result in a total freezing of the body. The encephalitis lethargica patients' need to be activated by "outside" stimuli suggested to Sacks that auto-activation had been damaged by the neurological disease as it often is in Parkinsonian patients, albeit on a lesser scale.[29]

There is an important difference to be made between movement and auto-activation, especially if activation is linked to displacement. According to their own accounts, Sacks's patients do not associate the "catatonic" phase of the disease with a total loss of movement. What they experience seems to be closer to absolute movement—a degree-zero of movement—than to a complete stopping. Absolute movement as they describe it is movement without auto-activation. They feel movement, but cannot translate the feeling into displacement. In their "frozen" states, this absoluteness becomes severe inertia.

Inertia is the property of a body by virtue of which it tends to persist in a state of rest or uniform motion unless it is acted upon by an external force. Inertia does not imply a total loss of movement: it suggests an inability to activate a change in state. An inertial body is still moving, but its movement is absolute: movement without punctuation or change in degree. Absolute movement is the complete smoothness of movement, felt as a loss of differentiation of space or time.

In Hester's early years of post-encephalitic syndrome, she could be brought out of her inertia by "the merest touch . . . which served to dissipate these states, and to permit immediate resumption of movement and speech" (Sacks 1990, 95–96). At this stage in her disease, her inertia was in line with an extreme form of what most people experience at one time or another. All bodies tend toward a certain degree of inertia: it is not uncommon to find ourselves dazed by a television screen. Or to find it difficult to "snap out" of a daydream or get out of bed in the morning.[30] The difference between Hester's case and ours is the movement's ability to auto-activate change. Auto-activation—the habitual capacity to change direction, speed, state—is something we generally take for granted. Able-bodied people tend not to question their ability to take the next step.[31]

But people like Hester who suffer Parkinsonian symptoms as a result of contracting encephalitis lethargica can no longer take auto-activation for granted. Activation must come from outside, usually with someone else's assistance.[32] This can occur in different ways. For example, if you throw Hester a ball, she will catch it, even when apparently "immobilized." If you place her in front of stairs or other landscape affordances she may suddenly be able to climb. But place her in an open space and she will stay stock-still. On her own, especially where experiential space-time is "smooth," Hester cannot move.

As with all states of inertia, what is necessary is a force coming from elsewhere. In most of us, this "elsewhere" need not be initiated by someone else: it is embedded in habits of movement. It is important to distinguish here between the idea of willing movement (i.e., I want to move) and moving through habits of movement (i.e., moving through a future-pastness that is already welling in our capacity to move). Think of morning inertia. What gets you from your quasi-awake state out of bed? The thought of coffee likely gets you moving. Coffee propels you through the frozen state into auto-activation, stimulating something akin to the taste of being awake. You move without giving another thought to the challenge of taking the next step. Coffee's on your mind.

Not so with post-encephalitic patients. Nothing can make them think their way from absolute movement to displacement. Perception has been damaged such that a thought gets them nowhere. Rose R. explains:

> Whatever I do or whatever I think leads deeper and deeper into itself. . . . Everything I do is a map of itself, everything I do is a part of itself, every part leads into itself. . . . I've got a thought in my mind, and then I see something in it, like a dot on the skyline. It comes nearer and nearer, and then I see what it is—it's just the same thought I was thinking

> before. And then I see another dot, and another, and so on. . . . Or I think of a map; then a map of that map, and each map is perfect, though smaller and smaller. . . . Worlds within worlds within worlds. . . . Once I get going I can't possibly stop. It's like being caught between mirror, or echoes, of something. Or being caught in a merry-go-round which won't come to a stop. (qtd. in Sacks 1990, 76n54)

Thought implodes, getting in the way of the potential for release into movement. There is no past or future here. With thought constantly folding-in, the potentiality for an elsewhere folds into itself, becoming yet another fold in the process toward infinite infolding. In the end, there is not even the capacity to *conceive* of an "elsewhere." Absolute movement: the incapacity to experience the transduction from incipiency to activation.

When Hester entered Mount Carmel hospital in her thirty-sixth year, she descended into an almost constant "immobile" state. After meeting Hester in 1966, Sacks realized with dismay "that it [was] possible for Parkinsonism and catatonia to reach an infinite degree of severity" (Sacks 1990, 97). Sacks describes his meeting with Hester as a realization of the "infinite nature," "the qualitative infinity" of post-encephalitis under the most dire conditions. This encounter leads Sacks to theorize that the immobility of encephalitis lethargica is a kind of layering of infinitudes of inertial quasi states. He writes:

> It suddenly came to me that Parkinsonism was a propensity, a tendency—which had no minimum, no maximum, and no finite units; that it was anumerical from its first infinitesimal intimation or twinge, that it could proceed by an infinite multitude of infinitesimal increments to an infinite, and then more infinite, and still more infinite, degree of severity. And that its "least part," so to speak, possessed (in infinitesimal form) the entire, indivisible nature of the whole. (Sacks 1990, 97n63)

Because of the severity of her condition, Hester's "awakening" is particularly striking, not least because of her remarkable ability to articulate states unimaginable to those of us who have no trouble getting moving. One of the aspects of her disease Hester describes is the experience of the "smoothness" of space during her "catatonic" states. Smoothness for Hester is akin to having "no sense of process of forces or field" (qtd. in Sacks 1990, 112n71). Standing in for the propelling force of activation is a flatness, an uninterrupted vista of nothingness, an infinitely slowed-down movie experience that she can but watch passively "like a movie film which is running too slow" (1990, 112n71). Hester describes herself as inertially alive in her movie-world but incapable of relating to an "elsewhere." The only option left: to replay her movie in slow-motion in an inward-folding account of the same nowhere again and again to infinity.

Sensing is a topological activity. When we sense, we experience and create folds of space-time. We sense on top of senses, one sense-experience always embedded in another: cross-modal repetition with a difference. For example, when we walk toward a wall, we perceive that wall as limiting our potential displacement, but as we approach it, it also appears as being a certain color or texture. We sense its presence in ways both causal (directly relational) and perceptually nuanced.

The inertia Hester experiences in her frozen state is a topological implosion of perception without the causal relations that would connect her surroundings to an "elsewhere." To connect (to) environments is to directly perceive the environment's relation to our moving body. When implosion occurs—an inertia at the level of the infinitesimal—it becomes impossible to sense-with. There is no toward to which to relate. Frozen, encephalitis lethargica patients are in a constant, immanent state of sense implosion.

Hester describes this imploding universe as akin to looking through a stained-glass window refracted at odd angles in an infinity of opaque layers. What Hester describes is the immanence of the absoluteness of movement infolding. Sense-presentation takes over, relegated to a regressive passivity, a taking-in that becomes an observation of infinite refraction. Causal links are increasingly distant. Taking the place of relational networks is a kind of memory of sense, a "pure," undifferentiated sensing rather than a sensing-with. There is nowhere to go but in.

In their process of "awakening," especially when it becomes apparent that levodopa (L-dopa) is not a wonder drug that will unproblematically continue to work long-term, many of Sacks's patients begin to invent techniques to keep the infolding at bay. In their "immobilized" states, as described earlier, their experience of space is one of overwhelming smoothness. This smoothness curtails their ability to find or create landmarks. To counter the encroachment of smooth space, they devise ways to create an experience of striation that assists them when they feel the encroachment of inertia. These techniques are modes of bringing space-time into relation.

The key to auto-activation is change. To move, we need space-time to appear, to make itself felt as such. The danger of infinite smoothness is precisely that there is no appearance, no "standing out." Without it, nothing can be felt as such: the field of perception flattens. In this eternal smoothness, what is left is hardly more than the "nothing" of Rose's "just the same thought as I was thinking before. . . . Worlds within worlds within worlds" (qtd. in Sacks 1990, 76n54).

The question is: what activates perception in such a way that it incites us to *take* the next step? Whitehead has an answer. He believes that what activates our capacity to world is *causal efficacy* as completed through what he calls *symbolic reference*.[33] Causal efficacy is the stage of perception that refers to the immanent relationality of all experience. When Hester talks about her sense of there being no space-time in her frozen state, she is referring to a lack of the immediacy of relation. The motivation for taking the next step is relation: there has to be a force toward which to connect. This force is not a decision in the sense of an individual wanting to move. It is a relational encounter with the immediacy of pastness working in the present. To move is to move-with the experience of movement moving. It is to feel-with the incipiency of preacceleration.

Relation in its incipiency is a field of force. This force acts causally on the sensing body in movement, dispersing its inertia. Relation is causal in the sense that it preempts a connection. Hester cannot walk in a "smooth" open space because there is nothing to preempt auto-activation. But when there is a boulder in front of her, she can climb over it. This is because the boulder striates the otherwise open or smooth space, provoking auto-activation by bringing space-time into focus. The boulder makes the injunction to move felt in a way that open space cannot.

In their frozen states, such activators are necessary for post-encephalitic patients. The causal efficacy at the heart of activation seems to have gone missing. While they know how to move, they have no capacity to *get moving*—they are missing the relational field that brings motion into action. They sense, and yet their sense perceptions seem to know no bounds. Inwardly convulsed within absolute movement, their prehensions of sensa fold into themselves. Neurologically, the "with" seems to be blocked. Without causal efficacy, moving-with the world worlding is impossible.

Causal efficacy activates the how of experience. It is non-sensuous in that it builds on pastness: it is "heavy with the contact of the things gone by, which lay their grip on our immediate selves" (Whitehead 1927, 44). This experience of pastness folds into a relational presentness that gives experience the breadth that opens it to activation. Through causal efficacy, we immediately feel our connectedness to the world in its present appearance. This explains why, for most of us, taking the next step is not an issue. We know the ground is there: we trust our capacity to gauge space. We walk easily with the implicit knowledge of the intrinsic relation between body, ground, and space-time. We move through movement moving. The pastness of experience has taught us how to feel the approach of a wall, to immediately know whether there is room to continue moving. We don't have to consider where the ground is. We feel the cliff's edge coming into appearance. We intuitively know how to field space-time because space-time appears to us as a fold of relation. This fold makes sense to us: we find our movement through it. This does not mean that we don't make mistakes—sometimes our sense of space skews, and we walk into a mirror, or we miss a step and fall, or we trip over a wrinkle in the carpet. But generally, causal efficacy provides us with an immediate sense of how things go together.

When causal efficacy is missing, as it seems to be with post-encephalitic patients, there's nowhere to go but still. It is impossible to gear into activation without the causal relations that make space-time tangible. Sacks's patients are overwhelmed by an undifferentiated otherworldliness that takes in the complex qualities of experience without being able to connect them to one-another—otherworldly, because the frozen state occludes the very concept of worlding. With L-dopa, the perceptual experience of causal efficacy suddenly seems available, and displacement becomes possible. Neurologically, L-dopa seems to return to the patients this lost ability to field relation. But without first being "awakened," this capacity of Sacks's patients to activate relation is limited to the infinitely nuanced but, for them, infuriatingly timeless experience of what Whitehead calls *presentational immediacy*, the state where perception is ensconced in the perception of perception.

Presentational immediacy works at the perceptual levels of complexity and subtlety, gauging patterns and contrasts. By itself, it *does* nothing.[34] "This mode of perception, taken purely by itself, is barren, because we may not directly connect the qualitative presentations of other things with any intrinsic characters of those things" (Whitehead 1927, 23). To reach the stage of full perception, presentational immediacy must recombine with causal efficacy: "Every actual thing is something by reason of its activity; whereby its nature consists in its relevance to other things, and its individuality consists in its synthesis of other things so far as they are relevant to it" (Whitehead 1927, 25). In presentational immediacy, activity is restricted to self-reference.

Symbolic reference, the culmination of perception into relational synthesis, occurs when the modes of causal efficacy and presentational immediacy overlap and intertwine, when the direct action of relation is experienced alongside the qualities evoked through perceptual morphogenesis. The folding of presentational immediacy into causal efficacy and vice versa captures the eventness of experience both as that which participates in the nuances of sensing and as the immediateness of relation. Causal efficacy provides the datum for presentational immediacy, and presentational immediacy propels the immediate givenness of the causal event toward the complexity of lived experience.

Without the two together, we cannot fully participate in experience. The world flattens when causal relationality falls out of it, becoming "stained glass windows." What is experienced is not a worlding but an infinite refraction of colored glass. It's like a sensory overload without anywhere to fold but in, infinitely. Miss T explains: "I can do nothing alone. I can do anything with—with music or people to help me. I cannot initiate, but I can fully share . . . The moment you go away I am nothing again" (qtd. in Sacks 1990, 61). What is missing in this case is the capacity to auto-link sensation to worlding. Techniques of recombination fail to extend beyond the infolding sensa enveloping her.

In the state of "awakeness" or activation, symbolic reference appears fully functional in Sack's post-encephalitic patients. "By symbolic reference the various actualities disclosed respectively by the two modes are either identified, or are at least correlated together as interrelated elements in our environment" (Whitehead 1927, 17). Key to symbolic reference is the overlapping of perception and relation. The overlapping of perception and relation can be conceptualized as the force of habit, as long as we consider habits to be event-forming. Habits are not pure reiteration: they are repetition with a difference. Through habit, we move through movement again. This moving through movement always brings with itself a new series of relational networks. Conjunctive potential mixed with sense experience makes every perception an event.

"Awake," post-encephalitic patients are clearly within the complex realm of symbolic reference. This is demonstrated through the patients' capacity not only to articulate the astonishing aspects of their various states but also to invent ingenious techniques to bring causal efficacy into presentational immediacy such that they can continue to benefit from symbolic reference. Frances D. describes one such technique. She explains that even on L-dopa, she has a tendency to refreeze in certain spaces, such as the long corridor of the hospital. To de-freeze herself,[35] she carries a supply of small paper balls. As she feels herself begin to slip into inactivation, she drops a ball. The ball has a double function: it striates the long, otherwise "smooth" corridor, bringing the corridor into the space-time of relation that permits her to take the next step, *and* it allows her to keep moving in the awakeness of the reacquired state of symbolic reference. One ball can act on more than one step.

Smoothness does not carry within itself the possibility for change. When perception works, smooth space is "constantly being translated, transversed into a striated space; striated space is constantly being reversed, returned to a smooth space" (Deleuze and Guattari 1987, 474). When it doesn't, as with Frances D., only the feeling of smoothness remains. This feeling is associated with "an amorphous, nonformal space" that "one occupies without counting," a space without break or module, "an intensive rather than extensive space, one of distances, not of measures and properties" (Deleuze and Guattari 1987, 477–479).

Frances D.'s space-striators awaken her to the complexity of space striating, triggering causal efficacy: their "tiny whiteness" immediately "incite" or "command" her to take the next step (Sacks 1990, 63). But these striators by themselves do not cause her to move. They create the conditions for the relation movement-body-space to rejig into activation. This propels into motion the inertia that is beginning to set in, transducing absolute movement into preacceleration into displacement. Space striators are techniques for moving through movement for those who have lost their capacity to world. They can take the form of music, a loud-ticking watch, horizontal lines drawn on the floor, balls thrown, an obstacle course, a boulder, stairs. Anything that intercepts the seeming emptiness of smooth space potentially works. Because to freeze, according to Lillian T., is "to freeze in empty spaces" (Sacks 1990, 63n47).

Smooth space feels empty: it mimics the infolding space-time of extreme Parkinsonism. "Many of the symptoms and features of Parkinsonism, especially 'freezing,' are due to getting stuck in a Parkinsonian emptiness or vacuum. Stuckness gives rise to more stuckness, or paralysis, or entrancement of attention—on there being . . . no proper object for attention" (Sacks 1990, 63n47). There being no discrete appearance for perception is the felt-effect of dwelling in presentational immediacy, where infinities of nuance take hold and go nowhere. To feel without the capacity to do is to be imprisoned in the midst of sensa without the capacity to make connections. Connections come from past recombinations activated in a present. These recombinations are techniques for relation that activate experience even as they add to it.

When symbolic reference occurs, a worlding takes place. This worlding can lead to false premises: the very fact that it *can* be delusional is a key aspect of symbolic reference. Perceptions can mislead us—the bump on the floor may turn out to be a cat. This capacity for delusion gives our worlds shape. Within the flatness of smooth space, delusion is non-existent. What takes over is a repetition of the same, an overwhelming nowness that becomes a nothingness. Because nothing ever changes, nothing ever develops. Rose calls this the "flatness of nothing." This nothing is the effect of presentational immediacy folding in on itself absolutely, resulting in an affectless layering of bare sensa. In a dialogue with Sacks, Rose explains.

Sacks: But how can you possibly think of nothing?
Rose: It's dead easy, once you know how. . . . One way is to think about the same thing again and again. Like 2=2=2=2; or, I am what I am what I am what I am . . . It's the same thing with my posture. My posture continually leads to itself. Whatever I do or whatever I think leads deeper and deeper into itself. (Sacks 1990, 76n54)

Without symbolic reference, experience empties. It is not only nothing: it feels like nothing.

When auto-activation ceases, time stops. Infolding toward emptiness, the frozen Rose feels no link to a past because to feel that past, it would have to be activated. She would have to think new thoughts. But this is precisely what she cannot do. She can only re-think or re-feel the absoluteness of her inertia. The vastness of that smoothness lulls her into an even deeper nothing in which sensa are present but not directly perceived. Process without event.[36]

In presentational immediacy there is neither past nor future, which is why Whitehead stresses the need for the continual interfolding of causal efficacy and presentational immediacy. "The how of our present experience must conform to the what of the past in us" (Whitehead 1927, 57). Symbolic reference takes us back to the relation out of which a symbol is created. This return is "almost automatic but not quite . . . The imperative instinctive conformation to the influence of the environment has been modified" (Whitehead 1927, 66). Symbolic reference connects thought to experience, creating a field for auto-activation. "Such symbolism makes connected thought possible by expressing it, while at the same time it automatically directs action" (Whitehead 1927, 66).[37] Symbolic reference brings relationality to the fore through direct, symbolically conditioned action akin to the taste of being awake coffee provokes.

"Symbolically conditioned action is action which is . . . conditioned by the analysis of the perceptive mode of causal efficacy effected by symbolic transference from the perceptive mode of presentational immediacy" (Whitehead 1927, 80). To perceive is not simply to get to know the world but to activate it and to field it, in one and the same motion. If all we have is presentational immediacy, we are stuck with a portion of presented duration with which nothing can be *done*. We sense to sense to sense. There is nowhere to go, nothing to do. "The conscious analysis of perception is primarily concerned with the analysis of the symbolic relationship between the two perceptive modes" (Whitehead 1927, 81). When nothing new can be thought, negative knowings abound. Rose explains, "I think a thought and it's suddenly gone—like having a picture whipped out of its frame. . . . I have a particular idea, but can't keep it in mind; and then I lose the general idea, and then the general idea of general idea; and in two or three jumps my mind is blank—all my thoughts are gone, blanked out or erased" (qtd. in Sacks 1990, 76n54).

To "know negatively" is to proceed backwards from presentational immediacy into its infernal decomposition toward nothingness. It is to experience presentational immediacy without the relationships set up by causal efficacy, to apply the disparate onto the disparate, the qualitative onto the qualitative, ad infinitum. This infinite infolding means that there is never any "satisfaction" of the actual occasion. Never any completion to an event. What is sensed is sensed as bare sensa without altering the body-world relation, and thus without limit. All event means no event.

When you take the next step, something has happened. Movement has shifted from incipiency toward displacement. The event has taken form, leaving an opening for the next actual occasion. The next actual occasion will build on certain aspects of what just happened, even while it recomposes into new configurations. The causality of perception does not mean that the next actual occasion will be the same. It means that the event of taking the last step makes ingress into the experience of taking the next step. It means your walk moves through movement moving: symbolic reference. To take the next step, you need to feel the experience of relation recomposing beyond the inertia of being. Taking the next step gathers force for becoming.

Dancing the Technogenetic Body

4

Explorations of new technologies and dance, led by Mark Coniglio, Scott de Lahunta, Antonio Camurri, and others, have often focused on the difficulty of locating gesture-as-such. One key to developing sensitive software is understanding—and embedding into the software program—what a gesture is. In a 2006 paper, Scott de Lahunta suggests that the best way of coming to an understanding of gesturality is to work collaboratively with dancers such that "the choreographic and computational processes are both informed by having arrived at this shared understanding of the constitution of movement."[38] A similar tendency is expressed by Mark Coniglio when he suggests that live performance work must "delve beyond direct mapping and the metaphor of a musical instrument; to building systems that could better sense qualities of movement; to represent something of the 'gestalt' of movement."[39]

An engagement with technology and dance demands an encounter with the syntax of the moving body. For the practitioners of dance and technology, the exploration of movement is intrinsically related to how to locate where a movement begins and ends in order to map its coordinates within a sensitive system. Yet the questions "What is a gesture?" and "How can the computer recognize one?" may not actually lead in the direction proposed by Coniglio and de Lahunta. Rather, it may direct the techno-dance process toward establishing a kind of grammar of movement that would—paradoxically—be more likely to tie the body to some preestablished understanding of how it actualizes. "Mapping" gesture risks breaking movement into bits of assimilable data, replicating the very conformity the computer-dancer interface is seeking to get beyond.

Instead of attempting to map gesture, this chapter therefore begins somewhere else. It explores the potential of the *wholeness* of movement, including its "unmappable" virtuality. The unmappable—within a computer software program—is the aspect of movement I call preacceleration, a tendency toward movement through which a displacement takes form. Due to gesture's implicit relationship with displacement, vocabularies of gesture tend to overlook preacceleration. A focus on gesture (defined as extensive displacement of body parts divisible from a wholeness of movement) tends to lose sight of movement's incipiency, thus overlooking the virtual opening these sensitive technologies wish to encounter. If a vocabulary of gesture is to be reclaimed as part of what can be stimulated in the encounter between dance and new technology, I believe it must be done through the continuum of movement, through the body's emergence in the realm of the virtual becoming of preacceleration. Rather than molding the body to the measure of motion-detecting technology, I propose we begin with pure plastic rhythm, situating the sensing body in movement in a mutating matrix of technological becoming. Let's call this body-emergent technogenetic.

Scene 1: The Dance

A dancer walks across the stage. She wears sensors on her arm. Behind her is a large screen. Connected wirelessly is a software program that orchestrates input and output according to a computational relationship between displacement and its convergence into sound and video. As she moves, the software generates a reaction in the environment. To be detected, the movement has to actualize. The movement must be registered by the program as a gesture-in-itself. It must become a displacement. Preacceleration cannot be detected by the software. An extensive movement is therefore necessary, usually a displacement either of a limb or of the whole body across space. Depending on the software, this movement triggers an image or recomposes a sound (slows it down, speeds it up, generates it). This usually happens in the "real time" of the dancer's movement. The spectator is thus invited to participate in an intermedia experiment.

The challenge is how to keep the participant's attention on the quality of the movement. In a situation where the dance modulates sound and image in real time based on extrinsic movements of a dancing body, attention tends to shift from the qualitative to the quantitative. Because of the system's prosthetic apparatus and its emphasis on subjecting the dancing body to its predefined parameters, the participant's attention tends to be drawn to the workings of the system rather than to the movement's microperceptual qualities. We catch not the dancer's preacceleration in its present-passing, but the ways in which her movement stimulates a transformation of the video image. We want to know when and how the music is modulated and due to which kind of displacement. We watch the dancer for this shift, trying to locate the specificities of the technology and its gestural syntax. This concern for the technology soon situates the dancing body on the techno-dance stage as a preformed organism onto which the technology is grafted. The question shifts from "what can a body do" to "what can technology do." This experience of the dance performance is directly related to the limits of the system. The body movement is reduced to bits. Gestures become data for technology rather than contributing to movement's experiential wholeless. Attention is distracted from the subtleties of pure plastic rhythm. What stands out is actualized displacement in the service of the software.

Such a dance-event is typical of many of those situated at the nexus of dance and new technologies.[40] In such cases, technological experimentation involves a body whose movements trigger a system that can read certain kinds of displacements and translate them. These technological systems operate prosthetically and are often attached to the human body. They operate on the basis of the more-than, "enhancing" a dancing body's capacity to create space-times of experience. These dance/new technology experiments emphasize how digital technology can foreground previously untapped dimensions of the moving body, creating a body that is sensually emergent, alive with image and sound. But are these new technologies really opening up the body to its technogenetic potential? Can the vocabulary of the prosthetic re-generate the moving body toward sense modalities otherwise untapped?

The prosthetic suggests a vocabulary of the more-than. Within this vocabulary, the "than"—the body, usually—tends to be thought as an already-formulated entity. Concepts such as the machinic (Deleuze and Guattari[41]), the Body without Organs (Artaud[42]), the posthuman (Hayles[43]), and originary technicity (Derrida[44]), explicitly challenge the notion that the body could be reduced to a "thanness" that would need to be supplemented to create a body that was "more-than" its organic envelope. They suggest that a body is always already more-than, refuting the logic of the "than" that would need to be prosthetically enhanced to reach its more-than state. Refuting the thanness that supposedly becomes prosthetically enhanced, such concepts as these suggest that the "more than" *is* the very condition of the becoming-body.

What we see in dance/new technology performances is often a prosthetically enhanced body where the prosthetic "makes the difference," contributing technologically to the stage-space.[45] The idea is that the prosthetic brings the body to a new level of sensation through movement. But this transformation tends to occur at the level of representation. We perceive a change in space (the image shifts), but do we *feel* space differently? The logic of the prosthesis as it is mobilized in this kind of dance trend rarely moves beyond the limits of interactivity.[46] It does not move the relation: it foregrounds mediations between different systems whereby one portion of the system is necessarily preconstituted. In most cases this means working with a stable body-concept. From stable to unstable and back, but never really metastable. New ecologies of experience are rarely created under these conditions.

Experiential transformation is rare. It depends on the capacity to create events that are "new" enough that they catch our attention, and graspable enough that we can relate to them. "Relate" is the key word here: we must feel these occasions of experience in their eventness. To simply watch an event—to remain a passive spectator to its inner workings—does not result in experiential transformation. Transformation entails a shift in affective tone such that the participating spectator feels the performance, responding to it through an emphasis as much on its duration—its capacity to create experiential space-times—as through its content—its micromovements in the making. New technology and dance performances do suggest the capacity to produce platforms of relation that call forth new kinds of process that create new kinds of events. Yet they too often remain limited by the dimensions of the software. This tends to call forth a docile body, both in the software-conformist dancer and in the technologically attentive spectator. Affective transformation depends on evolution in the machinic system such that both bodies and technological systems are altered. Technogenesis requires transduction.

The technogenetic body is infinitely more-than, but not within the confines of the prosthetic. It takes the body as pure plastic rhythm. Bringing transduction into the mix means provoking a change not only of state but of dynamic. Nudging a process to a new level suggests making the body-as-event the subject of the composition. This can only occur through an embedding of some kind of analog process into the dimensions of current technology's potential.[47] The analog is key to this process because unlike the digital, the analog always has virtuality embedded in its open system.

The digital—the locus of the "techne" in most new technology—operates in a much more stable manner than does the analog. Its parameters are preset, even when change in state is what is at stake. The result: you had to know in advance what could happen. This effect of preknowing what a body could do limits its technogenetic potential. For technogenesis to occur, what must be sought is a way to foreground the effects of unknowability that are virtually present in all movement. The incipiency of movement's emergence must be tapped. This access to virtuality is not yet available to digital computation, which must conform to actual ones and zeros. By bringing the analog into the digital mix (by intermixing new technologies with dancing bodies such that the dancing body is emergent with the technology rather than simply added to it), the technical system might tend toward ontogenesis, toward technogenetic evolution.

Evolutionary systems that build on accumulation are emerging. Still, too often the "emergent" quality of the system depends on how the body moves with the software. Here's the paradox: moving-with the software means learning to move the software. Whether you plan it this way or not, the choreography becomes determined by the software, which qualitatively limits what a body can do. Where technology was supposed to open the body to a wider relational potential, it actually reduces the body's capacity to create experiential space-time through micromovements in the making. The dancer learns to traverse space rather than to create it. For technogenesis to occur, the dance must surprise even the dancer—it must move toward relational eventfulness. For this to take place, recompositions of potential (movement taking-form through virtual recombinations shape-shifting into displacements) are necessary, activated not simply by or in relation to an external source but in tandem with the co-composition of an event in the making.

This is not a plea to return to a pretechnologized body, or to abandon a technologically enhanced dancing body. It is an invitation to explore the potential of technogenesis for the sensing body in movement. For this, a vocabulary of process is necessary. Process here means working with enabling constraints that create the conditions for ontogenetic emergence. To experiment with a digitally enhanced post-technologized body beyond the dichotomy of the organic/prosthetic is to ask what a body can do such that it is not the prosthesis that enables it—as a tool supplementing the imposed thanness of the body. The very more-thanness of pure plastic rhythm must come to the fore. We must move beyond the prosthetic as an external category toward an exploration of the originary technicity that technogenesis taps into.

Technogenesis—ontogenesis of the bio-technological not as a technical additive to the biological but as an emphasis on originary technicity—suggests a working vocabulary. Here, the body is posited not as a stable category but as a creative vector of experiential space-time. Foregrounded is the body in movement: pure plastic rhythm. Such a body cannot be dissociated from the flux of micromovements of which it is composed. To think a body in movement is not to locate the body in a preformed world but to conceptualize moving worlds as instances of interrelating bodies. Technogenesis defines bodies as nodes of potential that qualitatively alter the interrelations of the rhizomatic networks of space-time in which they are ephemerally housed. These networks are not distinct from the bodies they instantiate: they are themselves sensing bodies in movement. Sensing bodies in movement are open systems that reach-toward one another sensingly, becoming through these relational matrices. As these bodies individuate relationally, they evolve beyond their ontological status, becoming ontogenetic. Technogenesis is the dynamic becoming of the sensing body in movement.

Scene 2: Whitehead Begins to Dance

To move is to create (with) sense. A body perceives through difference. A change in environment provokes a sensory event. Whitehead suggests that perception is both sensuous (sensed) and non-sensuous (a direct perception of pastness in the present). To perceive is not simply to accumulate sense-data: it is to directly sense relation as the virtual activity inherent in the taking-form of objects and worlds. It is not that a "subject" perceives a world but that the world is pulled into experience. This activity of "pulling" suggests that there is no subject-position that precedes experience. Without an initial perceiving subject, a preformed body cannot exist. Worlding occurs in the process of a world becoming subject, or a subject becoming world. Or, to extend the analysis, subjects are transitory individuations in a processual worlding whereby certain actualities take form in a nexus of "contemporarily independent" events.[48]

To understand the stakes in this argument, it is necessary to think actuality in terms of the stopgap of perception: about a half-second. What we perceive, we perceive always at a delay such that this perception is already composed of the holes of experience.[49] I do not perceive an object per se, the objectness is prehended (drawn out from a pastness in a way that is qualitatively new) as an event that space-times me. Through the prehension, "I" am subjectified as an instance of that particular object-event. This object-event constructs me—individuates me—as much as it is individuated by me. Such an experience is actively creative: "I" must assist the perception, fill up its holes, give it form. This giving-form happens as "I" (as individuating event) fill in the gaps of perception, giving the object a contour or a background (that "I" may not directly have perceived), situating it in a worldness that cannot be separated from it. As "I" do this, "I" am also individuating (moving beyond any kind of discrete "I-ness" or thanness) on a plane of becoming that Whitehead calls an actual occasion. "I" am not detached from this process, and yet "I" am only composed by it to the extent that it will initiate my infinite re-composition. I is an event.

To explain this strange refraction of experience, whereby "I" individuates in direct engagement with the individuating world, Whitehead turns to two concepts that sound very familiar—appearance and reality—redefining them through his vocabulary of process and event. He does this to attempt to dislocate the notion that experience is a subset of an already formed body-world. For Whitehead, the world only preexists in so far as its pastness (its virtuality) can be activated in the present. To appear does not mean to conceive the past as a world strangely available to an unsuspecting present. Appearance here is much closer to a Bergsonian concept of active recollection.[50] What we call the present is composed of strands of pastness recomposing and perishing through it. This does not mean that all presents are predetermined. Quite the contrary: the present is always new, but its newness is compelled in large part by experience as it is reactivated or re-collected from the past half-second of experience. To reactivate is never simply to relive. There is no world that will remain the same after reactivation. Reactivation will always, to some degree, mean invention.

Focusing on perception as an *activity* allows Whitehead to reconceptualize the vocabulary of preformation (where perception is contained by a preformed world). Prehension for Whitehead is perception as event. An actual occasion is the expression of a particular prehension—or set of prehensions—that eventually converges into a subjective form. The subjective form is not the form of the object itself. It is the coming-into-form of the ontogenetic process out of which its objectness—its eventness—comes to the fore. We never prehend an object as such. The objectness of the prehension forms in the eventness that is the actual occasion. Objects emerge in relation as events of experience. As an object begins to take form, its process concresces such that it becomes more stable (and recognizable as such). This (meta)stability (the object having reached its eventness or subjective form) is the beginning of the inevitable perishing of the actual occasion, which creates an opening for new experience to take form. As the actual occasion perishes, it populates the nexus of pastness. The nexus as such cannot be perceived. But parts of it can (and will) be reactivated in future actual occasions.

This virtual nexus is how Whitehead defines reality. As the actual occasion perishes to give way to the next actual occasion, the actual occasion melds into a reality virtually populated by all of the positive (having been actualized) and negative (having remained inactivated or virtual) prehensions that make up our experiential worlds. This nexus of perished actual occasions—reality—can be conceived as a wealth of potential out of which possible worlds emerge. Reality is therefore always more than and less than appearance: less than what appearance can be, and more than what appearance is. To be experienced, reality must be activated. Even then, it is not strictly "what it was" but "how it can become."

To think the body in terms of appearance and reality is to focus on the body's unactualized potential as an aspect of its becoming that cannot be realized as such, but can be called forth, adding novelty to its open system. The taking-form of an individuating body is an "appearance" of the body within a vastness of unrealized potential. Technogenesis occurs at the threshold of emergence of the becoming-body where reality is pulled into appearance, and something is added to the mix. This something is a movement-with that provokes a body to become in excess of its organ-ization.

Novelty—or creativity—occurs always in the present: novelty emerges through the time-slip between reality and appearance. Because the present takes form on the threshold of appearance and reality, the present must be conceptualized as operating in the midst of the virtual becoming actualized. Prehension catalyzes reality into the movement toward appearance. Reality contributes to appearance by bringing experiential pastness into the present. This experiential pastness transduced into the present brings a certain pre-experience to the event of perception. Whitehead calls this aspect of perception causal efficacy in order to remind us that what we perceive first is not an object but how it worlds. This causal aspect of perception is the directly perceived relation between objectness and experience. Activating perception means activating the relation that underlies the object's very capacity to be perceived. As outlined in the previous chapter, causal efficacy is the active link between objectness and experience that allows the object to take form experientially.

In most organisms, to causally prehend is only one aspect of perception.[51] The second phase is called presentational immediacy. In this second phase (though never quite second, since in higher organisms it is experienced in tandem with causal efficacy), perception is enhanced by the *quality* of experience. Whereas with causal efficacy we perceive the relation enclosure-safety upon entering a room, with presentational immediacy the color of the room emerges, a quality, strictly speaking, unnecessary to the experience of feeling safe, yet that subtly alters "safety's" affective tonality.

As demonstrated in chapter 3, presentational immediacy is lost without causal efficacy: despite the heterogeneity of its experiential dimensions, "pure" presentational immediacy cannot comprehend or delineate an event. Qualitative difference must be associated with causal efficacy's capacity to create a relation between event and world. Pastness is necessary for perception, even if that pastness does nothing but invite the creation of an object-world relation to be deformed in the next prehension. Novelty emerges from the productive constraints of the pastness of worldings in the present-passing. Presentational immediacy is what adds nuance to the mix. Without presentational immediacy, the world loses nuance. As with the intertwining of appearance and reality, what we know as perception is similarly a complex intermixing of causal efficacy and presentational immediacy.

Appearance is the active pulling out of experience from reality, the "giving form" of the nexus in the presentness of worlding. Reality must in a certain sense "precede" appearance: what appears is always less complex than reality itself. Yet reality can never be prehended as such, and, in this way, remains undifferentiated. Appearance and reality thus exist on a continuum: perception happens always for the first time through appearance, and yet appearance depends on the activation of reality. To experience is always to exist on the cusp of appearance and reality: it is to co-live the present as a pastness of emergence that will only be known in its future-pastness-becoming-present. There is no moment that precedes the prehension out of which perception occurs: the future and the past coexist through the present.

With prehension foregrounded as the key to the eventness of experience, appearance and reality can no longer be delineated as hierarchies of objectivity and subjectivity. We now begin to conceive the eventness of an actual occasion as that which embodies different layers of experience that lead toward nodes of perception. Sensing bodies in movement emerge ontogenetically from such durational interweavings.

Scene 3: Dancing the Ground

A dancing body is a sensing body in movement. A dancer actively perceives and moves worlds such that new kinds of experiential space-times are constituted. These worldings are pullings out of an experiential ground that shifts with each of the dancer's movements. The dancer senses and creates microspace-times in one and the same movement, individuating with each shift in ground. The ground becomes part of the shifting through which these individuations develop, emerging as a key aspect of the series dancer-movement-ground.

As it enters into movement, the ground is reconstituted as novelty, intertwining with the capacities of what a gravitational body can do. The ground is one of movement's enabling constraints: the dancer will always reach the ground again. Yet in the series dancer-movement-ground, it is *how* the ground plays into movement moving that is at stake. Grounding need not be a strictly vertical proposition: with the inflections of movement moving, ground can become a vorticality, a horizontality. Actively prehended, the ground moves (with) the dance.

Now we find that the ground takes part in the creation of the becoming-form of dance (a curve, a spiral, an arabesque), that movement's subjective form is always intrinsically related to a moving ground. The ground contributes to the dance as a form-finding element in the dancer's shape-shifting process, operating not as a stable entity but as an active determinant in the process. The ground is a compositional aspect of a dancer's movement, reconstituting the ways in which space-time potentializes the moving body and vice versa. The ground does not simply ground—it dances.

A dancing ground is a technogenetic element in the dance. A technique of composition, the ground becomes a condition of emergence for the ontogenetic body. Techniques conceived this way are technologies composed with, for, and through a dancing body. They foreground the more-thanness of pure plastic rhythm. Grounding is a key aspect of technique: even without being told, the dancer learns to continuously relocate the ground as an element of experimental space-time, creating momentum with and through the ground toward gravity-defying re-vectorization.

To ground, when dancing, is to alter the composition body-floor such that the ground actively relocates in relation to dynamic movement. Movement here is never simply movement-in-space. It is movement-with-space that qualitatively alters the duration of experience. To say that the ground is "beneath her feet" is to misunderstand the very mobility of groundedness.

There is a link to be made here between the dancing and the walking-to-the-bus-stop body, even if the same kinds of technique are not emphasized. The shiftiness of ground may be less palpable with respect to a walking body rushing to a bus stop, but it is nonetheless virtually present: you might, for example, experience a "loss of ground" due to a shift in the level of the sidewalk that causes you to lose your balance. The dancer is trained to defy the ground as stable surface, whereas the everyday walker tends to depend on the ground's stability. But that does not mean that the ground necessarily conforms to the expectations of the walker.

Shifting grounds are but one technique through which a body creates space-time. Dancers can—like all other movers, only more obviously—breathe space,[52] folding the space into the duration of a textured tactility that moves the air, creating a sense of a clearing. Dancers can walk space, such that the dimensions of space-time seem to compress. They can sound space, such that the vectors of space-time seem to inflect, curving experience. By creating such occasions of experience, the sensing body in movement alters experiential space-time such that space-time is felt in its emergence.

This coming-into-emergence is a technogenetic experience. It is technogenetic because it recomposes the body. This recomposition takes form through a multiplicity of techniques. For Simondon (1969), a technique is a technology of emergence (an ontogenetic technology or a technogenesis) through which new complex systems are composed. These techniques can be thought as associated milieus of potential. Associated milieus are ecologies that emerge through the very technogenesis that gives them form. Associated milieus are compositional matrices for the machinic body, in-forming the body through transductions that open the body-becoming to the metastability that provokes it to become in excess of its organism. Techniques matter form such that bodies become experiments in the making.

Can digital technologies create techniques capable of such technogenetic transduction? Transduction is a durational process whereby what is transformed becomes a worlding rather than simply an effect on an already-constituted system. Transduction alters the conditions of a process. Can digital technologies create ontogenetic conditions for emergent body-worlds? Is it possible for new technologies to perceive the virtual effects of force taking form in the virtual-actual passage from reality to appearance, to feel the incipience of movement, to sense-with sensing bodies in movement, "catching" pure plastic rhythm in its passing? Can new technology engage the virtuality of pastness, making its effects felt? This is not simply a question "of the superiority of the analog,"[53] but a question to technogenesis itself. Can technology *play* the virtual?

The virtual is played by a dancing body through preacceleration. Yet it bears repeating: virtuality is not something digital technologies are yet able to tap into. How to create functioning parameters for software development on the basis of something that cannot be known, that can only be felt in its effects? Technology becoming technogenetic involves inflecting the digital with virtual potential, bringing to the fore movement's incipiency and its relational matrix. How does a movement that cannot yet be seen make itself known?

Digital technologies must work at the level of perceptual emergence. To do so, they must harness resources where they can. Technology has to become ontogenetic. By working ontogenetically—toward technogenetic emergence—rather than prosthetically, technology must become capable of actively *making* sense such that it creates new sensing bodies in movement. No longer held back by the limits of the software, movement might then be able to make the technological process *appear* rather than simply moving to its parameters.[54] To add nuance to these experiential experiments, technology must also make its failures felt, its lagging behind, its system collapse, its loss of ground. Making the digital analog is not the goal: technogenesis becomes evocative when it works at the level of invention, when its techniques make transduction felt, foregrounding the metastability of all moving systems.

For such technogenesis to take form, Whitehead's distinction between appearance and reality must be taken into account. The appearance of a technogenetic body cannot be based on a body (an organic body, a dancing body) that preexists its emergence. The body must not be danced and then supplemented: it must dance its supplement.[55] It must dance its novelty such that it introduces within the movement the mutability of the body's rhizomatic networks of actuality and virtuality. We must never forget: a body is never wholly actual. It is always virtually what it will have become as it interweaves the organic and the technogenetic, where the organic is as much a technology of the senses as the senses are technologies of the organic.

To sense—to experience the world amodally[56]—is a key way to activate the body's relation to the world and open the body to its technogenetic potential. This already occurs in the dancing body when the movement causes the room to space differently through an accumulation of tactile sensations coursing through the air. Felt affectively as a change in the dynamics of the emergent environment, this kind of experiential space-time takes form with and through the dancer's body as a molecular reorganization of duration such that the dimensions of the felt are re-experienced in conjunction with the reassembling of a dispersing, re-cognizing becoming-body.

The sensing body in movement also feels time. This feeling of time happens through the activation of past movements in the present. Whitehead calls the direct perception of pastness non-sensuous perception. Non-sensuous perception underscores the fact that perception begins relationally with an emphasis on the pastness that allows us to feel the world in the future-present. This pastness (which can be durationally as immediate as the present moment passing) enables the formation of causal relations between past events and current circumstances such that we feel the world ecologically before we know exactly what it is. To feel ecologically is to directly perceive the relations out of which space-time is composed. Perceiving ecologically does not imply giving meaning to form, but forming environmentally. To say we perceive non-sensuously—or ecologically—is to emphasize how the world creates modalities of perception even as modalities of perception world. Ecological durations are not linear—they are richly layered, their nexus ripe with reality, their actual environments populated by appearances.[57]

To think technogenetically, we must keep in mind that we perceive not an object-as-such but how the object merges with experience: the object *is* its experiential function. Objects are novel because their conjunctions are new, not preexisting them, but immanent to them. Objects, prehended, are individuations within an ecology of practices wherein perception is key. Non-sensuous perception is an activity of relation whereby the composition of an event takes place through a re-uptake of the virtual (immannce) into the actual (appearance). Through non-sensuous perception we directly perceive relation. In Whiteheadian terms, we prehend the affective tone—the relational concernedness—of an object-becoming-world.

A sensing body in movement is activated both sensuously and non-sensuously. Perception occurs on a continuum of relation. To make sense technogenetically, the coupling dance/new technology must ask how a technology can make relation felt. This means technology must operate both sensingly and non-sensuously, moving between the virtual (immanence) and the cusp of the actual (incipience). This may be done, for instance, by working with a delay through which the room is durationally recomposed. Imagine, for instance, a dancer cutting across the space, shifting space-time's tactile borders through a succession of movement-layers that compile a thick database that eventually alters the sound in the room. The sound is not altered by a given movement but by an overload in the system. The sound can now be perceived as a sensory experiment technogenetically emergent with perception's own half-second delay. Experience is overlaid rather than delineated through a representation of movement=sound in a distinct one-to-one relation. Now, the system recomposes the room even as the dancer composes with the system. The coupling causes the room to shift, to move, to breathe. As this happens, the intensity of a shift in space-time is felt. This is felt not through the sound shifting as such but through a slight difference in affective tone. The room reverberates around its color, its sound-quality, its becoming-form. Now, the spectator feels a concern with the space. This concern provokes a new kind of attention: a perception of the tonality of the interval. A new composition begins to unfold, one that may be related to an ontogenetic shift in the participating body of the spectator. Technogenesis: two bodies recomposed at different durations in the sensing spectrum.

If technology can recompose a body beyond the level of sensuous perception—beyond the directness of an operation that makes something seen, such as an arm movement translating into a video image—bringing the relational quality of experience to the fore, technology becomes technogenesis. In a technogenetic event, more than displacement or representation must be perceived. What must also be felt—by the dancer first and foremost, but also by those participating in the performance as spectators—are the microperceptions through which the displacement is activated. Many of these perceptions are non-sensuous because they work at the level of the barely there, below the threshold of sensuous perception. Rather than the sensory perception itself, we must feel the relation out of which the movement event emerges. This experience is affective and cannot be separated from the creation of space-times the technogenetic event calls forth.

Technogenesis contributes concern to the event that does not end with the performance: the affective tone's residue lingers, provoking adjacent forms of experience, many of which remain virtual. Technogenesis always involves more that the datum, more than the sense-presentation, more than the present. Technogenesis makes the process felt, foregrounding the duration of the individuating machinic body.

Technogenesis cannot be premapped. How then can it work alongside a technological system whose parameters are set? The ontogenetic coupling of digital technology with the originary technicity of the individuating body must take this into account. Rather than mapping the technology—as a prosthesis—onto a moving body, it is necessary to incite the movement to appear out of the technological process that is the machinic assemblage of individuation.

To make the movement appear does not mean to restrict the movement to the parameters of the technology. It does not mean to delimit movement to gesture. We require operations that traverse the spectrum of the technology's potential metastability in relation to a becoming-body. When technology begins to operate along this spectrum it forms an associated milieu with the interval that is the becoming-body. Technology not mapped-onto but emergent-with a body-becoming might make different durations felt along the stratum that is the sensing body in movement. This would happen first not at the level of reality but through the presentness of appearance. The technology would have to function not as a system that takes over the moving body but as a complex interface through which the technogenetic body can be moved to appear. The effect of this (dis)appearing body would eventually populate the nexus such that certain aspects of the technogenetic body could remain dormant, real yet virtual, embedded in a pastness accessible in the present through activation. There is no doubt this already happens—but still too rarely. Techniques for technogenetic emergence must become part of the technology's interface: we must develop techniques that create new associated milieus never distinct from the ontogenetic body. Technological recomposition must no longer be inserted into a body-system: it must be emergent with it.

Scene 4: Bus-Stopping the Ground

Let me return to my example of walking to the bus stop. Earlier, I suggested that the ground's recomposition of the dancing body was simply an extreme example of the everyday walking body's relation to ground. You might say: whereas the dancing body specifically dances the ground, walking to the bus stop is an activity that presupposes a stable ground. Is it so cut and dry?

While walking to the bus stop, the ground reconfigures the series into a focus toward a transportational vector. In advance of the walking, the bus stop already appears as the propulsion for the walk: the ground-in-itself is backgrounded in favour of transportational (bus-oriented) momentum. The prehension ground-movement in this case is directly intertwined with transportability. Yet the ground also contributes to walking, despite the fact that the transduction of ground into the steadiness of the walk involves a backgrounding of the ground in this instance. The backgrounded ground is a participant (rather than a coordinator) in the transportational vector that carries the movement. The ground appears only insofar as it is expressed as something else (steadiness of movement, for instance).[58]

The prehension "ground" is indissociably linked to the transportability of its becoming-function. It is not that ground *is* transport: it is that it appears in the function of transportability. As long as nothing gets in the way, the ground will continue to be backgrounded in the transportational vector ground-walk-bus-stop. But things are bound to get in the way: you smell the garbage in the alley, which causes you to lose your footing and trip. Through malfunction, you "lose" your ground and the ground appears, foregrounded, horizontalizing you, altering your sense of space-time. Suddenly, ground no longer contributes steadiness-in-movement. Facedown: the bus stop is momentarily backgrounded. The event has shifted and with it the ground. Now you see your reflection in the puddle, and this makes you feel self-conscious. You prehend a selfness that was part of neither the transportational vector nor the appearing groundness. And then: you recall your lateness, and a new actual occasion begins to take form where the ground is once more backgrounded. You quickly rise and resume your walk. The ground reenters the transportational vector, contributing to the hurriedness of the movement that will take you toward busness. The hurry is foregrounded now, but this does not mean that the ground is stable.

Each event creates a different ground. Space-times of experience are always linked to shifts in ground. Ground is part of the technogenesis that makes events felt. Every appearance grounds differently. And every worlding is ontogenetic: it creates holes through which we dance, opening the way for movements that technogenetically invent worlds.

What is real and what appears exist in a complex network of movement moving. How movement moves is relational. When we move the relation, we never begin with a gesture. We move into gesture. What a body can do is characterized by its capacity to make sense beyond a vocabulary of the already-there. An ontogenetic body has an infinite potential for technogenesis. New technologies must dance to pure plastic rhythm.

Interlude: Perceptions in Folding

Prehensions are events of perception. They pull what become actual occasions from the extensive continuum of experience. The extensive continuum is made up of the undifferentiated folds of the universe. The outfolding through prehensions of the infolding of experience propels the taking-form of an event. With its unfolding into an event comes the expression of life in the making.

Life is as complex as the actual events that compose it. These actual events are multiple, each of them composed of prehensions culled from the magnitude of pastness non-sensuously felt as the present passing. Non-sensuous perception is the activity of perceiving the tonality of pastness in the present. Non-sensuous perceptions shade the currency of futurity. Perception as the infolding of the potential for activation of the future-past is the relational nexus for life-in-the-making. Perception is not the taking-in of an object or a scene. It is the folding-with that catches the event in the making.

Every actual occasion has a physical and a mental pole. The physical pole is the datum for the event's actualization. The mental pole is the potential for abstraction. Actual occasions become conceptual through the ingression of eternal objects. Eternal objects are what give actual occasions their quality. The quality of a prehension will differ in accordance with the kind of eternal objects associated with it. An eternal object is the event's tonality—the whiteness, the hardness, the liveliness. This tonality provides a quality of relation for the event across the nexus of actual occasions.

Eternal objects are less objects than foldings-into. They make ingress into the actual occasion, lending the event its color. This folding is a multiplying of the singular. It folds not many parts, but many ways, to infinity. "Dividing endlessly, the parts of matter form little vortices in a maelstrom, and in these are found even more vortices, even smaller, and even more are spinning in the concave intervals of the whirls that touch one another" (Deleuze 1993, 5).

The corpuscular society that is the nexus of actual occasions is infinitely porous, each actual occasion a world fluid with the potential for relational deviation. This potential for deviatory foldings is the actual occasion's futurity. It is the way in which the occasion continues to resonate even after it has reached its satisfaction and become, for all eternity, what it will have been. The event has taken form and yet its form-taking folds with eternal objects that continue to populate the universe, not as objects, but as more folds, as elastic nodes in the process of becoming.

Eternal objects give taking-form its resonance. When an occasion culminates its process, it perishes. How a perished event can be regathered into experience depends on the ways in which its qualities extend into the future-passing of felt experience (via non-sensuous perception). Were perishing the absolute end of the occasion, there would be no futurity to an event, no becoming across experience. Whitehead's actual occasions are not closed in on themselves as are Leibniz's monads. Through the ingression of eternal objects, actual occasions remain virtually open to qualitative resonances across the nexus of becoming. Eternal objects continue to color events in the making even across their perishings, subtly altering how future events emerge. The perished occasion's fluidity of curvature is apparent in the ways in which it continues to provoke new kinds of individuation.

Color is an example of an eternal object. Color changes the hue of an event, giving it a tone that casts the event beyond its own satisfaction toward the future foldings of colors intermixing. Think of Robert Irwin's *Who's Afraid of Red, Yellow and Blue* (2007). The experience of this installation goes far beyond the memory of the six horizontally laid colored panels. It is an event *for* color. *Who's Afraid of Red, Yellow and Blue* reaches across the immediateness of its presentation of primary colors to actually color future experience.[59] The exhibit gives itself to perception, attempting not to "show" us color, but to allow color to appear for perception in its primariness and its secondariness (when we look through the yellow panel at the red one, we see orange, and the blue becomes purple). What we experience is a strange perceiving-with-color that colors our perception not only for this event but for all future instances of the active perception of red, yellow, and blue. *Who's Afraid of Red, Yellow and Blue* makes perception actually appear the way it already does virtually. Having experienced the extraordinary sensation of feeling space color in the active passage of primariness to secondariness, I will never again think I am seeing "just red."[60] What was virtual before this experience has now actualized in my experience of more-than-redness.

Eternal objects folds through contrast. The quality of the event is not simply its redness, it is the hue of its neither blueness nor yellowness. It is how shades come together to create an affective tonality that folds into experience to make the event inseparable from its quality. What we perceive as quality is the activity of folding into perception.

"A 'relation' between occasions is an eternal object illustrated in the complex of mutual prehensions by virtue of which those occasions constitute a nexus" (Whitehead 1929/1978, 194). The sharing of qualities opens the world to relational potential. Each event is contemporarily independent from all other events even as it holds within itself—via its infinite foldings—the potential to create an associated milieu. This associated milieu does not change the actual form of the occasion, but it does alter its resonance. It foregrounds a quality that would otherwise be backgrounded. These kinds of mutual prehensions give life to the already-quasi-formed, emphasizing the capacity for morphing inherent in all events of the future-past.

Contrast in Whitehead does not mean the equal juxtaposition of two extremes. It is "that particularity of conjoint unity which arises from the realized togetherness of eternal objects" (Whitehead 1929/1978, 229). Contrast is the activity of foregrounding or backgrounding that makes certain qualities stand out, creating what Whitehead calls *emergent evolutions*.

Emergent evolutions are the individuation of relational fields composed by the activity of small perceptions [*les petites perceptions*] folding. These microperceptions are perceptions without objects: hallucinatory tendencies in the sense that they express nothing but the emphasis on the quality of becoming. They do not give us a body fully formed or an object-in-place: they fold perception into a becoming-body of movement creating the emphasis of quasi formation that is relation in the making. Small perceptions move the relation event-nexus into infoldings of perception.

"Small perceptions are as much the passage from one perception to another as they are components of each perception" (Deleuze 1993, 87; translation modified). Small perceptions are like what Arakawa and Madeline Gins call imaging landing sites: they qualitatively site perception beyond the register of perceptual actuality. They are virtual recomposings of the force of perception. They feel the world worlding, and they contribute to it, this contribution altering the dynamics at work in the relations they call forth. They regather perception, recomposing the body toward its appetite for seeing-with.

Eternal objects fold into an event as its qualitative differential. They inflect the event's final form without necessarily changing its content, creating nuance within it at the level of small perceptions. "It is the differential relations among these infinitely small actuals that draw into clarity; that is to say, that constitute a clear perception (the color green) with certain small perceptions, obscure, and evanescent (the colors yellow and blue)" (Deleuze 1993, 90; translation modified). They determine the character of perceptions in folding.

Perception operates on the threshold of consciousness. The eternal objects folded through prehensions act as perception's differential, opening the event of perception to an associated milieu of nexus-occasion that in-gathers its quality. Conscious perception acts on the quality of perception's relational potential. What we perceive is not the thing as such but its capacity for relation. Perceiving first and foremost the capacity for relation means that a stone is perceived, not as an object-as-such, but as the feeling of hardness in the hand. Perception is the feeling-with of an event forming.

This is key to memory. Remembering a feeling involves activating relation by bringing into appearance a feltness in the present passing. A memory is not an unfolding of the bottled past in the neutral present. Remembering is the activation of a contrast that inflects the differential of experience unfolding such that the then is felt as an aspect of the nowness of experience. This is a relational event: it foregrounds the presentness through the past, emphasizing the quality of difference in their contrast. The event of the memory is how it takes form in the present, its hue activated through the contrast past-present, then-now.

Perception folds in an infinite play of foregrounding and backgrounding. Eternal objects are nodes of relation for this elastic process of pulling in and out of experience's continuum. Perception moves-with these openings toward changes in nature occasioned by "minuscule folds that are endlessly unfurling and bending on the edges of juxtaposed areas, like a mist or fog that makes their surface sparkle, at speeds that no one of our thresholds of consciousness could sustain in a normal state" (Deleuze 1993, 93). Unfolding is never the opposite of folding. Unfolding is intensive movement. Perception is the activity of making this intensity felt in the taking-form of worlding.

Folding into perception is moving-with the virtual resonance of force taking form. Perception is in the folds, not of the folds. It has no object as such. Folding into perception is sensing-with the world worlding. Perceiving pulls out singularity: this is what we identify in its passing as an object. What we perceive is the object's capacity to create contrasts, to differentiate the nexus: "It is that the perceived *resembles* something it forces us to think" (Deleuze 1993, 95; translation modified). The quality of perceptibility—the whiteness, for instance—calls forth a feeling for white. I think cappuccino foam. This perception creates a feeling for coffee.

Perception infolds thoughts in the making. It does not reflect the world, it ingathers its relational fact into a feeling for its future infolding. An object becomes the threshold for thinking feeling. The event is not "seeing an object" but folding the "objectile" that contributes to perception's infolding. We perceive-with objects, catching the edges of their contours, participating in the relations they call forth. Eternal objects make ingress into this object-world individuation, creating the potential for future relation. The objectness of the object is how it is felt relationally, rather than simply its actual matter-form. How it takes form on the nexus is how we prehend it. This quality of relation is what gives an object-event its potential infinitude. Perception is the force for the world's infinite unfolding.

Grace Taking Form: Marey's Movement Machines 5

Force Taking Form

Étienne-Jules Marey (1830–1904) spent his life inventing machines to measure the imperceptible.[61] He began this exploration of perception in the late 1850s with graph-writing instruments. These machines were concerned with measuring the body's inner movements, calculating, for instance, the almost-invisible movements of the pulse's rhythms and the blood's flow by tracing them onto the surfaces of smoke-blackened cylinders. Over his research career, he developed many such experimental machines ranging from inscription instruments to photographic apparatuses.

Marey's focus was explicitly positivistic. His concern was to create machines to make visible what until then had remained invisible. This interest in invisibility led Marey toward an investment in the machinic, where the machinic is defined as an agglomeration of potential processes that exceed the limits of a particular mechanism. One of the most compelling aspects of Marey's work is how the exploration of different modes of movement led him to devise techniques for perception that in turn became new kinds of sensing machines. Never quite satisfied with the results of his experiments, his life was dedicated to invention: he continuously created new experiments for which he had to build machines, and then built new machines based on the results of his experiments.

Marey's focus on the invention of machines and processes to measure the imperceptible invariably led his research to become invested in the experiential.

Despite his desire to secure results for publication in scientific journals in the name of the advancement of knowledge—something his early graph-writing machines allowed him to do with processes such as measuring the pulse—he quite soon found himself ensconced in a universe of movement for which there was no adequate source of measure. As the movement experiments focused more on the processual (especially those of gases, but also his experiments with locomotion), he began, despite himself, to delve into the exploration of incipiency, graphing not only curves *of* movement but curves *in* movement.[62] These curves are a radical change in Marey's approach in the sense that they cease to work solely as representations of movement-passed and become fascinated with movement-passing. By the end of his life, although still committed to measuring movement in quantitative scientific terms, what stands out in his work are photographic images of experiential flows, elastic forces, quasi-virtual perceptions not of the movement as content but of the incorporeal surfacing of the microperceptual.

This chapter looks at how plotting movement "actually there" but imperceptible to the eye was slowly transformed in Marey's work toward the invocation and mapping of forces. As forces that could not be seen (but could be felt) emerged, instead of denouncing them as unviable for quantification, he created new techniques for their measurement. "How does a bird's flight interact with the resistance of the air?" he might ask. The machine devised to inform his curiosity would answer this first question, only to propel him to explore further and inquire how force could be visualized. This desire to measure in turn expressed itself in a continual reworking of *perceptual* techniques. Machines that began as simple mechanisms for the study of a particular movement became instigators for creating new machinic processes to sense movement's force. This compulsion to make the force of movement-passing appear would then propel the construction of yet another movement-sensitive machine. This fascination with the machinic processes of experimentation situates Marey's research along an uncanny continuum between positivist analysis—the exploration of an object of study divorced from its environment, and what William James calls *radical empiricism*—a pragmatic investment in the *relation* between objects and worlds.

In true positivist form, Marey believed in the mechanics of what could be proven. "Science has two obstacles that block its advance, first the defective capacity of our senses for discovering truths, and then the insufficiency of language for expressing and transmitting those we have acquired. The aim of scientific method is to remove these obstacles" (Marey, qtd. in Braun 1992, 12–13). Experimentation through visualization always preceded documentation for Marey. His first concern was to find ways to develop insights into movement through representations made visible early on by his graphic machines, and later by chronophotographs. His aim was to find quantitative modes of analysis to make us see what seeing obstructed. This paradoxical investment in vision is one of the astounding aspects of Marey's work on movement. Although he never explicitly mentions the role of perception in his experiments, his work specifically brings to the fore the complexity of mechanisms of perception as linked to movement. The images Marey creates are both given to and engaged in perceptual experimentation.

Marey's legacy, I believe, is the invention of perception machines that, in Paul Valéry's words, "draw vision drawing."[63] In this chapter, I focus on the progression in Marey's life from the creation of machines that perceive bodies moving to experimentations with "drawing perception drawing." I am interested in how Marey develops modes of experimentation that play with the very mechanisms of perception, and how he creates machines that captivate perception's endurance across states of durational becoming. Uncannily, what Marey's experiments foreground is the very mechanism of perception itself: that to see is not to re-compose an already-composed form. His work makes apparent that to see is to create-with the force of a movement taking-form, where what we see is a composition of holes (intervals) and wholes (pure experience,[64] duration[65]) that together create a field of forces around which perception takes form.

Perception's force-field is a complex surface of as yet undifferentiated experience. We see not an object but its activity of relation. We see holes: contours, edges, active intervals moving. We feel wholes: experiential duration not yet divided into actual objects. We see not only what we actually look at but what we remember ourselves seeing. What we remember ourselves seeing is actualized through non-sensuous perception, which refers to how an experience of pastness—past seeings—finds its way into our present as a force of potential. It's not just that we see what we've already seen—it's that what we've already seen contaminates what we feel we see and re-composes what we're actually not seeing.

When we feel the force field of perception what we (virtually) see is an interval. We cannot actually perceive the interval, and yet there is no perception without it. The interval is a relation not yet actualized for actual perception. To see is not to see the interval—it is to see-with it, to compose-with relation.

"The eyes never take in a scene at one go. They rove over objects, detecting edge. The gaze must pass and repass to hold the edge, because edge is actually in continual variation, constantly struck by variations in light and shadow which in any given instant blur its boundary" (Massumi 2006). Co-constituted by a turbulent worlding, vision is not a capturing of the world but a captivating by it. "Even under the most stable of conditions, the eyes add variation through their own micromovements, which never cease. Sight comes of the *duration* of these variations. Vision finds the edge over and over again, through its variations. The edge's constantly returning to the eye under variation is what draws out the constancy of its form. Visual constancy is of variational return" (Massumi 2006).

To see is to feel-with movement moving. Vision is not a passive receptive surface—it is a duration expressed. "The retina is an *active surface* gathering durational variations into the clarity of a line *which was never seen as such*. In any given instant, the line receptively speaking was a blur. Its clarity *emerges* through duration as a function of variation" (Massumi 2006). Vision produces the very novelty Marey's animated images also seek to convey. The experience of the imperceptible is exactly what vision plays with, animating not a stable surface but creating-with the very potential of the not-yet. There is no seeing that is divorced from movement.

Marey's experiments with movement are thus always also experiments with perception. By experimenting with the body in movement, Marey actually provokes the *sensing* body in movement, inventing machines for the transduction of feeling into sensing. He wants to perceive the incorporeal, and to do so, he must push the senses to the edge of what they can do. He must create techniques through which the senses' virtual tendencies are transformed into actual processes for re-visualization.[66] What we virtually feel must become actually sensed. Marey's machinic experiments do not teach vision to see that which is imperceptible. They foreground the activity of perception that is at the heart of vision. Marey's movement experiments are, in the end, experiments with sensation.[67]

Techniques of Relation

Marey's machines are techniques of relation. As open systems, they do not simply measure preconstituted bodies moving, they invent techniques of relation for the creation of becoming-bodies of movement. Marey's machines produce margins of indeterminacy that call forth new machinic processes. How we see what we sense is Marey's main concern, resulting in a generative practice of creating assemblages that generate open passages between sensing bodies and machines: an ecology of practices.

Machines such as Marey's are more than the combination of their parts. What is at stake in these kinds of machines is their technicity, the ways in which they create associated milieus—active intervals—that open experimentation to evolution. Each experimental process creates an evolution toward a particular relational series—that of the blood-heart-graph, that of the foot-sensor-ground—that incites Marey to devise yet another technique, not only for the measuring of actualized movement, but for the stimulation of virtual movement.[68] Each experiment also contains a measure of unpredictability—since new combinatory series are always taking form—that makes novel demands on the machinic process. While machines might otherwise be understood as passive mechanisms for the measuring of activity, I believe that Marey's machines are relationally entwined with the experiments he devises. In fact, the machines become his mode of experimentation such that what he devises through them itself becomes "machinic."

Deleuze and Guattari define the machinic phylum "as materiality, natural and artificial, and both simultaneously; it is matter in movement, in flux, in variation, matter as a conveyor of singularities and traits of expression" (1987, 409). To render something "machinic" is to inscribe it in a process that couples it with the environment out of which it emerges. The sensing bodies in movement Marey studies are not conceived as separate from his experiments. They are integrally connected to the machines he creates. As a key aspect of the living process of experimentation, movement thus becomes an interstice of body and machine in a practice of continual invention of what a machinic body can do.

The tweaking of systems to create experiential evolution that informs methodological processes is a form of radical empiricism. It creates novelty out of relational matrices. This "adaptation-concretization is a process which conditions the birth of a milieu that, instead of already being conditioned by another already-given milieu, is conditioned by a milieu that exists but virtually before the invention" (Simondon 1969, 55; my translation). Invention is not simply the creation of a new machine to better capture movement in space but a jump to a different register whereby the machine begins to operate ontogenetically. More than a sum of its measuring parts, the machine generates potential, registering not simply data on movement but ontogenetically adding to itself such that it is always intrinsically in the process of reinventing what a machine—or a technique—can do. "We could say that concretizing invention creates a techno-geographic milieu . . . that is a condition of possibility for the functioning of the technical object" (Simondon 1969, 55; my translation). Marey's technical objects are co-constitutive of experimental process. They create an associated milieu of body-movement-machine whereby new conditions for experimentation are invented.

Marey's machines are evolving techniques, themselves open to experimentation, working not to fulfill goals already written into their functioning but toward the invention of new milieus. These new milieus are in turn conditioned by the experimentations they provoke, always reconstituted according to the results toward which the experiments are geared. For example, when Marey seeks to understand the movement of the walk, he discovers that in order to get a clear picture of the movement itself, he must background everything except the walking. To do so, he develops various techniques of appearance/disappearance. He calls this simplification, situating movement in these cases as an extraction from the surrounding environment. In this series of experiments, Marey narrows the body-apparent to its simplest form for rendering its movement, choosing to highlight only certain points of the body as it moves, allowing the actual (the visible body) to slide into the virtual (the body unseen), such that what is actually perceived is the incipiency of movement moving. As the quasi virtual takes shape perceptually (the movement foregrounded instead of simply the body moving), what we experience is far from a dialectic of inside/outside that would separate environment and body: Marey creates an uncanny dance of appearance disappearing. We feel the palpability of the imperceptible. Body, movement, and environment have become one. Here, the trace of preacceleration is almost actualized, felt through the visualization of the flow of movement moving. It is as though he had not simply foregrounded how movement works but given movement back to movement, "drawing vision drawing."

Marey does not immediately arrive at "drawing vision drawing." Early experiments show a more restrained experimentation. "Study of a Man's Walk with a White Rod along His Spinal Column (1886)" is an example of an experiment that does not go beyond displacement's representation. In this experiment, Marey backgrounds the human body such that the vertical lines of regular, cadenced intervals of movement's displacement in the walk are foregrounded. He does this by placing a white rod at the body's back to foreground the movement of that one area. This experiment results in a series of vertical lines organized in an equal cadence, emphasizing that walk's displacement. The representation

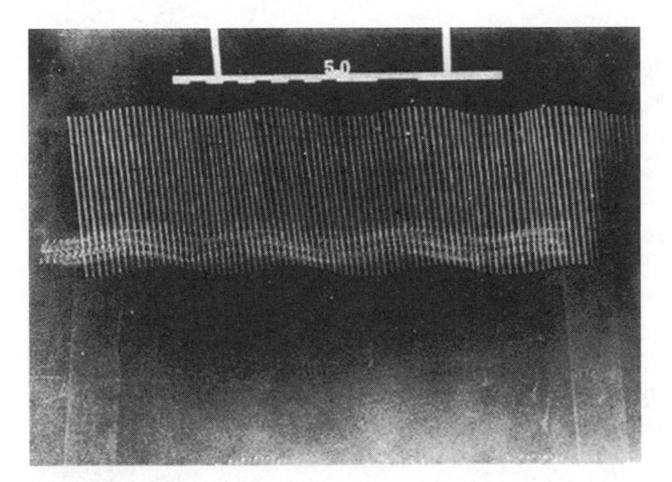

Figure 5.1
Étienne-Jules Marey, *Etude de la locomotion humaine: Homme marchant avec une baguette fixée le long de la colonne vertébrale*, chronophotographie sur plaque fixe, vers 1887, Musée Marey, Beaune, France.

that results can easily be plotted onto a graph, but movement's preacceleration cannot be felt.

But Marey does not stop there. He continues to experiment with the walk, producing a completely different image eight years later. This one, called "Trajectory of the Pubis during Human Walking (1894)" is an undulating line, curving in an elastic zigzag from right to left. This time what we see is not a grid but a rhythm. For this later experiment in locomotion, rather than using a vertical rod to measure movement, Marey places bright points on the body's hips, thus capturing the spiral of movement moving. Without the rods holding the body to a straight line, the curve of movement's spiral makes itself felt. The line does not simply represent movement: it creates the *feeling* of movement. We are moved by what we do not actually see. The elasticity of the image feels like a drawing of vision drawing.

Felt movement is more difficult to plot on straight lines. Measure, or cadence—as opposed to rhythm—produces graphically equidistant formations along which a line can be plotted. Rhythm, on the other hand, is produced through inflection—the infinite folding of a line provoked by vectors of force that alter its trajectory in time and space—and operates in the register of elasticity. A tension

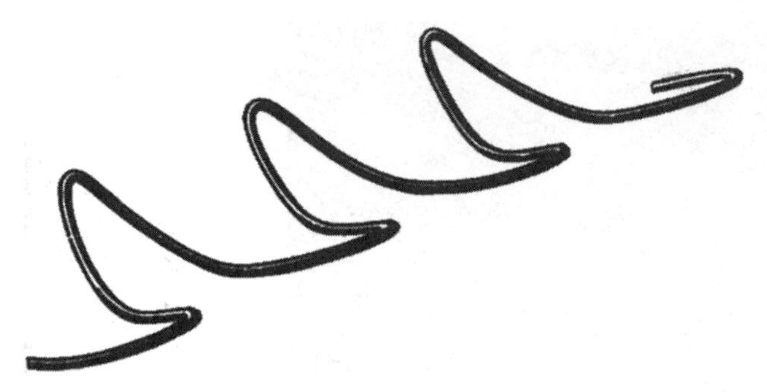

Figure 5.2
Étienne-Jules Marey, *Trajectoire du publis pendant la marche humaine*, p. 150, figure 79, *Le mouvement* (courtesy Jacqueline Chambon).

between measure and rhythm is always operative in Marey's work, particularly in the rift between his writings and the ways his chronophotographies express intensive movement.

The chaos that measure attempts to colonize is what rhythm feeds on: "From chaos, Milieus and Rhythms are born" (Deleuze and Guattari 1987, 313). Chaos is not the opposite of order. What we experience—the event of force taking form—is always prehended from a certain quasi chaos: the indeterminacy of the not-yet-actual. As the virtual passes into the actual, in this in-between passage where force begins to take form, a chaos of incorporeality can be felt. This chaos is the intensive magnitude of potential. Positivist science seeks to overlay potential with order, imposing measure from the outside. Radical empiricism works from the quasi chaos of the not-yet, beginning in the rhythmic middle of a becoming event. As the events reach what Whitehead calls their subjective form—their completion or concrescence—the quasi chaos of their taking-form is overlaid by the factness of their completion. But events always in some sense remain invested with this quasi chaos, for they have been prehended from the indeterminacy of the forces that compose them. This indeterminacy is a living aspect of the event. It is what rhythm feeds on.

Rhythm is active in the associated milieu of this quasi chaos. It is not rhythm added onto measure but relational movement in its incipiency. Associated milieus are vibratory with states of becoming. "Every milieu is coded, a code being defined by periodic repetition; but each code is in a perpetual state of transcoding or transduction" (Deleuze and Guattari 1987, 313). Rhythm passes through, qualitatively altering the milieus it creates that, in turn, generate it. "Transcoding or transduction is the manner in which one milieu serves as the basis for another, or conversely is established atop another milieu, dissipates in it or is constituted in it" (Deleuze and Guattari 1987, 313). The early image of the man-rod walking imposes measure onto movement. The movement is territorialized into coordinates that tend to close down its operations. The constraints of the walk—one foot on the ground at all times—become coded in a regularized space-time, which closes down all potential for the walk to evolve beyond its initial normative constraint. The resulting perception of the image is a perception *of* movement rather than a perception *in* movement. In the later image of the walking undulation, the walking transduces into curvilinearity, producing an associated milieu of body-movement-environment. Here perception participates in the quasi chaos of preacceleration. The associated milieu of preacceleration vibrates with the potential of polyrhythmicality. The walk as such is not transformed, it is what is emphasized that is different. This time the walk is more than a regularization of coordinates. It is a line of force, an elastic pulling and pushing through movement's intensive magnitudes. What is felt

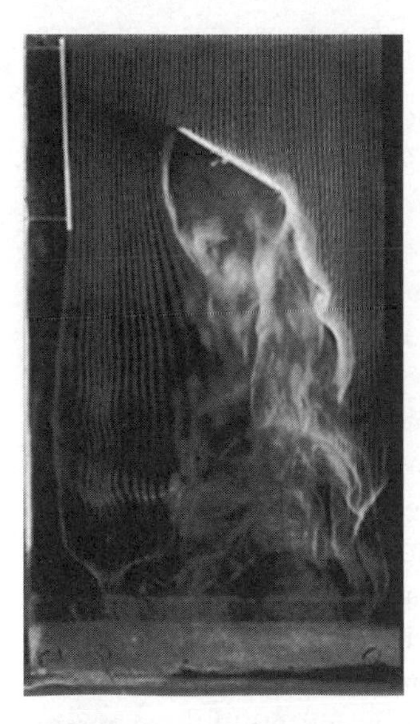

Figure 5.3
Étienne-Jules Marey, surface courbe inclinée, angle 36 degrees, tirage d'après plaque negative sur verre, 10 × 5 cm, 1901, Musée Marey, Beaune, France.

in this second image are the microperceptions at work in the event of moving through movement. Vision suddenly sees more than the walk it has come to expect through visual representations. It sees the expression of movement's curvilinearity.

Foggy Expressions

The images of air and smoke Marey creates at the end of his life (1898–1901) build on this curvilinearity of movement moving, taking it to an even higher level. These are images of movement disturbance that play with the timeline of form's composition. These movement experiments with gaseous fluids are perhaps the best evocation of the poetry of the almost-seen in its many stages of microperceptibility. Two images stand out. In the first one, the smoke is traversed by a trapezoid shape that causes a violent undulation of the linear smoke-lines, transforming the composed grid-like surface into a fire-like feeling. To compose a form into a feeling is like making the holes felt even while conserving the whole of undifferentiated perception. To simply say we perceive a shape—a distorted trapezoid—would be to work at the level of deduction. I believe what Marey does is qualitatively different: this work makes the quasi chaos of sensation felt.

To experience the feeling of a form is to experience force taking form. In the 1901 series of movement experiments with air and smoke—using the machine with 57 channels[69]—Marey moves different shapes through smoke. Each movement of the shape through the smoke strands produces a different current. Through these images of forms-passing, we actually see air taking shape. We see the air and feel the form. Marey is once again inventing ways of seeing.

Despite his concern that the senses "often conceal the essential [and] lead to mistakes," Marey's final experiment captures sensation in the making. As always, his interest in the amplitude, force, duration and regularity of the shape of movement lead the way toward new techniques for the foregrounding of the otherwise imperceptible. The whole of his work until then had been concerned with showing how forces could be deduced by a movement-curve in order to relay back to the visible the trace that is imperceptible of movement taking form. In this 1901 series the turbulence of preacceleration is most resplendent. In these images, moving-through shifts from extensive to intensive passage. These are among the most graceful images, where movement-through feels like movement-with. The

Figure 5.4
Étienne-Jules Marey, surface courbe inclinée, tirage papier original, 8.8 × 5.2 cm, 1901, Musée Marey, Beaune, France.

Figure 5.5
Étienne-Jules Marey, *Mouvements d'un cheval blanc*, chronophotographie sur plaque fixe 1886-6, Musée Marey, Beaune, France.

smoke and the object dance together, creating an gaseous plane of consistency. Particularly beautiful is an image where what looks like an oblong object has been moved-through the smoke-lines, leaving an undulating braid in its passage, calm and curvilinear at once.

In the passage from graphic machines to chronophotography, Marey's movement work tends toward expression more than representation. Expression and representation are at two ends of the spectrum of perception. Representation is the coming-together after the fact of an event already constituted. Expression moves-with the very act of perception. The event of expression does not allow for a schism between the event and its perception. The eventness of perception can be felt in the horse experiments, for instance, in the expression of movement galloping. The smoke experiments express movement dancing. The becoming-body of movement is in-formed by the expressions it makes possible. Oblong object becomes winding veil becomes turbulent whirlpool. This is not a metaphor: it is an actual feeling of the almost perceptible virtually seen. In these becoming-bodies of movement, what expresses and is expressed makes manifest the virtual node of the in-between. What we see is not an object, a person, an animal. What appears is the expression of body-movement relation—the interval—brimming over with microperceptions, with microexpressions never quite actualized. What is expressed is the variational field of movement. What is produced is sensation or feeling, affective tone.

To look at Marey's photographs is to feel them. Feeling is an amodal experience that is a passing-between of sense-modes. Perception is constituted by feeling-tones. Perception lures feeling, coalescing visual experience into a force of feeling. Affectively, feeling works on the body, bringing to the fore the experiential force of the quasi chaos of the not-quite-seen. This not-quite is the quality of potential we perceive in many of Marey's movement images.[70] These images do not represent movement, they move-with the movement of the feeling taking form. They are affective because to see is to feel-with, to participate in the intensive passage from the virtual to actualization. What is amodally felt, perceived-with, is the microperceptual appearing at the threshold of sight, but not actually seen. Working at the limit of a body's capacity to actualize, this perceiving-with affectively reworks what a body can do.

Affect passes directly through the body, coupling with the nervous system, making the interval felt. This feltness is often experienced as a becoming-with. This becoming-with is transformative. It is a force out of which a microperceptual body begins to emerge. This microperceptual body is the body of relation. While affect can never be separated from a body, it never takes hold on an *individual* body. Affect passes through, leaving intensive traces on a *collective* body-becoming. This body-becoming is not necessarily a human body. It is a conglomeration of forces that express a movement-with through which a relational individuation begins to make itself felt.

Affective duration is felt in Marey's experiments through the image's force of composition. This composition is not a translation: it is a transduction of movement into sensation through the prism of the image, foregrounding the quasi chaos of movement's incipiency. This mode of seeing is not strictly a looking-for—a looking "for" the form passing through, for instance—it is a looking-with. It is a looking-with because not only do we feel the movement of the images, we feel the holes through which the images leak. In the smoke images, it is as though the smoke were still filtering through our experience of looking. This is what Bergson means when he says that "a world well perceived is a world that never ceases to move" (1990, 343–344). A world well perceived is a perception of the (w)holes of vision where movement commingles with experience to produce expressions of novelty.

From Image to Intensity

When we see-with, what we perceive is the feeling of intensity. We feel intensity without seeing its actual form. The feeling of intensity coexists virtually with what actually appears. Intensity is of duration, not measure. Intensity has no extensive magnitude—it cannot be conceived as separate from pure experience. Positivism's shortfall is its tendency to attempt to capture intensity's extension for a quantitative system of measure.

> In the idea of intensity, and even in the word which expresses it, we shall find the image of a present contraction and consequently a future expansion, the image of something virtually extended, and, if we may say so, of a compressed space. We are thus led to believe that we translate the intensive into the extensive, and that we compare two intensities, or at least express the comparison, by the confused intuition of a relation between two extensities. (Bergson 1910, 4)

Intensity is anathema to quantification. It concerns the elasticity of movement. Intensity in-gathers the imperceptible toward a movement-feeling. This movement-feeling is the experience of force taking form. Bergson writes, "At first [grace] is only the perception of a certain ease, a certain facility in the outward movements. Since easy movements are the ones which prepare the way for others, we are led to find a superior ease in the movements which can be foreseen, in the present attitudes in which future attitudes are pointed out and, as it were, prefigured" (1910, 11–12; translation modified). What we experience as grace is an emergence of future ease in the present movement. A graceful movement is one that feels like it already carries the fullness of the movement-passing within the preacceleration of the movement taking form. Time collapses into an intensity of process, and what we feel is not the object of the experience but the flow of experience itself.

Marey's images of the smoke filaments are capsules of intensity that foreground the process of perception taking form. The movement of the air emerges for perception as a graceful dance that couples the outlines of the forms passing through the smoke with the sensation of their passing. We feel the grace of this passage. The future of movement moving feels like it is taking form in the present. To create an experience of the future in the present requires a foregrounding of the immanence of movement within sensation. Grace taking form is not an experience-of but an experience-with that takes on the color of the inquiry even while it invents new uses for it. Weaving novelty into the very act of perception, Marey's images produce incorporeal becomings, imbuing the experiential process of worlding with the grace of a movement-with that would otherwise remain virtual. Vision curves into its own potential.

"If curves are more graceful than broken lines, the reason is that, while a curved line changes its direction at every moment, every new direction is indicated in the preceding one. Thus the perception of ease in motion passes over into the pleasure of mastering the flow of time and of holding the future in the present" (Bergson 1910, 12). Intensity cannot be measured because it cannot foresee how the future will inhabit it, what qualitative magnitudes will divert it, how elasticity will alter its process of taking form. Intensity is never the object of an experiment: it dwells in the milieu of its process. Grace emerges out of this milieu, not as a marker of a knowable future in the present, but as a calm carrier of future's quasi chaos in the present-passing. Grace is the feeling of being in the eye of the storm, where calm reigns. Grace is out of measure and yet completely in sync with the future passing.

Compulsion to Invent: From Rational to Radical

An experimental result translated into quantitative fact is always judged according to external standards. It is read according to predetermined parameters that stabilize the inquiry by assuming that what is measured can be dissociated from the whole: positivism takes for granted that at least part of the system is stable. In Marey's case, what seems at first not to be open to experimentation is the body itself: in his book on movement, he never questions the givenness of the body. And yet, what is fascinating about his research as it progresses is how the body *does* become part of the inquiry. Over the course of his career, he ends up inventing modes for visualizing individuation, a practice of processual intervention into what constitutes a body in movement. His research becomes one invested both in measuring movement and creating modes of perception for the ineffable: the body-becoming. This unresolved tension in Marey's work between the rational and the radical leads to a constant tinkering with the mechanics of invention such that quantity and quality become intermixed and their complex environment—their associated milieu—actually becomes the object of study.

The radical empiricism of Marey's machinic experimentation can be felt in his continual reinvention of techniques not only for the capturing of movement-passing but for its ghostly evocation in its various quasi-chaotic states of becoming. William James defines radical empiricism as "an empiricism [that] must neither admit into its constructions any element that is not directly experienced, nor exclude from them any element that is directly experienced" (1912, 42). For James, radical empiricism is radical because it begins with the actually imperceptible—relation—and asks how relation produces events of knowledge. In radical empiricism, there is nothing prior to direct experience, and no way to work outside of experience's incipient relationality. "For such a philosophy, the relations that connect experiences must themselves be experienced relations, and any kind of relation experienced must be accounted as 'real' as anything else in the system" (James 1912, 42). In Deleuzian terms, this means that what is foregrounded is not the object, the word, the concept but the assemblage through which ecologies of practice emerge.[71] This process of assembling is never individual—it is collective. Speaking of enunciation as an assemblage, Deleuze explains, "The utterance is the product of an assemblage—which is always collective, which brings into play within us and outside us populations, multiplicities, territories, becomings, affects, events" (Deleuze and Parnet 1987, 51). Radical empiricism experiments with assemblages such as the associated milieu, an environmental in-between that never preexists the force of its taking form. "This is assembling: being in the middle, on the line of encounter between an internal world and an external world" (Deleuze and Parnet 1987, 52).

For Marey, there seems to be no contradiction in the pursuit of positivism through experimentation: Marey sees experimentation as a necessary tool for the production of quantifiable results. The criteria of positivism—"a rejection of metaphysics and in its place an affirmation of facts derived from observation; the proposition that science constituted the ideal form of knowledge; and the understanding that scientific explanations of phenomena would, by definition, lead to one or more laws of which an individual phenomenon is an observed instance" (Braun 1992, 13)—are amply met by the experimental methodology he pursues. And yet, as is becoming apparent, there is also within his work a fascination with the milieu itself and the intensities it is capable of producing. This can be observed in his magnificent sculptural rendition of the seagulls, *Flight of the Seagull: 25 Images per Second* (1887), which brings to life the in-between stages of the bird's flight. If Marey were interested only in the quantitative analysis of the movement of the bird's wings, why would he have the resulting image sculpted in bronze?

Figure 5.6
Étienne-Jules Marey, *Décomposition du vol d'un goéland*, sculpture en bronze, 1887, Musée Marey, Beaune, France.

As the co-arising impulse to measure and experience coalesce within Marey's work, what increasingly emerge are movement machines—machines that do not strictly represent movement but create new modalities of perception. These machines produce more than results. They produce novelty, which sparks thought, which leads to more experimentation. Movement research that may have begun as an exploration of an already-constituted reality becomes a machinic intervention into the not-yet-seen. While Marey-the-positivist continuously strives toward creating more accurate techniques for the measuring of movement, Marey-the-radical-empiricist creates speculative assemblages that induce complex sensations in the name of the perception of perception. The irony: the degree of precision he seeks in the production of quantifiable results contributes to the creation of event-based machines that provoke an active coupling of movement, bodies and milieu.

Multiplicities are evoked in Marey's work both quantitatively and qualitatively. They figure as quantities-for-measure and intensities-in-process. Intensity can never be measured since to measure would immediately interrupt duration, transforming force into form. Yet in the experience of the elasticity of the almost, the virtual resonance of intensity can be felt as movement moves through an actualizing form. While the intensity of passage is not present in the final concrescence of the form, it remains part of the feeling co-arising with the constitution of that particular form-taking. Quantitative results could arguably take the co-arising of intensity and form-taking into consideration in the refashioning of subsequent experimental processes: producing quantitative results need not preclude the experiential. This is the case for Marey, whose experiments create the conditions for the quantitative to be sidetracked by the qualitative. This passage from quality to quantity introduces novelty into his experiments, inciting him to create evolving forms of inquiry. A key question emerges: can there ever be "pure" positivism, or is positivism always moved by the forces of intensive magnitude?

Numbering Numbers

Numbers express this productive tension between positivism and radical empiricism. Counting is one way to understand both the difference and the continuity between measure and intensive magnitude. Bergson explains:

> It is not enough to say that number is a collection of units; we must add that these units are identical with one another, or at least that they are assumed to be identical when they are counted. No doubt we can count the sheep in a flock and say that there are fifty, although they are all different from one another and are easily recognized by the shepherd: but the reason is that we agree in that case to neglect their individual differences and to take into account only what they have in common. On the other hand, as soon as we fix our attention on the particular features of objects or individuals, we can of course make an enumeration of them, but not a total. . . . Hence we may conclude that the idea of number implies the simple intuition of a multiplicity of parts or units, which are absolutely alike. . . . But now let us even set aside the fifty sheep themselves and retain only the idea of them. Either we include them all in the same image, and it follows as a necessary consequence that we place them side by side in an ideal space, or else we repeat fifty times in succession the image of a single one, and in that case it does seem, indeed, that the series lies in duration rather than in space. (1910, 76–77)

The question of how numbers number is central to Marey's experimentation. On the one hand, his process is one of counting as a collection of units. Each movement is mapped so as to be identical (in time and space) to the preceding one. What is measured is not the intensity of the flow but its calculated significance as located on a grid that maps space-time as preexistent. Interesting information can result from such measuring, such as the fact that at one point in time during the gallop, all four of the horse's legs are off the ground, or that in a bird's flight the resistance of air plays a key role.

But this is not the only kind of numbering, nor is it the only counting at work in Marey's experiments. Marey also works with intensive magnitudes, where what is numbered is individuation rather than self-identity. When the trapezoid moves through the smoke, it qualitatively alters the shape of the trapezoid, the smoke filaments, and the air in the surrounding environment. It creates atmosphere, altering the experience of space-time. The counting here is not a quantification of elements. The air can only be known in its transformation. What is measured is as much beauty or feeling as it is shape. This is a transductive operation, whereby different endurances take hold, inviting different kinds of processes to take form.

Marey's work can be seen as engaging actively in the study of movement as divisible (quantitative measure) *and* as indivisible (duration). Different kinds of numberings produce different results. As Marey's work demonstrates, both the quantitative *and* the qualitative are necessary for the invention of new processes for experimentation. While Marey only chooses to give academic credence to one aspect of his method, the intensive magnitude felt in his visual results definitely seems to play a role in the subsequent designing of new techniques for measurement.

The issue of intensive magnitude (multiplicity in duration) versus extensive magnitude (quantitative multiplicity) is akin to the question of divisible and indivisible movement in Bergson. When movement is counted, and when its counts are considered equal to one another in both form and content, it is rendered divisible by the fact of its being pulled out from its previous durational indivisibility. This is necessary for all quantitative research. The difference between positivism and radical empiricism is not necessarily to do with the act of counting (radical empiricism can also seek results) but with the issue of how the point of departure is conceived. Whereas positivism begins with the divisible number as a given, radical empiricism works from the premise of relationality that foregrounds the indivisibility of duration (as pure experience). When radical empiricism counts, it begins in the middle (*milieu*). "We must distinguish between the unity as experienced and the unity which we set up as an object after having thought of it, as also between number in process of formation and number once formed. The unit is irreducible while we are thinking it and number is discontinuous while we are building it up: but, as soon as we consider number in its finished state, we objectify it, and it then appears to be divisible to an unlimited extent" (Bergson 1910, 83).

This is Marey's quandary. On the one hand, he is drawn to the satisfying results of concrete division. On the other hand, he is moved by the interval. His work posits clear distinctions between movement and body. And yet he never begins the process of experimentation from outside the experiment: he experiments from the middle. He posits the body as preconstituted, and yet creates experimental devices that foreground the body's permeability to forces, its transitions coloring its becoming-states.

Marey's crossing-over from positivism to radical empiricism and back can be felt most strongly in his chronophotographic images, which experiment with the idea of overlapping states of transition. Even as Marey defines his results according to precise coordinates of movement in time and space, he continues to devise ways of perceiving the transition from incipiency to displacement as the interplay of relational movement, thus creating a moving space-time in a durationally multilayered environment. Through his chronophotographies, Marey ultimately explores the animation of space-time where different layers of bodies in transition interweave. This experiential overlapping of states is what Bergson calls *pure succession*, an interplay of fields of intensity and qualities of movement melding that produce the feeling of the force of form.

By now it is apparent that Marey's work provokes a tension between radical empiricism and positivist science. His images invite a seeing-feeling of how the drift between measure and duration takes hold. Although he begins with measure, the feeling of duration lingers long after the viewing. Duration is endurance in and of the present-passing. In the smoke images, it is felt at the elastic point where the object and the smoke meet, where the becoming-gas of their passage is experienced. The present-passing is not of the object: it is the affective tonality of the becoming-form of the experience. In Marey's images, this sense of becoming is felt through the ghostly imprint the movement moving leaves on the living trace of the present-passing.

I see Marey vacillating between creating a body of work that begins and ends where movement stops (quantitative analysis based on measure), and creating a practice that works from the milieu of experiential experimentation (qualitative exploration working through duration). Marey in essence creates an associated milieu of positivism *and* radical empiricism. Associated milieus can never be distinguished from the techniques of their functioning: they operate and develop through the relations out of which they are constituted. In Marey's case, his strategies for developing and documenting processes are key both to how results are mapped for scientific publications *and* to how processes are enhanced through the creation of new experiments. Through this singular associated milieu, Marey's research alters the ecologies of practices out of which it builds. His work pushes the limits of positivism *and* brings complexity to the exploration of the concept of relation that is at the heart of radical empiricism.

Since relations are always of different degrees of intimacy, measure does not suffice to make them known. What is necessary is a technique of the in-between that does not seek to assess only the form-as-such (the object, the body) but that is also invested in the milieu through which it comes into emergence. All of Marey's work operates through this tensile environment between measure-representation and rhythm-relation. This is a productive tension, fascinating in the way it challenges Marey's commitment to positivist science and its modalities of measure. He produces, it seems, a continual doubling of experimentation, where he posits the result as the culmination, even while he continues to rebuild the machine that in its next rendition will open incipient movement toward new vistas of unmappability. If Marey were content with measure as such, there would be no need for a new machine, or a more complex technical system. Yet he keeps devising them, creating not only new machinic processes but new techniques of relation, plotting not representational movement in its discrete elements but relational movement, expressed through its incipiency.

Lines of Flight

Marey wanted to learn how to fly. In 1869, he developed his first graphic machine to explore the flight of birds. His main concern was to understand the mechanisms of the wing of the bird in space and the intermittent effects of air on the moving wings. Already in these early graphic experiments, he was attentive to how the combinatory milieu of air-flight-movement reveals operations of force. His research question was to what extent the quality of being airborne depends on the muscular apparatus, and whether the air itself works as a force of resistance to produce an intensive movement that keeps the bird in flight. This question was directly associated to creating a flying machine, an interest that led to many years of experimentation with how flight itself creates the conditions for the bird's movement, and how air resistance rather than simple musculature keeps the bird aloft.

The first machines were quite simple: Marey placed a small sensing apparatus on the edge of each wing that measured the bird's flight. This apparatus's function was to graphically measure each received movement. With a thin cable

Figure 5.7
E. Valton, *Vol des oiseaux, transmission des mouvements de l'aile de l'oiseau aux appareils inscripteurs*, aquarelle, vers 1869, d'après les travaux de Marey, Musée Marey, Beaune, France.

attached to each wing, the graphic machine and the bird were able to communicate. Measuring frequency of wing movement in flight, Marey discovered that "the duration of the lowering of the wing is generally longer than that of its elevation" (Mannoni 2004, 18). As he had presumed (against all scientific speculation at the time), the movement of the bird's wings was not directly regulated by the musculature—it was in fact intrinsically dependent on the resistance of the air acting on the wing. This discovery would have consequences in the field of aviation. But not before Marey stopped attaching birds to machines! As can be surmised, creating the conditions for measuring movement was quite a challenge as long as the bird continued to be restricted to a predetermined circuit. This was the impetus for his later move toward chronophotography, a practice that would allow Marey to develop a sense of the bird's movements that was more closely linked to its actual tendencies *in flight*.

"The veritable perfecting of machines, that which we can say elevates the degree of technicity of a machine, corresponds not to a production of the automatism, but on the contrary opens up a margin of indetermination within the machine itself" (Simondon 1969, 11). The dynamic ground out of which Marey's work evolves is an associated milieu for the rethinking of the rift between the sensuous and the non-sensuous, between the sensing experience of the present-passing and the non-sensuous future-feltness of the past. Each of Marey's experiments evolves out this dynamism. The processes for vision he creates are platforms for relation for the perception of perception. Perception becomes machinic in the sense that it is no longer a stable given in the process of exploring movement, but itself becomes a milieu through which experimentation takes place. In the exploration of margins of indetermination for the machinism of perception, what Marey continuously foregrounds is the imperative to make the machine sensitive to change. From experiments of movement to experiments with movement, Marey's work begins to foreground how perception fields the relation between incipiency and displacement.

Techniques of relation such as those Marey invents are abstract machines,[72] abstract because what they can do is outside the realm of the prethought. Marey's abstract machines for perception operate through the emergences they provoke, forecasting futurity in the making. "When we speak of abstract machines, by 'abstract' we also mean 'extract' in the sense of extraction. These are montages susceptible of putting into relation all heterogeneous levels that move through them" (Guattari 1995, 55). Marey's machines extract the imperceptible, bringing it to the fore not as material for measure but as ephemera for experience. We will never actually see incipiency passing through preacceleration to the interval of movement moving, but we can experience it. This is the richness of Marey's images, which extract the unknowable and force its recomposition with the actual such that a becoming-form begins to act on the incorporeality of its recomposing. Abstract machines do not impose form onto matter, they are processes (of) in-formation, continually, rhythmically recasting the heterogeneous processes out of which they themselves are emergent.

Marey's flying machines never actually manage to fly. This does not seem to dissuade him. Still convinced that he will find a way to transform a bird-like instrument into a flying machine, in 1874—as vice-president of the Société française de navigation aérienne—Marey opens his laboratory and materials to Victor Tatin, a young engineer who had already built a few flying birds propelled by elastic springs (that crashed to the ground). Due to his earlier graphic experiments measuring the movement of air in bird flight, Marey knew that the faster the bird, the more air resistance on its wing, the more solid its trajectory through the air. Slower birds have to move their wings faster to increase the force of resistance. Marey continued to believe that this was key in the development of a flying machine.

Marey's deductions on air resistance in flight influenced Tatin's aviatory experiments. In his 1876 paper entitled "Travaux du laboratoire de M. Marey" (Braun 1992), Tatin presented his most successful flying machine, which operated from the principle that the force of movement in flight is directly proportional to the force of resistance. Eventually, however, in the way of transmutation that took hold of each of Marey's inventions, Tatin's flying machines evolved beyond their originary concept (and the firm belief of Marey's that flying machines would be close to birds in their form) and moved toward what Alphonse Pénand already knew: the best flying machines would not be big birds but aeroplanes.

Although his research on birds did not ultimately lead Marey closer to creating a flying machine, it did invigorate his work on movement, producing some of the most extraordinary photographs of his career. In 1883, with the help of a photographic gun (a precursor to his chronophotographic apparatus), which revolves at different speeds on a stable axis, Marey deepened his research on the movements of birds. The series he eventually develops out of these experiments is well known, entitled *Flight of the Seagull: 25 Images per Second* (1887). Later sculpted in bronze (see earlier image), this series is particularly remarkable in its ability to bring to life the intensive passage from form to force. Working with

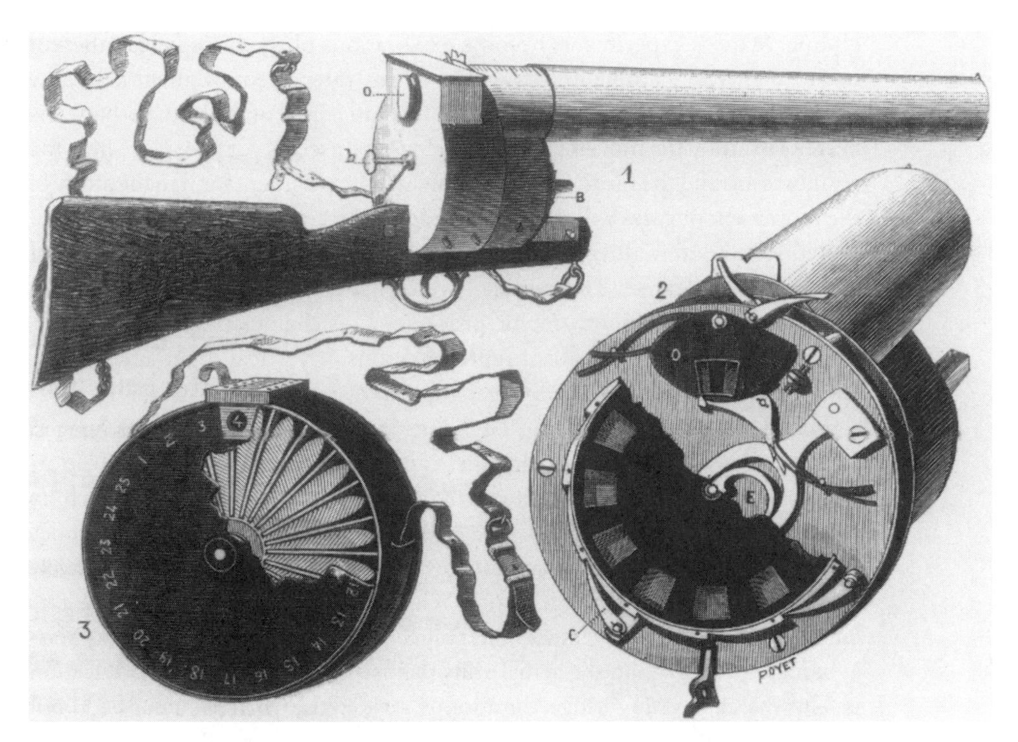

Figure 5.8
Étienne-Jules Marey, fusil photographique, 1882, pp. 131, 132, figures 69, 70, *Le mouvement* (courtesy Jacqueline Chambon).

Figure 5.9
Étienne-Jules Marey, *Vol du goéland*, chronophotgraphie, 50 images par seconde, 1887, Musée Marey, Beaune, France.

gliding, Marey's experiments become explorations of the force fields inherent in the intensive relational movement of flying. Intensive movement is key, he thinks, to understanding how gliding relates to the flight of the bird. Perhaps it is best not to study the movements of the wings themselves but to explore how the air moves around the bird? This transition in his experimentation to the study of the movement of gases will take another decade to come to fruition.

Representation in three dimensions becomes central to Marey's approach at this point in his career. This period—which marks a shift in his practice from graphic machines to photographic processes[73]—is characterized by his dissatisfaction with two-dimensional representations of vertical flight and his fascination with Eadweard Muybridge's rapid-movement stills,[74] which he finds reprinted in a magazine entitled *La Nature*.[75] Stunned by Muybridge's images, Marey decides to create a machine that can capture the in-between of "true attitudes of movement, those positions of body in unstable balance for which no model can pose" (qtd. in Braun 1992, 47). Despite Muybridge's clear influence on Marey at this juncture, what emerges from Marey's process is qualitatively very different from Muybridge's work. While Muybridge's images look like cinematic stills, it is the movement's interval and duration that is palpable in Marey's images, rather than the actual stills themselves. In Marey's work, duration is felt, whereas in Muybridge, duration is divided. Muybridge's images do not incorporeally flow into one another, and are in fact often shuffled for narrative purposes.

Open images produce open systems: Marey's process cannot be stalled. With his developing chronophotographic methods, Marey continues to create image-event after image-event, each richly textured and durationally rhythmic. Sketches of futurity emerge from the chronophotographic processes. More and more, they do not represent movement: they live it. The life of movement Marey experientially captures chronophographically is increasingly movement's virtual passage, its momentary stoppings always elastic, its intervals intensive, felt in the transitions from preacceleration to preacceleration.

A singular written expression of Marey's approach to incipiency and intensive duration, and with it a slight admission of his interest in aesthetics, appears late in his career. He writes: "Sometimes, this superposition of images can be used; it gives a larger intensity to the images that represent moments of lesser velocity of the object in movement" (Marey 1894/2002, 58). In contradistinction with Muybridge's photographs that are divisive multiplicities standing still, Marey acknowledges that his images are concerned with altering durations: "The multiple

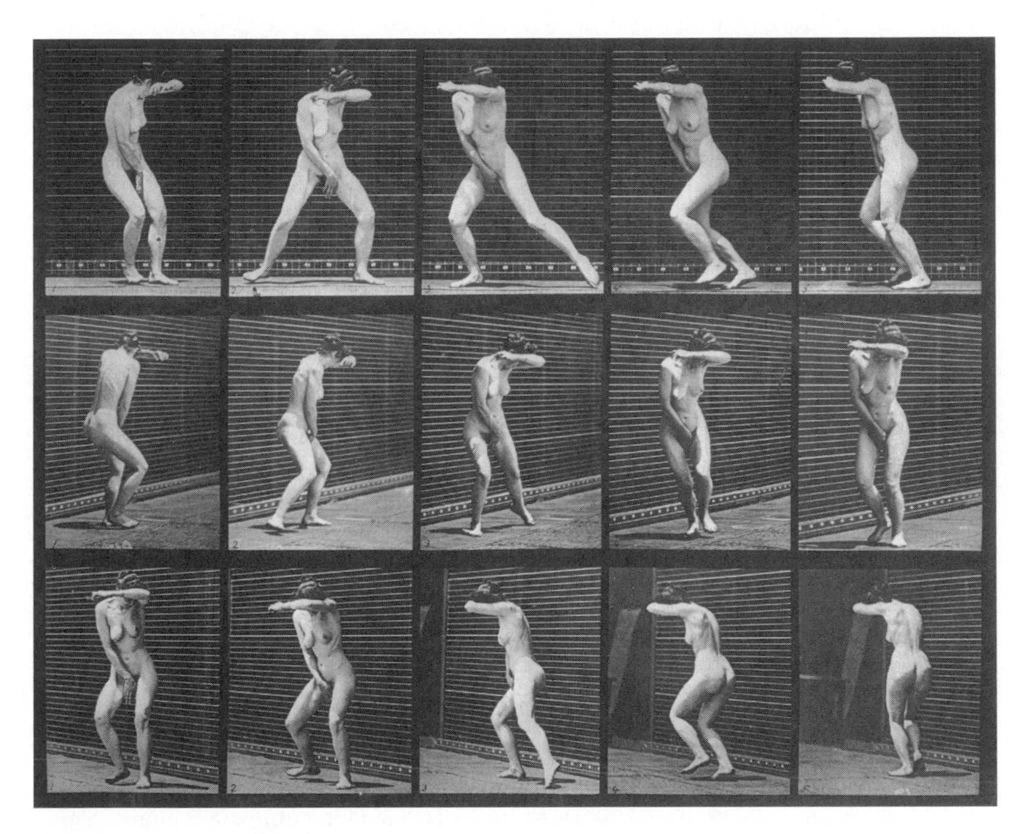

Figure 5.10
Eadweard Muybridge, "Turning Around in Surprise and Running Away," Plate 73, 1884, University of Pennsylvania Archives.

co-present images—imbricated images—in a chronophotograph do not all have the same status, despite the fact that their intermittent measure, their shutter speed, stays uniform" (Didi-Huberman 2004, 239). In this brief passage, it seems as though Marey himself considers his images as potential planes of duration. They are not simply sequences but sequential machines.

"It was been said that my work is 'always the same old thing.' This assessment . . . is the greatest reward for my efforts," writes Marey (qtd. in Dagognet 1992, 63). Marey's perception machines for movement in the making are repetitions with a difference. Each machine does something new, yet retains a similar problem: to map the invisible. The combination of elements tends to be quite similar from one machine to another: a sensor attached to the object of study or used to measure the force of movement, a conductor, and an inscriber. Yet "the same old thing" is more a force of transduction than it is a crude repetition of the same.

> Consider . . . the repetition of a decorative motif: a figure is reproduced, while the concept remains absolutely identical. . . . However, this is not how artists proceed in reality. They do not juxtapose instances of the figure, but rather each time combine an element of one instance with *another* element of a following instance. They introduce a disequilibrium into the dynamic process of contraction, an instability, dissymmetry or gap of some kind which disappears only in the overall effect. (Deleuze 1994, 19)

Marey's process of repetition and difference leads to transductions where movement machines become movements of thought, which in turn become machinic perceptions. Just as his ten seagulls flying is an intimate conjunctive play of what air and bird can become, his machines are associated milieus through which previously unthinkable assemblages take form. The machine becomes the event for the next rendition of movement's elastic curvature, a technique for the co-constitution of the technique-feeling-thought series that is the foundation of experimentation.

Blanchot speaks of "releasing the part of the event which its accomplishment cannot realize" (qtd. in Deleuze and Parnet 1987, 73). Marey does not simply create movement-events: his movement experiments create experiential space-times. He operates on more than one level of experience at once, working with the virtual becoming of elastic forces and with the actual becoming of curvatures of movement. Marey creates out of a dynamic ground that propels eventness to take form visually. His work offers a bringing-to-expression that continuously exceeds its original parameters for measure.

Hesitation

When duration makes itself felt, a hesitation occurs whereby we perceive the fluid force of the world's becoming. Whitehead calls this force of feeling presentational immediacy. This perceptual experience is a relational movement that worlds even as it culls from its worlding the qualities and effects of this dynamic process. Presentational immediacy is perceptually felt duration. What is felt is movement's lingering, its hesitation. This is what we actively perceive in Marey's smoke-filled images: the strange, ethereal passings-through, foggy expressions of movement's potential to linger.

We feel the elasticity of perception. We feel the nuance, the *n*-dimensionality of the elastic that propels the experience toward the very unknowability of future sensations. Agitations, excitations, contractions are felt in the feeling of force taking form. To look at Marey's images is to feel the microperceptual: the perceptibility of the almost.

The elasticity of the almost that is felt so palpably in relational movement as two bodies dance together reemerges here as an activating trace of what perception can do. Perception and representation are no longer a sustainable dichotomy: they are different rhythms of a singular event of relation. What moves as a relation in relational movement moves as a perception in Marey's images.

Intuition is the connecting thread. For Bergson, intuition is a mode of knowledge that distances itself from measure, asking not how something can be divided but how it can be experienced. Intuition relates one concept to another, finding threads, for example, between the becoming-movement of relational movement and the becoming-image of Marey's chronophotography, seeking not to tie them together but to intensively connect them in their capacity to open thought. Openings of thought create movements of thought. Marey's opaque transparencies move with perception. From imposed curves to immanent curvature, perception becomes elastic, and the image becomes graceful. Virtually present, grace makes perceptible the preacceleration inherent in all movement. The grace of Marey's images is their capacity to make the interval felt. We feel the preacceleration through which movement takes form. We feel elasticity even though we cannot see it as such. We experience the imperceptible.

Interlude: Animation's Dance

1. Animation is not the art of DRAWINGS-that-move but the art of MOVEMENTS-that-are-drawn.
2. What happens between each frame is much more important than what exists on each frame.
3. Animation is therefore the art of manipulating the invisible interstices that lie between frames.

—Norman McLaren, qtd. in Pierre Hébert's *Corps, Langage, Technologie*

The art of movements that are drawn is animation's dance of the between. When animation dances, it foregrounds incipient movement rather than actual displacement. Norman McLaren works with movement's incipience, creating techniques to animate this virtual quality of the in-between. His techniques are many, including those he invented: the pastel method, which he first used while creating *Là-haut sur ces montagnes* (1945), and the stereoscopic three-dimensional technique used in *Around is Around* (1951). Each of the techniques for animation McLaren invented or used involves making the virtual interval of movement's preacceleration felt.

Like Étienne-Jules Marey before him, McLaren's experimentation with the incipiency of movement involves creating new techniques to catch movement in its passing. His interest in technique is an exploration with the technicity of the "how" of movement moving: "How it moves is as important as what moves" (McLaren 2006). The how of movement moving is movement's virtual becoming, its preacceleration. Movement's preacceleration is expressed in animation through the active interval between frames. Thanks to the persistence of vision, the interval between frames remains imperceptible as such, the moving-image apparently a seamless unity across the cuts of the frames. Yet the interval is nonetheless active in the watching: it is a virtual event in which the spectator unwittingly participates. We do not actually see the interval, but we do feel its force as it infolds into the perception of movement moving.

In his work, McLaren explores the feeling of movement moving. He asks: How do we activate this feeling, and keep it active in perception? To make incipiency appear, McLaren privileges movement over "content": "For me, the 'purest' cinema is that which communicates the essential of information, thought, and sentiment by movement itself, and allows no other factor or almost to intervene" (qtd. in McWilliams 1990, 17; my translation). To allow no other factor to interfere ensures that movement remains the subject of animation.

The interval is never neutral. It holds in abeyance the traces of movement-passing and prepares movement-coming. That we do not see movement as such in the interval suggests that to experience the feeling of movement is not to view a displacement. It is to sense the force of a movement taking form through its preacceleration. This is what McLaren means when he says he seeks to "film the essence of movement" (qtd. in Bastiancich 1997, 102; my translation).

McLaren draws movement such that it takes consistency not on the frame itself but across frames. Thus, movement is felt not in a pose but in its experiential taking form across time and space. Keeping such a complex process of animating alive involves creating different techniques for different animating scenarios. McLaren was very pliable in this regard, creating forms of animation that evoked the complexity of the kinds of movement he sought to create. Sometimes he drew directly on the film stock; sometimes he filmed the processual traits of a painting in progress; sometimes he filmed with stereoscopic techniques; sometimes he used an optical printer. Each of these and many other techniques were used to explore the consistency of the virtual interval—movement's preacceleration—as it expressed itself through the experiment of the "how" of movement moving.

Animating movement is not restricted to drawing in McLaren's work.[76] For McLaren, sound plays an equally important role, often providing the rhythm for the moving intervals he draws. "For myself, indeed, with an abstract film the most pleasing forms are those which come closest to the music. There must be

Norman McLaren, *Begone Dull Care*, 1949, National Film Board of Canada.

visual equivalence" (McLaren 2006). *Begone Dull Care* (McLaren 1949) works this way, its sound animating the surface of the film. In this eight-minute short, the music of the Oscar Peterson Trio carries the becoming-forms of the images shifting across frames, themselves folding into the musicality of the sound. The visual forms are resonances of color and line more than they are figures. In one particularly evocative section, the colorful screen shifts to black and white, the complex colors morphing into the simplicity of a line. It is as though the consistency of the image were reshaped by the quietening of the sound. The minimalism of the foregrounded line is felt as an animation of the music's affective tonality. The line is perceived through the sound more than it is seen visually, shading into a dot, then reappearing as a line dancing with another line, melding into a musical singularity, then decomposing into the traces of its passing, the piano dancing its formation, the activity of the line appearing and dispersing over a black background with slight traces of color that momentarily dot the screen, only to disappear almost as soon as we've felt a change in tone.

This dance of the line's transformation evokes a quality in McLaren's work that resonates with his desire to make animation dance. His focus is never on the completed image but on the ways its transformation alters the process of experience. "It's constantly changing," he writes of the process of animation's dance, "You're repeating a drawing with change and it's the change that's the interesting part" (qtd. in Richard 1982, 32). Drawing-with, McLaren plays with the potential for animation to become *animate form*.

Greg Lynn defines animate form as the activity of force within movement's animation, distinguishing it from the action of movement's displacement. For Lynn, animate form "implies the evolution of a form and its shaping forces; it suggests animalism, animism, growth, actualisation, vitality, and virtuality" (1999, 9). The process of animating form involves working with the force of the incipiency of movement's preacceleration rather than with the addition of

Norman McLaren, *Pas de deux*, 1968, National Film Board of Canada.

movement to already-executed poses. Lynn uses naval design as an example, "where the abstract space of design is imbued with the properties of flow, turbulence, viscosity, and drag so that the form of a hull can be conceived in motion through water" (1999, 10). Animation is the *how* of movement's potential to alter the force of form.

Pas de deux (McLaren 1967) is the most evocative of McLaren's films on dance, and an important instance of animate form. Similar to Marey's later work on movement, in *Pas de deux* McLaren uses a chronophotographic apparatus to focus not on movement's poses but on the activity of the interval through which movement's preacceleration can be felt. "I had always been interested in the ballet in its purest form, stripped of narrative and anecdotal conventions. I like movement for movement's sake. Abstract ballet" (McLaren 2006).

Abstract ballet divests ballet of its fixity, foregrounding the experience of movement's taking form as accompanied by the techniques implicit in movement's execution. Abstract ballet does not devise a movement that negates ballet's precision. Rather, it foregrounds the quality of the interval that emerges between the rehearsed, ordered, precise techniques of balance, strength, and extension that define ballet. In this regard, McLaren's exploration of the affective potential of balletic precision is close to the work of the Frankfurt Ballet as choreographed by William Forsythe, where what is foregrounded is not the hold ballet has on movement, but its potential to use techniques to transduce the precision of pose into the qualitative open-endedness of force taking form. Foregrounding the affective tonality of ballet's technicity gives McLaren's film its grace. *Pas de deux* is an experience of grace taking form.

A few sequences stand out. In the first, a solo woman dancer is lit up against the black screen. Her body is outlined by the darkness of the background, the light almost piercing through her, lending to her form the quality of an evanescence.

She moves alone at first. Then, her alone is met with the trace of her movements evaporating. Movement emanates from the poses of her movement stilling, traces of her becoming-movement left behind. And then she leaves the pose of her stilled body to move somewhere else. At different time intervals, the posing body follows her continuing movement, creating a refrain of past movement in future becoming. Soon these traces of the surplus of movement passing begin to take over the apparent stillness, folding through the animation's dance, landing not into the next pose, but into the surfacing of its disappearance.

The solo dancer in *Pas de deux* dances her own form-taking, her displacements soon no longer discernable as such. Foregrounding the virtual event of movement moving as animate form, McLaren makes the process of force's contribution to form felt. Incipiency is perceived not in the execution of a movement per se, but in the elastic force of movement's decomposition, allowing "form to occupy a multiplicity of possible positions continuously within the same form" (Lynn 1999, 10).

For Lynn, the most important factor of animate design is the "co-presence of motion and force at the moment of formal conception" (1999, 11). Animate form is not about adding force to the already-thought or to the already-executed. It involves working with the force of potential that is co-constitutive of animation's dance. This is how McLaren works in *Pas de deux*. Rather than offering a filmed version of the ballet dancers' performance of the pas de deux, he opens the force of movement moving to perception.

Pas de deux animates movement's virtual preacceleration as it takes form. The pas de deux itself—a dance choreographed for two in which the male dancer

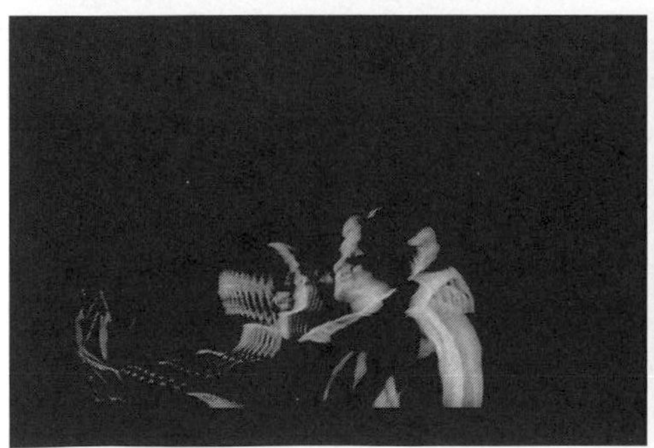

Norman McLaren, *Pas de deux*, 1968, National Film Board of Canada.

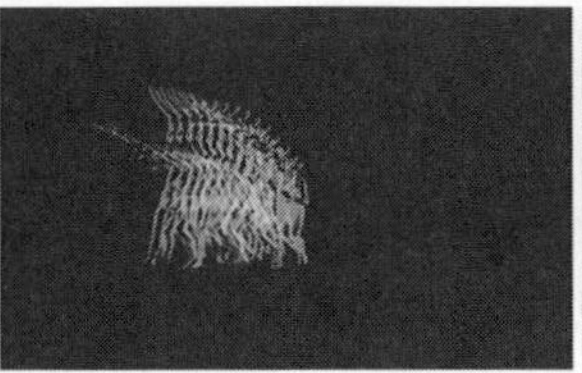

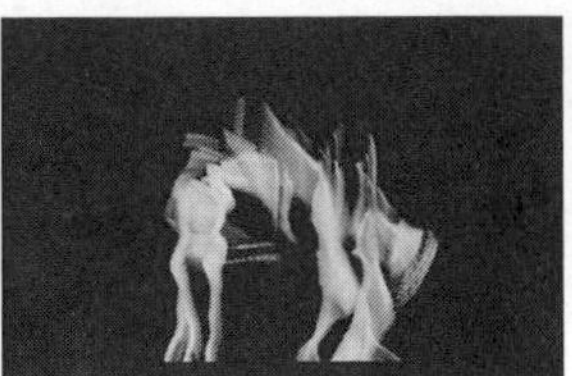

Norman McLaren, *Pas de deux*, 1968, National Film Board of Canada.

supports the ballerina in slow movements, a dance that involves a solo for each and a final coda in which the couple dance apart and together—traditionally represents relation through the choreography of the partner's coupling. The history of relation's role in the pas de deux is key to McLaren's exploration of the intensive passage from incipiency to displacement. Rather than foregrounding the representation of coupling in the dance, McLaren uses the relation between the dancers to make felt the rhythms of passage from the virtual to the actual and back. He plays with the beyond of coupling, making felt the way movement moves the relation. By the end of the film, the feeling of relation has become so intensive that the separateness of the bodies no longer stands out. The individual dancers have melted into the interval, relation itself foregrounded.

In traditional ballet the coupling often feels choreographed and standardized. What McLaren achieves in *Pas de deux* is the transduction of the coupling into the force of individuation taking form through the quality of movement tracing its future-anteriority. This individuation is not the taking-form of a single individual. It is the essence of movement felt as the becoming-body of dance.

In the last section of the short film, after the coupling has disintegrated into the intensity of relation, the incipience of movement becomes so intensified that what is foregrounded is no longer dancers dancing, but the interval itself. We watch as becoming-bodies of force taking form individuate, emerging through the traces of blurring movement meeting movement. Animation's dance becomes crowded with preaccelerations, intervals of movement forming not held to the precision of the balletic pose, but fluid in the transformation of the actual into the virtual. In a steady rhythm of transformation, the choreographed pas de deux morphs from an ordered geometry into a fluid topology, the becoming-spiral taking over the shape of the dancers' bodies, proposing an individuating curvature poised on the cusp of becoming.

6 From Biopolitics to the Biogram, or How Leni Riefenstahl Moves through Fascism

The gesture which we would reproduce on canvas shall no longer be a fixed moment in universal dynamism. It shall simply be the dynamic sensation itself.
—Umberto Boccioni, "Futurist Painting: Technical Manifesto 1910"

Grass-Hoop-Sky

Olympia Part 1, Festival of the People (Riefenstahl 1938), opens with the credits etched into rock. As the credits give way to the first image, the frieze comes to life. Bodies in stone become bodies in motion, emerging in a slow dance as the camera circles the ruins of what looks like an early Olympic site. This slow dance of the camera is accompanied by a sense of rock coming to life. We perceive a double, even triple movement: the music plays the atmosphere that transforms the ruins into mutating forms that give way to a moody sky. The sky is a protagonist: it awakens slowly, the sun languidly piercing through the image's opacity. In tandem with this gradual transformation from dawn to day, the camera movements create a mood of metamorphosis. By the time we reach the structure of the Parthenon a few minutes into the film, a mood of lingering transformation has been etched into the landscape's permutations. We have been led along the uncanny passage of transfiguration. In the opening of *Olympia*, Riefenstahl does not simply show us a field of ruins. She brings it to life.

From the very first shot, as the camera breathes movement into stone, it plays with the dynamics of appearance. This is reminiscent of an earlier scene in *Triumph of the Will* (1935) where Riefenstahl films the approach of Hitler, Himmler, and Hess. As we watch the three figures moving toward us, the camera pans from behind large columns, repeatedly blocking our view. The paradox of this technique is that the momentary and repeated obfuscation of Hitler, Himmler, and Hess's physical presence has the uncanny effect of intensifying the event of their arrival. We feel the virtual force of their importance through the disappearance of their actual bodies. A similar effect is produced in the first scene of *Olympia* as the camera approaches the Parthenon.

In this approach, the camera pauses at the movement of the grass billowing between the stone ruins. We feel the Parthenon gaining on us before we see it. The grass catches the wind, its ephemeral movement lending affective tone to the stone surfaces. What we see is imbued with the feeling of what we cannot see: the image resounds with intensive movement. Then the ultimate appearance of the imposing remainder of a lost era: a long shot of the Parthenon in full center. The play here is between materiality and fluidity. The material is the density of the ruin, the fluidity of grace taking form in the intensive passage between appearance and disappearance.

Then a face, made of stone and yet almost alive, the almost-flesh of the sculpture caught in a dissolve as the music quietens. Trumpets sound and another stone face enters the image in close-up against a dark background, caught in the between of night and day. As though from below, the next stone figure appears, moving still, shifting into the disappearance of the face that came before.

Figures 6.1, 6.2
Leni Riefenstahl, *Olympia*, 1938 (courtesy Gisela Jahn).

Immanent movement transduced into the opacity of the stone surface. A physical transcendence.

Dawn begins to rise as the next body appears, the camera dancing around it and then panning out. The violins begin to play, lending an eeriness to the encounter between the statues. Bodies, face to face, seem to flow away from one another, meeting and dissolving. The next body makes itself felt in an atmosphere of smoke, as though rising from the ruins. From stone to flesh, the between of night and day, of appearance and disappearance, creates the first living being: the stone body of the discus thrower begins to move. We watch the magnificent transformation from incipiency to displacement as the discus thrower merges with and then detaches himself from the sculptural remains. The camera caresses this body-emergent, fascinated with its smooth surface becoming-flesh. The body has been created, and it is already more than one.

Throughout *Olympia*, the protagonist is not the body as such but its atmospheric coming to life in relation to an always emergent environment. Think of the discus thrower: slowly, the camera circles, the body's movements taking shape in the becoming-form of a spiral. The body isn't yet moving—*the earth is moving*. As the spiral opens, the body begins to move, its preacceleration tearing flesh from stone. He moves, but only insofar as the whole image moves: what we experience is a pure movement (what José Gil calls *a total movement*[77]), a movement that qualitatively alters a body's capacity to become.

The discus thrower moves the image, altering how body, flesh, and image interact. He provokes what we could call the first series of the film, the ball-javelin-discus series. Here as elsewhere, Riefenstahl does not foreground a particular Olympian body. She creates a mobile series that makes apparent how movement is infinitely more than its displacement, and how a body emerges from the incipience of movement moving. Bodies, for Riefenstahl, are what happens in the between of image and movement.

In this first series, we encounter a body-experience more than a body as such. This body-experience is created through a thrownness that makes preacceleration felt. Each shot in the ball-javelin-discus series focuses on the act of throwing. From one throwing movement to the next, we feel the incipient force of movement moving. The camera moves not from body to body but from throwing to throwing. This repeated thrownness keeps a single body from individualizing. Bodies moving co-individuate with a world that becomes thrown.[78] This force of becoming provokes an experiential shift that calls forth a becoming-multiple.

Figures 6.3, 6.4, 6.5
Leni Riefenstahl, *Olympia*, 1938 (courtesy Gisela Jahn).

We experience not the discus thrower, or the javelin thrower, but the very thrownness of experience in the making.

The next series begins with a shift in the music from an orchestral ebullience to a more tentative, lighter score. The thrownness of the last series now merges with the sky, a structural point for the next series. This structural point actualizes the intensive shift from thrownness to swaying. On the intensive background of atmospheric potential, the mood changes. The quality of the movement shifts from a line of flight to a textural surface. The flute is predominant now, playfully interacting with the women's bodies as they merge into one another, shots overlapping. Another multiple body begins to take form, an amalgamation of limbs becoming grass, becoming clouds, becoming atmosphere. The arms dissolve into sky, fading into the legs of a woman skipping, the movement appearing always as though in advance of the displacement it provokes. As with the throwing in the last series, preacceleration makes tangible the way in which total movement *creates* a body rather than simply representing one.

Series shape Riefenstahl's work, giving force not to individual shots but to multiplicities evoked across and in the between of shots. We watch not from shot to shot but from event to event.[79] The event of the second series is how the woman becomes earth becomes sky, moving in relation with an atmospheric becoming of nature. Watching her, we feel the delirium of another spiral emerging. As elsewhere in Riefenstahl, the creation of series opens the image to the transduction from immanent movement to the physical transcendental, where the physical connotes not how the image is represented but how it takes form in tandem with the shape-shifting of time and space. This shape-shifting is felt largely

Figures 6.6, 6.7, 6.8
Leni Riefenstahl, *Olympia*, 1938 (courtesy Gisela Jahn).

through the affective tonality—the atmospheric lightness, in this case—of the series. Affective tonality is key to how the series develop alongside the "content" of the film, allowing the film to take shape on multiple levels at once. Even as the shots glean their shape from images of the young, beautiful, strong Olympian body, what emerges through the multiplicity of resonant images is not a discrete individual but a becoming-shape of movement.

Riefenstahl creates the becoming-body of the second series out of a transduction of consistency into shape, grass + arms. Hers is the creation of a dance transcendent and yet immanently material. Throughout, this immanent materiality is foregrounded, a materiality that takes form as a body-becoming. This body-becoming evokes a physical transcendentalism—physical in its materiality, transcendental in its immanence. What dances is not the body as such but the between of the series, its interval. This interval—what I will call a biogram[80] –shapes the form of Riefenstahl's work.

Olympia never introduces a stable body. Rather, she foregrounds a body that provokes relations between nodes of appearance-disappearance that take form through images intense in their capacity to shape-shift. The body always appears in its splendid materiality at the very cusp of its disappearance. This body-becoming is as alive as the light dancing in the arms-grass-hoop series, and as virtual as the fluid movements of stone, embodying an aesthetics both terrifyingly fascist and biopolitically inventive. This fascism is not "ready-made," not located in the body as already-formed. In *Olympia* we encounter a much more evasive fascism: the fascism of the in-between where biopolitics calls forth a biogram.

The Biogram

What holds the series together? Ball-discus-javelin and arms-grass-hoop are held together by the becoming-body of a biogram. The emergence of a biogram is not the creation of a static body. It is a virtual node out of which a bodyness can be felt. This feltness of a body is an affective experience. It is the tendency of a body to become that the biogram makes palpable. With the appearance of the biogram what is foregrounded is the affective tone of the event rather than a body as such. The becoming body has no fixed form—it is an exfoliating body. It creates space through both intensive and extensive movement, appearing as such only momentarily in its passage from incipiency to the elasticity of the almost. The body in Riefenstahl's work is not given but produced—produced not in its entirety but in passing, in movement, not from one shot to another, but from one series to another.

The biogram is closely related to Deleuze and Guattari's concept of the diagram. The diagram is defined as the conjunctive force that in-gathers an artwork's intensity. Deleuze and Guattari build on this concept of the diagram, suggesting that a diagram is in fact an abstract machine, that "constitutes and conjugates all of the assemblage's cutting edges of deterritorialization" (1987, 141). By this, they mean that a diagram is a technique or series of techniques for the open conjugation of intensities. The diagram is not content driven—it operates at the interstices of composition where the virtual is felt as a force of becoming. From diagram to biogram is a passage through a different abstract machine, one connected to the techniques of appearance and disappearance of a becoming-body. In the case of Riefenstahl, I foreground the biogram because the abstract machine of recombination in her work is one that works specifically on the body.

The series in Riefenstahl are conjugated by biograms that provoke body resonances. They introduce new ways of composing a body. The biogram is what conjugates rhythms of appearance-disappearance for the becoming-body. These are rhythms of speed and slowness, rhythms alive in the nuances of movement moving. Riefenstahl's biograms move across consistencies, creating textures rather than forms. Through the biogram, we experience exfoliation, not a ball; flight, not a javelin; tangles, not limbs. We feel the quality of elasticity before we experience form. The biogram is the becoming-body's intensive edge that makes bodyness felt at the conjunction of image and movement.

The biogram makes itself felt in the intensive passage from one intensity—one series—to another. This shift is never a passive transition that leaves two series intact. It is a transmutation, the biogram the virtual node between the series. The biogram carries the movement of the event even before the event has expressed itself as such. The biogram cannot represent anything because it has no pregiven form. It creates out of the plane of consistency that it preempts. It is diagrammatic because it has not yet determined its function. It resides on the plane of consistency because this is the plane of incipient relationality. The biogram propels a process of determining that always resists final form. It is a relational concept that operates at once from within the series and at the edges of its deterritorialization.

The biogram works in a strange paradox of time. Take the series javelin-ball-discus. This series connects to itself through the repetition of the act of throwing. This repetition is already a difference, not only because of the different bodies or because of the different objects, but because each preacceleration of the throwing body qualitatively alters both what a body can do and what an image can do. Thrownness becomes body. Yet the becoming-body takes form only retrospectively in the biogrammatic conjunction of the series. What conjugates the series is the fact that a body will emerge. Composing the image while keeping its potential for flow alive is one of Riefenstahl's remarkable strengths.

Figure 6.9
Leni Riefenstahl, *Olympia*, 1938 (courtesy Gisela Jahn).

Music is central to this process. The music in *Olympia* is visual as much as the becoming-body is musical. Music is never backgrounded: it is the intensive connective tissue for the physical transcendental.

The merging of series is as essential for the biogram as are the series themselves. Returning to the discus-thrower in *Olympia,* we watch the becoming-body merge with the thrownness and then with the becoming-sky becoming-earth of the women dancing. We soon find we cannot feel where one series begins and ends. The atmospheric sky-landscape becomes the throwing body becomes the dancing body, a multiplicity. This becoming-multiple is not necessarily the becoming-human of the multiple. It is also the becoming-hoop of the thrownness, the becoming-grass of the dancing, the becoming-sky of the arms moving. Bodies culminate as intensive surfaces that intertwine and fold one into another intensively, extensively. Then the becoming-body that was never quite man nor woman, yet also singularly both, becomes fire in a transformation that recalls the phoenix. We perceive not the representation of the phoenix but the becoming-fire itself, the plane of experience of movement in the making.

Thresholds of Appearance

The conjunctive force out of which a body is created is a biogram because of the ways in which it transforms what a body can do. Biograms work on the becoming-body. The biogram must not be thought as an image of the body. It is always deterritorialized. It holds nothing. It is a principle of conjugation, of consistency. It creates a texture before it coagulates into form. Better to say that the becoming-body "biograms." To biogram is to create a virtual resonance that expresses the conjunction between series that prolong what a body can do. Not what movement *is*, but what movement can *do*.

We do not see the biogram: we feel the force of its appearance. The biogram provokes invention through its capacity to conjoin, or create new relations. According to Whitehead, appearance brings forth novelty. "In all appearance there is an element of transmutation" (Whitehead 1933, 214). Transmutation from appearance to disappearance is a shift in phase as well as a shift in mode. From the virtual to the actual, from the biogram to the becoming-body, is not a linear transport. It is a transmutation of process-becoming-form. In this intensive passage, the biogram constitutes active points of creation and potentiality through which body-worlds emerge. The biogram itself does not transmute. The biogram is an operational vector in the transmutation from one series to another. As an agent of recombination, the biogram is not actually *in* time or *in* space: it is a force through which the imperceptible appears as a feltness of time spacing. The biogram has neither form nor content. It is the intensive passage from force to force that moves a body to express its durational intensity.

Biogrammatic movement in Riefenstahl is a thrownness felt as the preacceleration of a body-becoming. Alive in the virtual nodes of the between that composes the images as series, the biogram functions like the persistence of vision in the unaccountable shift from force to form. It makes the interval felt. "On account of the persistency of an image upon the retina, moving objects constantly multiply themselves; their form changes like rapid vibrations, in their mad career" (Boccioni 1970a, 27–28). The mad career of Riefenstahl's art is its incitement to transduce, to become-across in a shattering of the absoluteness of the frame.

Physical Transcendentalism

Futurism's echoes populate the beginnings of cinema and resonate in Leni Riefenstahl's work. Boccioni and Riefenstahl both explore how a wholeness of movement (movement as indivisible) challenges the idea of preexistent space. This is a Bergsonian problem: how to think of space as not preexistent without spatializing the potential emptiness of time's passing. For Bergson, the problem is that if space preexists movement—if space is the container for movement—then movement must be seen as coming in and out of existence. This would mean that discrete movements of time are connected through a process of spatialization. In the vocabulary of the cinematic, this would translate to movement operating only at the cut where one image meets another on the spatializing frame of the celluloid.[81]

For Bergson movement is distinct from space covered. Space covered is divisible whilst movement is indivisible. While neither Bergson nor Boccioni extrapolated their theses on movement toward the cinematic, it seems that Riefenstahl takes up their challenge, creating a durational vocabulary of movement for the cinematic that far exceeds Bergson's ideas about the potential of cinema. Riefenstahl's films make clear that cinematic movement does not only operate at the cut, or at the frame, but makes itself felt in and through audio-visual series.

Riefenstahl's images move. They move both intensively and extensively, always connected to the atmospheres they co-create. Like Boccioni's claim that "our bodies penetrate the sofas upon which we sit, and the sofa penetrates our bodies" (1970a, 28), Riefenstahl insists on thinking the image relationally, foregrounding the role of movement in the very creation of the image-concept. She underscores this important stylistic device by refusing to simply add movement—as a secondary operation—to a preexistent image. For Riefenstahl, interpenetration of strata is key. Boccioni's becoming-sofa functions like Riefenstahl's becoming-body. They both work with the idea of movement as topological transformation, a folding-in and through.

Riefenstahl's images foreground dynamic form. Dynamic form is not movement-of but movement-with. Boccioni uses sculpture to explore the potential of dynamic form. Even a material as seemingly opaque and dense as marble, he suggests, can become-movement. This becoming-movement occurs first within the matter-form itself. Boccioni's investigations into sculpture explicitly challenge hylomorphism, the belief that form is the finite element in the shaping of matter. Hylomorphism's claim: once shaped, matter stills—immobile cut. Boccioni resists this view, exploring instead how what seems immobile may instead be engaged in a kind of absolute movement, a virtual becoming that has its own velocity, a velocity felt not only in the infinite transgressions of both matter and form (in their continual becomings) but also in the dynamism of their coming together. In his "Technical Manifesto of Futurist Sculpture 1912" he writes: "We must take the object which we wish to create and begin with its central core. In this way we shall uncover new ways and new forms which link it invisibly but mathematically to an external plastic infinity and to an internal plastic infinity. This new plastic art will then be a translation, in plaster, bronze, glass . . . of those atmospheric planes which bind and intersect things" (1970, 52). He calls this physical transcendentalism.

Physical transcendentalism is not the annihilation of matter. What could be more material than sculpture? Physical transcendentalism is a way to think matter in movement. It decries the tendency of stabilizing matter into finite form. In physical transcendentalism, movement becomes the plane of immanence through which the becoming-body emerges physically. This physicality is transcendental because the body transcends the immanence even while the movement itself remains immanent. Physical transcendence is a way of conceptualizing the mattering of immanence, the cusp of its becoming actual when what appears is not the body as such but its biogram, the becoming-body at the threshold of appearance/disappearance.

When movement is conceptualized as an add-on to the sculpting of matter—when environment, atmosphere, preexists the sculpture—movement becomes indexical to space. We are left with movement as defined only by the actual bodies taking a stroll around the sculpture. To say that a sculpture moves is to say something entirely different: it is to suggest that form becomes matter in the mattering of form. It is to say that dynamic form is the molecular transduction that creates space rather than inhabiting it, physically transcending matter as precomposed form. Sculptural exfoliation. When the sculpture physically transcends its materiality, it does not become any less material. A becoming-body takes form that is neither strictly sculptural nor strictly physical: physical transcendence.

Physical transcendence involves transmutation from force to form, where the force field continues to be immanent to the experience of the taking-form. Transmutation produces not simply a change of state; it invents a new process. Physical transcendentalism for Boccioni is immanently material, material not in the sense of material stability (if there were such a thing) but in the sense of the becoming-molecular of matter's virtual tendencies. An event is physically transcendental when the virtuality of force is felt in and through the material stratum, such that its materiality exposes and makes felt the virtual potential of its force. The physical transcendental is the mobile cut that produces "mysterious affinities which create formal and reciprocal influences between the different planes of an object" (Boccioni 1970b, 61).

From Movement to Movement-Image

Deleuze's notion of the movement-image is one way of thinking the wholeness of movement in conjunction with the becoming-molecular of matter. When movement is conceived as transmutational, it is no longer derivative. A movement-image is no longer the image "of" something else. Movement no longer foregrounds a part-object—it transmutes the image. Movement as image reveals force not as a discrete element of form but as its operational envelope. Holding force in abeyance, the image foregrounds its experiential nature. This experiential wholeness of movement moving-with and moving-within the image is always at once actual and virtual. It is actual when it is prehended. Otherwise it remains virtual, backgrounded in the imperceptible wholeness of its infinitude. All of movement can never be prehended: prehension is a pulling out of portions of duration—events—out of which a nexus of experience is composed. This nexus is not an "out-there" that predates the event. The event is the movement of the image, its withness of movement moving. Wholeness of movement upsets the linearity of time: planes coexist and intersect.

The Deleuzian movement-image provides a vocabulary for thinking the indivisibility of movement cinematically. Movement in the movement-image is not image + movement: it is mobility-becoming-image. Thinking the movement-image sculpturally through Boccioni provokes a movement of thought that encourages us to conceive the surface as a fold rather than an area. "Sculpture must . . . make objects live by showing their extensions in space as sensitive, systematic, and plastic" (Boccioni 1970b, 61). Mattering form implies a becoming-plastic that, in Boccioni's words, is sensitive and systematic. This pliability of experience is one with the sculptural matter, with its becoming-movement: sculpture becomes a moving-image. If we insist on thinking the image sculpturally—which does not necessarily mean to give it three dimensions, but rather to give it plasticity or topology—the mobile cut can begin to be conceived topologically as well. This allows us to make the shift from a linear action line of shot-cut-shot or frame-movement-frame to the interpenetration of series. It is important to remember that even poses are mobile—movement moving need not refer to extensive movement. As with Boccioni's sculptures, the mobile cut moves intensively, creating rhythms between rest and movement. Movement-images catch mobility in its passing.

On a topological surface, all cuts are mobile: the mobile cut defies strict succession. A mobile cut demands of the surface that it be infinitely mobile. It does not presume that movement begins only once the frames meet, assisted by the projector. Movement is folded into image, becomes image: there is no fold that cannot be folded again. Pastness envelops futurity, bleeding time into movement and movement into time. The duration—the space-time—of a topological surface is intensively extensive, continually recomposing along new curves.

Dynamic form is not of an order of poses or privileged instants. Dynamic form is produced through the spectre of immanent movement. Yet dynamism, it bears repeating, is also material. It is force felt— incorporeally material, physically transcendental, intensively mobile. Virtually there. For Deleuze, the cinematic image foregrounds dynamic form. This is because the image can never be fully constrained: it moves, and it will continue to move, even beyond its actual movement. It is virtually there long after the prehension of its poses. Any pose, any stilling of the image, is simply another durational stratum in the complex experience of a lived perception. What the image can do is never exhausted. This is also what Boccioni is trying to say. Although the sculpture seems to give in to the pose, the pose is in fact given to the sculptural movement. You create the pose by prehending it. You actualize it. But its actualization is only as real as the intensive movement that backgrounds it. Any actualization can produce a pose, but this pose will have been created by a mobile cut that is a becoming intensive of extensive movement. The pose is never the starting point. It is what Deleuze calls a *crystallization*. What you think is stable is only as stable as your capacity to hold it to itself. This is not to suggest that the flux is outside, in excess of, the prehension of a pose. It is simply to say that the event—even the pose—is dynamic, actively becoming in a Spinozean flux of rest and movement. Rhythm is key.

Becoming-Rhythm

A contemporary of Boccioni and Bergson, and a great influence on Leni Riefenstahl, Émile-Jacques Dalcroze developed a taxonomy of rhythm out of which he created Eurhythmics, a pedagogic tool for movement central to the work of many modern dancers, including Mary Wigman, one of Riefenstahl's early teachers.

Dalcroze began his research with an interesting question: how is rhythm felt? In the course of his exploration into the varieties of modes of hearing and feeling rhythm, Dalcroze discovered that rhythm is not solely of the ear. It is amodal, and even more than that, it is virtually physical. This discovery led him to question how rhythm was taught. Too often, he observed, rhythm is conceived as an external meter for an internal process. Yet rhythm, he writes, "call[s] for the muscular and nervous response of the whole organism" (Dalcroze 1921, vi). Developing an early vocabulary for kinaesthesia and proprioception, Dalcroze noted that "sufficient attention is not paid to the determination and analysis of the relations undoubtedly existing between sound and dynamics, between pitch and accentuation, between the varying tempi of musical rhythms and the choice of harmonies" (1921, 6).

For Dalcroze, rhythm is not cadence or measure. It is not external to experience. To extrapolate from Dalcroze, this means that rhythm moves through elastic points on durational planes. These planes are milieus of transmutation. They are not locations as such: they always exceed what Whitehead calls *simple location*. This means that they have no discrete spatio-temporal coordinates and do not fill a definite region of space. Rhythm exfoliates, creating movements out of associated milieus that work as thresholds for the becoming-body. At these thresholds, potential is stored. To say that potential is stored means that not all that is proper to rhythm actualizes.

Rhythm can never be measured as such: it operates conjunctively. It is the and . . . and . . . and . . . of the rhizome that never finds a final territorialization. Rhythm provokes a milieu that is capable of accelerations and decelerations beyond the control of the apparatus that would seek to structure it. For Dalcroze as for Riefenstahl, rhythm becomes body. Dalcroze writes: "It is impossible to conceive a rhythm without thinking of a body in motion" (1921, 82). Movement produces rhythms as rhythms produce bodies. The biogram in Riefenstahl is the becoming sculptural of rhythm that creates a body-becoming. Rhythm: the durational modulation out of which a biogram is born.

For Boccioni there is an implicit connection between rhythm and force. Force-lines are what bring materiality to life. In Riefenstahl, they move intensively, folding topologically, transmutational across series—from grass to hoop, from thrownness to sky—expressing the potentialities of matter. Matter becomes force before it becomes form. Modeling the atmosphere is not about creating an outside for a sculpture. The inside-outside dichotomy must be dissolved: with rhythm there are only folding surfaces. Transmutation is vital to this process, because rhythm is not about content: "Rhythm is not on the same plane as that which has rhythm" (Deleuze and Guattari 1987, 313). Rhythm is a force for mattering on the cusp between the actual and the virtual, felt both actually and virtually in the between of the series, causing a change of direction, a jump, a syncopation. Rhythm is that which *propels* the force of movement (the energetic throwing—of the discus, the javelin, the ball) and not the displacement as such. Rhythm takes hold in *Olympia* not where the bodies can be differentiated as individuals but where movement becomes body and body becomes movement. Rhythm in Riefenstahl is the *n + 1* of the body in movement, the more-than that creates—tangibly, affectively—a becoming-body.

Take two scenes. The first is the one in *Triumph of the Will* mentioned earlier. This scene opens on the stone eagle of fascism, blending slowly into the swastika that is its base, and then reaching behind to the moody backgrounded sky. The orchestral sound builds and conjoins with a long shot that captures the dense straight lines of the standing soldiers choreographed expertly in the name of the fascist machine of organization. A wide central path is left open and down this path we watch as three bodies walk toward the flames, Hitler, Himmler, Hess.

The shot of these men is first taken from above and behind and then slowly pans toward stone columns where a delegation awaits. As it reaches the columns, the camera alters its trajectory and begins to move across the shot to film intermittently from behind stone. This shift in the camerawork alters the composition of the shot. What we want to perceive is momentarily eclipsed by the stone columns. The image of the three men's approach is one of appearance/disappearance that brings their grandeur into focus while catching in its intensity the stone-coldness of the perched eagle amid the immense swastika-clad flags that compose the militarized space.

In this play of appearance/disappearance, the rhythm of the image is interlaced with the marching cadence of the orchestral music. We prehend the scene in quick bursts, our perception of the juxtapositions of various verticalities polyrhythmic. The cadence does not take over: the measure is more than one. The provocation is affective. The audio is not outside: we feel its movement as part of the image's force. Polyrhythms of appearance-disappearance shift the affective tone of this experience of almost-seeing. Riefenstahl intensifies this affective tone as the scene progresses by alternating rhythmically from Hitler's body to the military bodies and the crowd. The one-many is achieved through quick succession: the crowd grows in consistency while Hitler's body defines itself as the locus of singularity.

The military measure of the disciplined marching is predominant and overpowering without being the only rhythm at play. There is a fissure here between what we hear and what we see, a strange cadence in step with a rhythmic

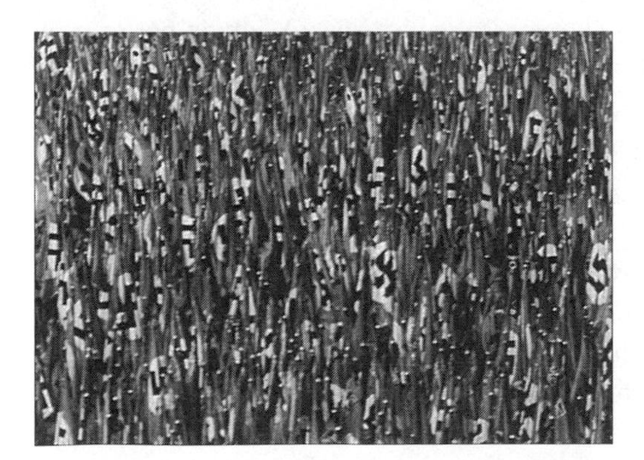

Figure 6.10
Leni Riefenstahl, *Triumph of the Will*, 1934 (courtesy Gisela Jahn).

disequilibrium, provoking a slight fissure in the interval between the planes of composition and organization. And then an incredible shot: a sea of flags. A rhythm all its own, the flags create a moving landscape, a play of texture and force that never quite takes form as a unified entity. In the creation of this plane of consistency, the image is immediately transported onto the plane of physical transcendence. As the camera pans out, we feel movement marching to the rhythm of pure charisma.

There is a tension here and elsewhere in Riefenstahl's films between the God-infused transcendence of the fascist era—which is an opening onto an idea of a body beyond all bodies—and the physical transcendence proposed by Boccioni—the incorporeal body-becoming. While the Hitlerian transcendence seems to take hold through the filming of the large choreographed compositions, forcing a continual recasting of the plane of consistency into a plane of organization, thereby combining transcendence with disciplinarity, a resolutely *physical* transcendence also operates in Riefenstahl's work, dominant by the time she makes *Olympia*. In *Olympia*, rather than moving between the choreographed disciplined body to the overbody of the decisively non-Nietzschean superman, the biogrammatic plane of consistency for the most part shifts toward a transcendence that excites or expands matter rather than reorganizing it into an immanent disciplinarity. And yet these two tendencies do sometimes overlap in her films, generating a complex intertwinement of her work with the Aryan superbody ideology of the fascist regime.

A similar shot a few years later from the second part of *Olympia* underscores this tension between disciplinary transcendence of physical transcendentalism. This scene focuses on dancers choreographed by Mary Wigman performing movements inspired in part by Dalcroze's Eurhythmics. The scene begins with the camera focusing on a few women dancing, their arms waving as their bodies seem to dissolve into one another. The plane of consistency appears through the dancing arms moving in contrapuntal rhythm with the sky. The swaying of their arms gains in consistency as the camera begins to pan out first horizontally and then vertically. The bodies become atmospheric in a way reminiscent of the earlier arms-grass-hoop series, the immanent movement of arms holding pins swaying together not unlike that of the flags in *Triumph of the Will*. Women-dancing-with-pins merges into the swaying of a multiplicity. Like the earlier shot of the moving flag series, this series is constructed on a plane of immanence that moves toward physical transcendence. Its movement moves us beyond the material into the physicality of its virtual tonalities even as it remains material.

Figures 6.11, 6.12, 6.13, 6.14
Leni Riefenstahl, *Olympia*, 1938 (courtesy Gisela Jahn).

And yet, as though called back by the transcendental of fascist doxa, the body suddenly becomes disciplined, all subtlety cast aside. As though in direct contact with the transcendent disciplinarity of the absolute state, the undulating series of pins-bodies dancing organizes itself in firm, straight lines. From flow to square, from becoming to being, the camera reveals a sudden materializing of the plane of organization. Physical transcendence always risks being captured by the war machine of the totalitarian state.

Riefenstahl's films develop the concept of dynamic form in Boccioni and the mobile cut in Deleuze/Bergson to arrive at a reassertion of the ways in which movement privileges expression over content. The foregrounding of dynamic form suggests that Riefenstahl composes *with* fascism but does not compose *a* fascist (disciplinary) body. What she composes is the expression of a becoming-body symbiotically linked to fascism but in excess of its disciplinarity. Riefenstahl composes-with. She begins with the beautiful, the young, the strong, but what she composes is never a particular or individual body. Movement is the commanding form of her work.

Commanding form is how the virtuality of a work connects to the manner in which a work reiteratively takes form.[82] In music, it refers to what sustains a work in the repetition of its playings. When we experience Riefenstahl's work, it is important to ask how it takes form today, how its reiteration over more than a half century sustains itself, how the shape-taking and the form-finding of her images continue to resonate. A work's commanding form is not associated to a moral imperative. Riefenstahl's images will never be disconnected from fascism. The point is not to attempt to do so but to evolve with them to connect to the force of their physicality within the transcendence her work forecasts.

Boccioni writes: "Let's split open our figures and place the environment inside them!" (1970b, 63). The commanding form of a work makes felt the effects of the virtual by making the inside-out of a work felt. Work becomes environmental, no longer distinct from the "where" of its taking form. The environment becomes embedded in the work, foregrounding new centers of activity through which the work continues to evolve. This evolution is less an actual taking-form than a virtual shape-shifting that alters the qualitative dimensions of what an image or a work can do to shift with and through time. From content to line of force. This is what Boccioni means. Make the environment "part of the plastic whole" (1970a, 18). Not environments of but environments with: worlds for the taking whose force lines produces infinite surfaces that fold, drawing out not the form as such but its potential for transformation.

The becoming-body in Riefenstahl is a force to be reckoned with, not least of which because it reinvents space-time. It is a force for the future. Certainly, its dynamism remains imbued with the charisma of Hitler's fascism. Yet it is also more-than: it becomes beyond the boundaries imposed by the era of its inception. It is more dangerous, more powerful, more evocative than what has been called a "fascist body" or an "aesthetic of fascism" because it is infinitely more malleable even than the regime itself. While the regime instantiates rigid planes of organization onto its population, thereby creating a continuous shift between the biopolitical and the disciplinary, Riefenstahl's bodies barely require the disciplinary. She begins there, certainly, working with the trained bodies of the military and of Olympic athletes, yet departs from their individuality as bodies of a certain time and space toward the creation of a becoming-body of absolute movement. The body she creates is beautiful, but not only in its human dimensions—it is a body-becoming-sky as much as a body-becoming-limbs. It is a plane of consistency of swaying grass opening onto sculptural flesh, the becoming-body emerging in the between. The becoming-body of the not-yet.

Take a later image of Riefenstahl's: the Nuba woman, black, statuesque, glossy, photographed against a blue blue sky, captured slightly from below. This is another instance of the extraordinary physical transcendentalism with which Riefenstahl creates and out of which no straightforward disciplinary or state racism can be delineated. There is a racism, I believe, but one that is immanent to the becoming-image, to a space-time without predetermination, a racism active on the biopolitical plane of populations, affective tones, and compositional series. What emerges: a becoming-multiple of the body that does not normativize a body before calling for its physical transcendence.

In Riefenstahl the body becomes "an involuntary medium for the expression of thought" (Deleuze and Guattari 1987, 85). The movement of thought Riefenstahl creates around becoming-bodies foreshadows a new aesthetic that is immanently political in its consequences. Riefenstahl is right to say she does not stage ideological political encounters. Her politics are not of the ready-made kind. They are affective politics. Through the shifting biograms of her work on the body-becoming, Riefenstahl opens politics to affects that resonate through bodies not unlike contemporary political tendencies. Such affective politics draw from certain aspects of fascism, but are much more powerful in their creation and mobilization of images than is Hitler's so-called fascist aesthetic. Unlike Hitler's aesthetic, the affective politics in Riefenstahl's work do not have to concern themselves directly with disciplining the elusive body. Riefenstahl creates (with) affect. She creates with affect's incipient movement. Riefenstahl thus creates a becoming-body that transcends its simple location, continuously moving toward an infinity of recombination. Conjunctively, biogrammatically, Riefenstahl creates the ultimate body without organs. Pure plastic rhythm.

This pure plastic rhythm is an immanent form in every sense. Rarely portrayed in its complete organicity within the frame, the body in Riefenstahl moves across milieus through conjunctive rhythms that create movements of thought. These movements of thought are not metaphorical. They are virtually present in each biogram, in each recomposition of shifting series. They are much more potent than any content-driven politics. Whereas content-driven politics offer the opportunity to stage resistance by producing or reacting to an object of contention, Riefenstahl's work propels thought into recombination. Affectively, her work draws us into space-times of experience that are not yet composed around a specific body. It becomes our task to compose from the edges of expression to the body's virtual center.

Micropolitics of Movement

Affective politics are not moral politics. An emphasis on movement does not promise an emancipatory politics. Affective politics are what we preconsciously make of them. They are of us and with us: we recompose with them. In this way they are much more dangerous and much more powerful than content-driven politics. They are politics for the making. Affect makes bodies even as it is made by bodies. It preempts what a body can do. In this way, Riefenstahl's work is prescient: hers is a contemporary political vision.[83] This is a politics affective in resonance, imagistic in content, polyrhythmic in style, a politics that has long left behind the figure of Kant's rational modern subject. This is not a politics already territorialized by the sovereign state. It is a micropolitics of the body through which force-lines create biogrammatic tendencies that beg the question of what politics can do. What politics can do in Riefenstahl's work is a question of affective tone, of expressivity, much more than it is a question of content. The politics of movement Riefenstahl's work proposes is a politics of futurity where the notion of the to-come remains unknowable. Such a politics works at the edges of a biopolitical tendency. To think this edge—the extreme topological surface where rhythm becomes body—it is necessary to think the active passage from biopolitics to the biogram.

From Biopolitics to the Biogram

Michel Foucault defines biopolitics not as that which replaces the disciplinary but as a series that works conjunctively with the notion of the disciplined individual while it moves beyond it toward a body-becoming. In the biopolitical episteme, movements of bodies work not at the level of individual detail but with global mechanisms of equilibrium, of regularity, of normativity. To interject into the normativity of the body-politic does not imply an intervention within a particular body but an intervention within the micropolitics of movement itself. Riefenstahl's work emerges from this biopolitical tendency, yet already moves beyond it through the biogram. Riefenstahl's becoming-bodies preempt the next episteme, one that concerns neither what a single or a group body can do but how a focus on movement moving can create a critique of pure feeling.

The techniques of movement at work in Leni Riefenstahl's conception of the movement-image move from the biopolitical toward the biogram in the sense that they emerge in the interstices of a body-becoming from the question of what a body can do. They operate through forces that create. For Riefenstahl, it is not a question of the power of a particular body. The body emerges not fully formed but in relation to an associated milieu that is itself a body-becoming.

Riefenstahl's politics are affective because of their insistence on making conjunctions at the level of the incipiency of the preformed. What is expressed through her work are the rhythmic pulsations of dynamic form: her images work liminally from the edges of concepts and forms, folding them beyond their limits. Riefenstahl's aesthetic is a politics both dangerous and inventive, productive of the potential of the more-than that is palpable in the rhythmic planes of consistency biograms call forth.

Riefenstahl produces not specific politics or bodies as such but milieus of potential. The biograms she foregrounds are rhythmically created in an architectonic of audiovision where the sound never precedes the image, and where affective tone takes precedence over content. This is even the case in her editing: when Riefenstahl creates a work, she catalogues the film not strictly according to content but according to what she calls "atmosphere." Riefenstahl inscribes rhythm directly into the process of editing, already emphasizing in the precomposition phase the image's skyness, its laughter or sadness, its darkness. The protagonists in Riefenstahl's films are affective tone, lines of force, polyrhythms. Her techniques are never created outside or in addition to the body in movement. Her shots are events.

These techniques are also preinscribed in her camera work. In the marathon sequence in *Olympia*, for instance, Riefenstahl attaches cameras to the bodies of the runners to impart the sense of rhythm of their running and then overlays the image with an orchestral movement so quick and powerful that it seems to qualitatively alter the running: through the relation between audio and image, it feels as though the runners are moving more slowly. As the music increases in crescendo, the cadence of the runner dissolves such that a rhythm emerges that no longer conforms to the measure of the steps hitting the concrete. We feel a thrownness of experience that is neither the running as such, nor the music per se. What we prehend is their internal mixing, their infolding. This multiple rhythm creates an affective layering whereby sheets of time begin to coexist. This thrownness is a polyrhythmic preacceleration whereby what is felt is becoming-movement more than actual spacing. The race becomes the body becoming orchestral.

Polyrhythm is the capacity to become through movement on more than one plane at once. It merges becoming-movement with becoming-rhythm. Most of the time, Riefenstahl builds in polyrhythm, creating an architectonics through the montage while overlaying it with audio rhythms and bringing them together to create ever more complex rhythms. Durations layer and begin to move, the movement felt in its incipiency. This creates a sensation of cutting-across that prolongs the potential of one rhythm while adding to it, which is no doubt why capturing her images is such an uncanny proposition, each capture as evocative as the last.

Composition reaches the heights of commanding form when it exceeds the sum of its parts. This more-than must survive multiple repetitions and must produce difference each time. It must be open, yet controlled. In Riefenstahl, the sum is dense with rhythm. It is dense with the constraint of the structure of composition that will culminate in a polyrhythmic movement-image that works. To work, the polyrhythm must produce the effect of an overlayering, whereby the body expresses itself electrically even while it backgrounds itself atmospherically. The body-becoming is the protagonist onto which polyrhythmic surfaces expand, fold, bend, emerge, collapse. For Dalcroze, musical rhythms can be appreciated only in relation to the atmosphere and space in which they move, only in relation to silence and immobility. "Musical rhythmics is the art of establishing due proportion between sound movement and static silence, of opposing them, and of preparing for the one by means of the other, according to the laws of contrast and balance on which all style depends" (Dalcroze 1921, 149).

Rhythmic Ascendance

Riefenstahl works with the immanence of movement, biogrammatically rendering apparent time within movement. From within this process of making duration felt, she releases rhythm, actively pulling force out of the incipiency of movement, inciting it to appear. Through her play of appearance/disappearance, Riefenstahl creates a time-image of the movement-image, resolutely impregnating one with the other, creating superimposed, heterogeneous, divergent series that operate in polyrhythmic continuity within the same continuous movement. Every movement-with occurs durationally. In Whiteheadian terms, what Riefenstahl does is make time of the order of appearance without backgrounding movement.

The time of movement is dynamic form. Dynamic form appears in the relation not from body to body but from rhythm to rhythm. An open whole—an atmospherics—is what preoccupies each of Riefenstahl's images. This whole-which-has-no-parts cannot be divided without changing qualitatively at each stage of the division. Think of the diving sequence. As the women fly off the diving board, they emerge first as individuals, one after the other, named, but soon, and even more so when the sequence shifts to the male divers, a flying takes place where the bodies become-sky, dancing their folds and surfaces in a relatedness that exceeds their individuality. There is no foregrounded individual in these sequences. We take part in a biogram that is a becoming-sky that couples flight and falling, landing, and surfacing. Duration is felt not as measure but as ascending rhythms. The dive itself disappears, and what takes

Figures 6.15, 6.16, 6.17
Leni Riefenstahl, *Olympia*, 1938 (courtesy Gisela Jahn).

its place is a wholeness of movement that finds expression in the multiple body-becoming repeating differently each time. A becoming-bird appears that is unforgettable, uncanny, untimely. What moves are superimposed durations of body-becomings, biograms, rhythmically ascending and descending.

To work through an episteme that operates at the threshold where biopolitics becomes biogram is not to suggest a complete annihilation of the biopolitical. If the biopolitical is concerned with populations, the biogram is the virtual node that creates conjunctions of the body-becoming of these divergent populations. But where affective tendencies can still be relayed back to individual tendencies within a biopolitical paradigm, biograms do not individualize. Like the sea of flags moving, biograms call forth thresholds that qualitatively alter the recombinations they foreground. Biograms affectively recompose series at the virtual node that is their hinge. Biogrammatic politics are affective politics, operating at the cusp of divergent series, creating not a body as such but an affective tone of a becoming-body, a plastic rhythm, a transcendent materiality, a topological surface, a physically transcendent asignifying materiality. Riefenstahl's images are the precursors of such contemporary biogrammatic bodies that express before they symbolize. When the image operates on the becoming-body biogrammatically, the effect is dizzying: direct time on wholeness of movement. What appears: intensity, tonality, affect. Leni Riefenstahl works an architectonic of rhythm not onto the body as such but onto its appearance. And when bodies appear, politics begin to move.

Interlude: Of Force Fields and Rhythm Contours—David Spriggs's Animate Sculptures

We shall see the shape of the atmosphere where before was only emptiness.
—Umberto Boccioni, "Plastic Dynamism 1913"

David Spriggs's works are wonders in movement. They make you move. This is the feeling of what happens:

The glass box containing a work called *Blood Nebulae* (2002) stands before us. We look at the object to recognize its form as we move toward it in the gallery space. As with all objects, we tend toward a frontal view, giving in to the totality of appearance a frontal view usually provides. But the artwork doesn't appear in the way we expected. Its red feels blurry, its edges shifty. Yet it's there—we can feel it.

Curious, we move around to the side. We find the becoming-form of the work moves with us. What we feel: the force of perception. This force moves us to look again. The object is appearing now, but its appearance doesn't stabilize. We are moved to move again. Now we are looking from the side, where the hanging sheets of Mylar are exposed. The actualizing form eludes us again. Instead of the taking-form of the figure, we face the Mylar's plastic texture undulating with the color of almost-form. We are fascinated with the sheets: they seem to be the (un)making of perception. We move again, moved by the process of art taking form.

Allied to Boccioni's concept of dynamic form, David Spriggs's animate sculptures seem to create force lines for the emergence of perception. Boccioni

David Spriggs, *Incorporeal Movement* (courtesy David Spriggs).

writes: "No one still believes that an object finishes off where another begins, or that there is anything around us which cannot be cut up and sectionalized by an arabesque of straight curves" (1970b, 61). An arabesque of straight curves might be a way to speak of the affective tonality of the bursts of red on the hanging Mylar of *Blood Nebulae*. Whereas the front view gives us a sense of how the nebulae might appear, seen from the side, the hanging Mylar proposes a redness for the perception itself of nebulae. Taking a tour of the artwork becomes a trajectory in the force field of perception's animated exploration of vision's edge.

Let me explain: what we see when we look is the emergence of contour from an interplay of edges. We don't actually see an image—the image composes itself through the force of a relational dynamic. All vision works this way, our eyes at any given moment proposing nothing close to final form. What we experience as final form is in fact an appearance of the composed relation across moments. We see this composition, and even as we see it, it recomposes. Blinking, readjusting for saccadic bursts, reorganizing for stereoscopic vision, our field of perception is a play of movement yielding rhythmic contours. Stability is vision's illusion. The challenge is de-animation, not the contrary.

This paradox of vision is made palpable in David Spriggs's work. Think of *Paradox of Power* (2007). The paradox here is not the idea of the bull per se (and what the multiple bulls might represent) but the way the bull comes into vision. Let's begin with a side-view: what we see is compelling—a strange permutation of red through blue. Looking again, we find we cannot really differentiate the blue, the red, the light seeping through, the plastic hanging, the edges of the glass box. It's as though we see each of these qualities in their very emergence, caught in a prearticulation of the image. Blue is blue-on-blue, red is red-on-red-on-blue, colors intermixing at the edges of our vision, their inmixing singular, our perception of them continuously shifting through the amodal experience of seeing-feeling the rhythmic contours of the almost-image. We cannot quite bear this view—it pulls us toward another angle, toward the image itself as it comes to expression. We've moved again.

And this is what we see, standing in front of the image (although we are not sure now if this is in fact the front, or whether this is just another mode of appearance of the multiheaded bull): we see blue and red, lines gleaming into light, their edges melting into a kind of emanation. This is not simply a multiple-bull: it is an image extending beyond its coming to form into the light of its own quasi appearance.

David Spriggs, *Paradox of Power* (courtesy David Spriggs).

The blue quivers in a quietness the red does not propose. The blue calms the one side of the animate sculpture, inviting us to view again the inverted body-legs of the becoming-bull. But we can't distance ourselves from the red, which catches our eye in an incessant calling. We find the blue cannot be seen without the appearance of red. Red here expresses itself as an active multiplicity. This multiplicity rears its four heads, each head a play of forces of appearance and disappearance, a coming forward and moving back into the colored light of perception perceiving. We feel the threshold here, insistent and persuasive, between color, light, and movement.

David Spriggs's animate sculptures are experiments with the concreteness of abstraction. Their intensity is felt through the very evanescence of their almost-form passing into multiplicity, a concreteness allied always with mutations that are abstract, almost-there for vision, but not quite perceivable. This paradoxical relation between the abstract and the concrete, between the virtual and the material, between the perceptible and the imperceptible, is at stake in each of Spriggs's animate sculptures. The theory-in-movement of the work: abstraction is what makes them concrete. As concrete as a vision. Robert Irwin suggests we call this movement toward the concrete "the process of a

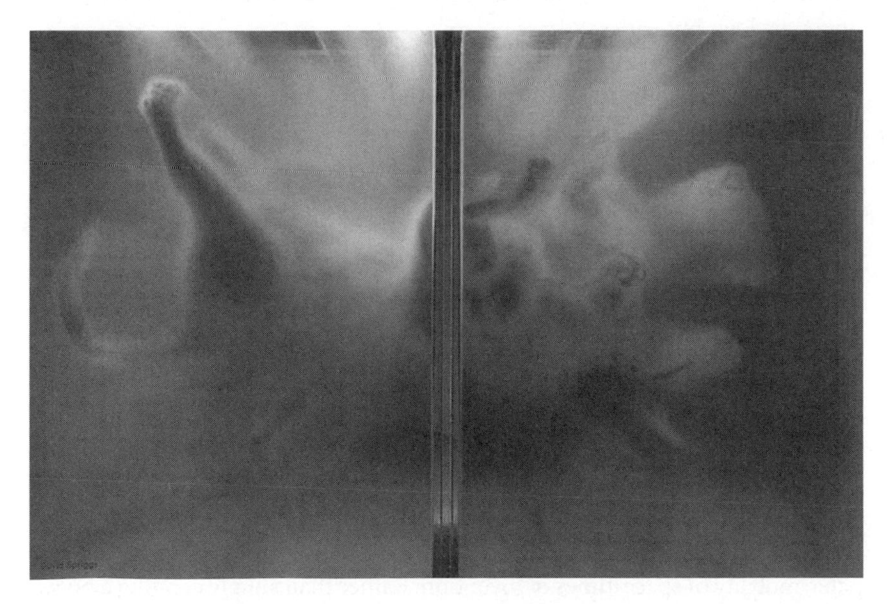

David Spriggs, *Paradox of Power* (courtesy David Spriggs).

complexifying abstraction" (1998, 33; my translation). In an attempt to formalize a vocabulary for the passage from art to thought, Irwin wonders about the process that allows perceptions/conceptions to take on a meaning entirely independent from their origins (1998, 33). He writes: "To try to construct [a model for perception] is at once complicated and theoretical, and the passage that follows must be as much a procedure or a set of procedures as an explanatory system. Concrete is as concrete doesn't"[84] (Irwin 1998, 35; my translation).

Spriggs's animate sculptures are concrete in the immateriality of their becoming. They make felt how movement propels objects into quasi appearance. Take *Incorporeal Movement* (2004). This sculpture animates light through the becoming-figural of a three-headed body of red. These three quasi figures are perceived not in their definiteness as three bodies but in a blurry relatedness that disallows a terse separateness. It is as much three bodies becoming one as one body multiplying. What Spriggs airbrushes here is not the final form but its becoming through the mixture of color, light, and shadow. The ethereal quality of the body-becoming-multiple is multiplied by our movement around the sculpture, a movement-with that strangely singularizes the experience (because we still try to focus the image into one head, one form). There is a perceptual play here of singularity and multiplicity, a play as much of light as of form. A play not *of* shadows but *with* shadows.

Creating with light and its absence is a way of asking us to move light. We feel the beckoning of light in our attempt to make the form concrete. *Incorporeal Movement* plays with light and shadow to create form, merging the concrete with the abstract. This does not happen by simply standing in front of it. Staying in place focuses the light, and with the imposition of stability, the appearance of form recedes.

Incorporeal Movement appears for perception. It appears if we actively perceive it. Virtually. It makes us move. We move to make it reappear. And as it reappears, we become aware of the ways in which it disappears. This disappearance occurs because the work isn't actually all there for the perceptual taking. It's there for the making, for the re-making through movement-perception. What we see: rhythms of color and light on the cusp of becoming shapes. Force-lines for perception in the making.

For Boccioni, force-lines emphasize the becoming-atmospheric of dynamic form. Becoming-atmospheric suggests a transduction from object to the palpable mobility of space-times of invention. Rather than simply creating a boxed animation, what Spriggs's work proposes is a creative engagement with the

David Spriggs, *Incorporeal Movement* (courtesy David Spriggs).

becoming-environment of the space-times of experience we cocreate as we move-with the sculptures' animate form.

This is not an easy task. An animate sculpture is a dynamic form that remains dynamic. To do so, it must keep moving (without moving). How? By creating a relational environment. Similarly to Irwin's *Who's Afraid of Red, Yellow and Blue*, whose vertigo of appearance gets people moving and talking, Spriggs's work creates openings for engagement. What his work proposes is that we create a movement-with that fosters the emergence of animate form. This play with emergence is an inventive pact between art and participant. It proposes relation without telling us in advance how to move.

Spriggs's work invites us to see-with what is not actually there and to move-with the constellation of what we're beginning to see. Moving-with perception composing itself, we experience the dynamics of form. We no longer simply observe—we are moved by the experience of watching, and we move with it. We note the contours but feel the colors. We see the lines but feel the rhythm. We see-with the becoming-work. We participate in the activity of plastic dynamism expressing itself through the emergence of a body-sculpture constellation. Plastic dynamism is not simply about how we see an object but also about how an object appears for our embodied perception: "Plastic dynamism is the simultaneous action of the motion characteristic of an object (its absolute motion), mixed with the transformation which the object undergoes in relation to its mobile and immobile environment (its relative motion)" (Boccioni 1970a, 92).

Entropy (2007). Look at it and feel its force. Your eyes refuse to focus. Even when you try to see the distinctness of form, what you see is blurriness—the becoming-form's absolute motion. Flatten your gaze, and what you feel is the relative motion of *Entropy*'s force. You feel its spiral as a centrifugal rhythm. You see the droplets of water as they recombine with the force of *Entropy*'s movement. You find it impossible to stand still. You move to the side, to where the sheets of Mylar themselves begin to curve. The animate form follows your movement moving: you realize your vision has curved in the process of feeling the force of the rhythm's contours. You see rhythm contouring.

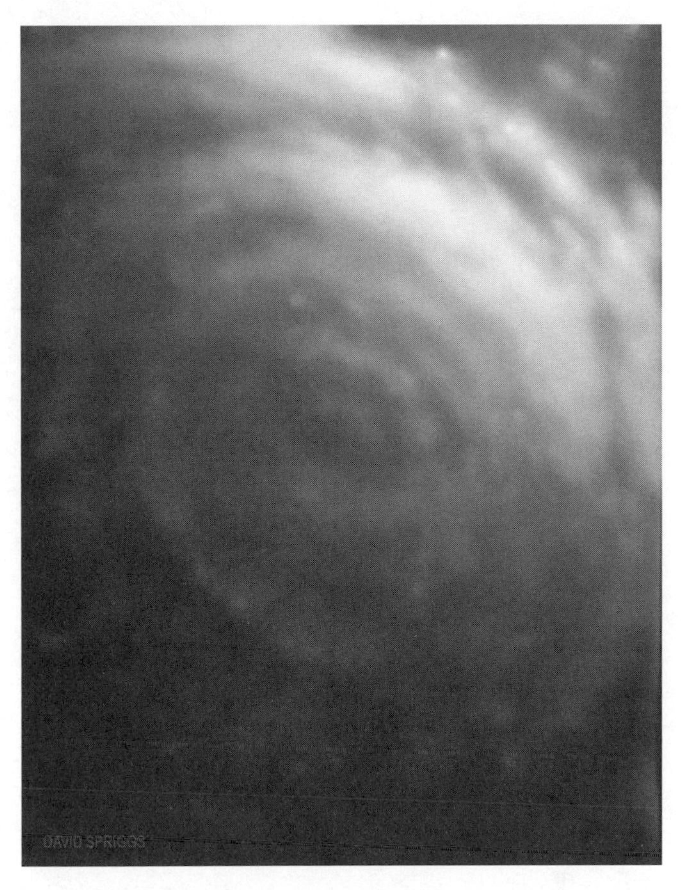

David Spriggs, *Entropy* (courtesy David Spriggs).

Relationscapes: How Contemporary Aboriginal Art Moves beyond the Map

7

Three Examples

1. Dorothy Napangardi's *Mina Mina* (2005) measures almost two meters in height (198 x 122 cm). Black on white, its white emergent through the black dots, *Mina Mina* encourages us to look-across, to move-with the fragile dotted lines that compose its labyrinths. "Looking at" is too stable for this shifting landscape that moves, already, in many directions at once. This movement-across is not a symmetrical one that would obediently follow a horizontal or vertical perspective: it is a vibrating movement, a resonance that forces itself upon our vision. How we see becomes a politics of touch: what the painting compels is not a static viewing but an activity of reaching-toward that alters the relation between body and painting, creating a moving world that becomes a touching of the not-yet-touchable. This touching is rhythmic. It occurs not on the lines or with the points but across the vista the painting elaborates, an experiential vista that is already more than the space of the canvas can convey. The dots and lines are more than traces, they are material becomings toward a worlding immanent to the experience of viewing. The becoming-world called forth by this black and white painting is the creation of an event of which my seeing-touch is part. It takes me not somewhere else but right where I can become, to a force-field that is an eventness in the making, an exfoliation of experience.

Mina Mina envelops space, creating new space-times of experience. It literally quivers with its dissonant becomings. This is not a metaphor. Space-time

Figure 7.1
Dorothy Napangardi, *Mina Mina,* 2005, Artists Rights Society, New York, NY.

is ontogenetically recreated through the process. The painting proposes new modes of viewing, a seeing-in-movement that incites us to move. We become part of the composition, part of the activity of relation through which the painting achieves its morphing form. We feel its limits even as its limits field us.

Deleuze writes: "We do not listen closely enough to what painters have to say. They say that the painter is already in the canvas, where he or she encounters all the figurative and probabilistic givens that occupy and preoccupy the canvas" (2003, 81). We look-with its diagram, the resonant force lines it calls forth. *Mina Mina*'s diagram comes together through the dotted black line on the upper right side of the canvas, a line that almost cuts off the corner from the rest, yet embraces the painting as a whole. This self-embracing gesture is more than a compositional device. It expresses the painting's withness, its immanent force. It creates a tensile elasticity that holds the experience of touching vision to the singularity of its own eventness.

Mina Mina speaks of salt lines, a mapping not of a territory but its passages, the traces it leaves in the landscapes it uncovers. A map is discovered here, not uncovered. We take part in the map's durational eventness, in an *activity* of mapping that directs our bodies not toward the representation of Mina Mina but toward its liveliness. This mapping is a creative vector of experience: it maps the future, not the past, leading us toward a recomposition of experience, a collaborative striation that smoothes the space of encounter.

2. Emily Kame Kngwarreye's *Alhalkere* (1991) covers the whole wall. Three meters wide, it is powerful in its vivid evocation of the land, dancing with both grace and force. Asignifying traits merge to create a non-representational, non-illustrative, and non-narrative field: "marks that no longer depend on our will or our sight" (Deleuze 2003, 82) Its diagram can be felt emerging from the deep reddish burgundy spilling from the top left-hand corner of the painting. It is as though the rest of the painting overflows from this dark corner, merging into a transformative activity of dot-painting, overpowered, finally, by yellow dots that transfuse with the surface, becoming surface, dense and airy at once. This quality of yellowness becomes the asignifying trait that propulses the canvas into an event. The event of *Alhalkere* is rhythmical: it moves in contrapuntal bursts that oscillate between red and yellow, creating a quivering of perception that dances the passage from the dot to the surface to the rhythm in between. Diagrams are "a chaos, a catastrophe, but . . . also, a germ of rhythm in relation to a new order

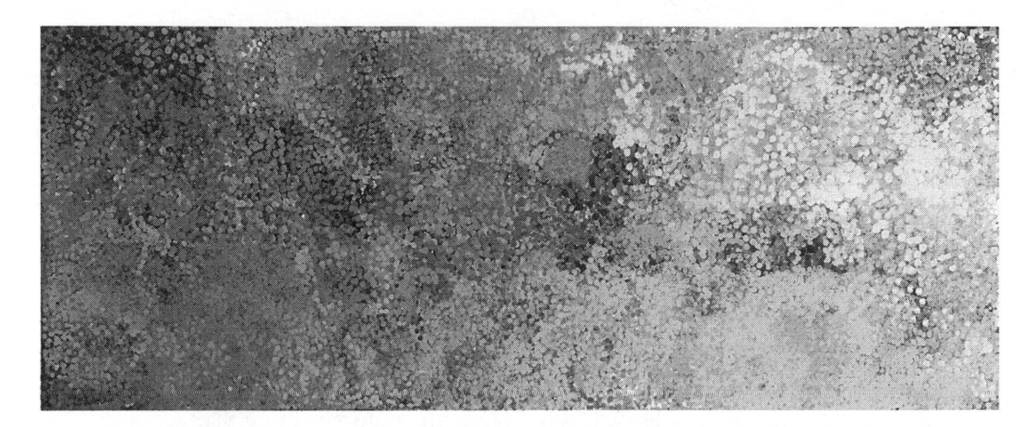

Figure 7.2
Emily Kngwarreye, *Alhalkere*, 1991, Artists Rights Society, New York, NY.

of the painting [that] . . . unlocks areas of sensation" (Deleuze 2003, 83). Felt in *Alhalkere* is the very act of painting, the materiality of rhythm.

Alhalkere's polyrhythmic quality activates timelines that are like plateaus of experience. Refuting the "purely optical," *Alhalkere* makes palpable the immanent materiality of color and shade, of movement and becoming-form. Demanding an active listening, it breathes surface and depth, noise and calm even as it carefully calls forth a minimalist gesture, a diagram of restraint that creates a sensation that is clear and precise. This precision is what allows the body—of the painting, of the viewer—to evolve with every encounter. It is what allows the painting to be both here and there, alive in its Aboriginal context in and beyond Australia. This precision, it seems to me, catches us by surprise in each of Kngwarreye's paintings.[85] It is felt like a color, but really it is a force that holds the painting to itself and while also inviting it to be much more than a painted surface. *Alhalkere* takes form through the activity of Dreaming, its diagram culminating in the almost uniform yellow that invites us to weave our own stories, to dance the eventness of the layerings of experience. A map? Only if we conceive it as a layering-in, a dotting-to-infinity, where the folding-in is also a folding-out. Not a direction but a dance, a palimpsest alive with the resonances it creates.

3. Kathleen Petyarre's *Arnkerrthe* (2001) speaks to the movements of a mountain devil lizard. But this square painting, asymmetrically symmetrical, also does much more than that. One meter twenty squared is a forceful enclosure

for a becoming-movement. Squares often call forth diagrams that conform to their limits. Petyarre resists these limitations, creating a becoming-body of movement-across that subtly emerges on the right quadrant, shading down through the otherwise almost-straight lines. There is a shadow here, a passage not yet quite actualized, that challenges the structure, bringing a fragility to its inner limits. On the lower left hand quadrant, the line thickens and there is a sense of reaching-toward a tremulous center point. This point is not fixed: it is a pulsation that envelops the whole painting. A meeting point, rather than a vanishing point. This point is what Deleuze would call haptic, evolving from a line to a touch distinct from its purely optical function. The mountain devil lizard's passage is not one simply to be followed. It must be lived via a politics of touch that remains a reaching-toward. This reaching-toward scrambles the painting's parameters, shifting the constraint from the square to the triangle, from the triangle to the parallel line, from the parallel line to the shadow, to the speed of the dots, to their fragile merging into new space-times of experience. Passages already traveled, actualized in their transformations, alongside passages set as markers for future explorations. The movement is squared with a difference, a differential becoming-elastic moving across the formation, a becoming-form barely visible yet felt. If this is a map, it is not a topography. Its diagram is the process active between directional tendencies and their textures. Its diagram is the evolution of a shadow of quasi perceptibility that moves-with, its lizarding creating relational matrices, circles in the square.

"That Dreaming Been All the Time"[86]

To paint the landscape with acrylics is a relatively new form of art for the Aborigines of Australia. Until the early 1970s, stories of land and spirit were evoked mostly through other media—sand, bark, wood. Today, acrylics produced in the desert are a voice of transition, marking the uncanniness of the future-past of the land, its mappings, its dreams.

Dreamings—Jukurrpa[87]—are an integral aspect of life in Central Desert society.[88] Stories told for more than 40,000 years, Dreamings not only speak about the landscape and its vicissitudes, they create space-times of experience. This creative alchemy sustains more than a reciprocal relationship to the land: it is also an enactment of the Law. Law creates-with life, setting operational constraints for the perpetuation of the creative nexus between Dreaming and life. As story, Dreaming evokes the lived landscape, a spiritual and lived experience.

Figure 7.3
Kathleen Petyarre, *Arnkerrthe*, 2001, Gallery Australis.

To dream is to take response-ability seriously. It is to operate at the threshold where culture and Law overlap, where the future-pastness of experiences in the making take hold.

For Aborigines, life is Dreaming in the sense that the coordinates of space-time out of which everyday lives emerge are significantly in line with the creation and recreation of the land and its Laws. But even this is too simple: the land is not an extension of the Aborigines—it *is* them. To be the land is to *become* in relation to it: in relation not to space itself but to the living coordinates of a topological relationscape that embodies as much the Law as it does the grains of sand that prolong it in real time. The land and the Law are not two, are not juxtaposed. They are not sustained in a present-future symbolism. They are one: a becoming multiplicity.

The Dreaming alters all dimensions of experience even as it embeds pastness in futurity. To simply locate a Dreaming as a story of creation is to touch on only one aspect of the concept. Dreamings are mythological and cosmogenic tales that are not simply stories of creation (with all attendant dramas and misunderstandings, love stories, and disappointments) in the Biblical sense: they are also stories of the creation of the future-present. Dreamings do not exist once and for all (although they also do that): they are tales for the retelling through song, voice, dance, paint. Dreams are for keeping alive.

All Dreamings are sustained by multiple guardians. Members from different clans are Kirda and Kurdungurlu for the Dreaming,[89] which means that while one person is responsible for the iconography of the Dreaming's location, another is responsible for parts of its story. An individual cannot single-handedly decide to paint a Dreaming, even if he or she is Kirda for that Dreaming. The Kurdungurlu must be included in the process: relation is already inscribed in the Dreaming before its story is told again. The same goes for the trajectories of the songs that populate and extend the space-time of the Dreamings. No one ever owns a complete trajectory. To sing the songs of a Dreaming, communities must be assembled, sometimes even intertribally. The Law is played out in this relationship of reciprocity. A sharing of the land is an experience of relation in its future-passing.

"To paint a Dreaming is at once to regenerate one's forces and to connect the object or the person to the earth and to the space-time of the hero who 'dreams' the life of people and their environment" (Glowczewski 1989, 83).[90] To dream is never an individual affair. Even night dreams in Aboriginal communities extend beyond the individual body: my dream may be your dream experienced through the vessel of my becoming-form. The earth-as-body is the support for the traces of ancestral bodies and the metamorphoses of experience in the present. It is a mnemonic for the Law of the Dreaming. To dream is to be in contact with others, to dream their dreams: "The agreement of others is necessary. An oneiric vision is attested as 'real' only on condition that it is connected to pictorial forms and narratives . . . that have been transmitted for hundreds of generations" (Glowczewski 1989, 151). There is never a single version that works for all Dreamings, but as many versions and contexts as are necessary for the story to be composed again.

Associated with the Dreaming is a certain birthright. In Aboriginal Central Desert society, you are born where the Dream enters you. To be born in Warlpiri is "palkajarri"—"becoming body."[91] A virtuality actualizes itself in the birth, a virtuality that is crystallized through a verse of a song that will be sung for generations to come. This song will "belong" to the becoming-body in the form of a Dreaming for which he or she will remain Kirda. To become-body is to materialize as song, as Dream, as rhythm.[92] It is not to materialize individually but to be sung again, to become as a multiple body of communal experience. "Warlpiri philosophy does not oppose images to the substance or the essence of things. The two are indissociable" (Glowczewski 1989, 212).

The cosmology of the Dreaming must be understood as both actual and virtual.[93] It is an overlapping of the two, where reality and dream are not opposed but superimposed. Aborigines of the Central Desert animate time in space. In their rituals, the present is ancestralized not as a nostalgia for the past but as a becoming-future. The past and the future, the actual and the virtual are traces of becoming whose dimensions are experienced in shifting continuity, as through the spiral of a Nietzschean eternal recurrence. When time is activated in this way what emerges is a timeline that is not linear. The present is always in the mode of an embodying withness not of a forgotten past but of a reexperiencing in the future-present.

Experiencing-with from Afar

Arnkerrthe, *Mina Mina*, and *Alhalkere* are prehensions of Dreamings. To prehend the Dreaming is to move with it, to compose with it. To prehend the Dreaming involves more than narrating an instance of it. It calls forth the activity of the land's eventfulness and pulls this eventfulness into the present-passing such that a new actual occasion—a becoming-world—emerges.

This is not a premapping of experience. Prehending the Dreaming, paintings such as *Alhalkere* feel the resonance of all that Dreaming can do, drawing its eventness onto the canvas. Transversally political, these paintings call forth a new way of feeling seeing, a seeing-with that moves the body. This elicited movement-with is affective: its tonality (its modalities, its resonances, its textures) alters both what a body can do and how the world can be experienced (Whitehead 1933, 176). To experience *Alhalkere* is to feel the recomposition of a living landscape that is not separate from the perception of perception that recomposes us. *Alhalkere* is the Dreaming insofar as it incurs concern for the event that is the shape-shifting of experience. Moving-with its own eventful becoming, *Alhalkere* is a metastable system that cannot be thought outside the experiential field it opens. Touching (with) us, *Alhalkere* asks that we have concern for the Dreaming.

Concern for the Dreaming is an ethics of encounter with the unknowable—an event in the making—that far exceeds the specificity of a particular piece of land. This is not to dismiss the importance of land claims in Aboriginal politics, nor to romanticize space as ephemeral. It is to take the immanent materiality of the Dreamings seriously and to note that what paintings such as *Alhalkere* do exceeds the parameters of their landmarks. Their concern is for the embodied eventness of land, not a predetermined location. It is not based on an identity politics that would promote an exclusive dialectics of inside/outside. Experience itself is at stake, *in the making*. The fluidity of experience of paintings such as *Alhalkere* does not limit itself to preinformed historical circumstances. It is radically empirical: it is an invitation to invent with the unspeakable, the imperceptible, the as-yet-unfelt. "Dreaming stories and 'icons' [do] justice to the force and effect of these paintings in the material terms they themselves effect" (Biddle 2003, 61).[94] The immanent materiality of these paintings calls forth an empiricism that is directly experienced, that is directly relational. And that is how they reach me, 10,000 miles away.

The relation the Dreaming proposes is not composed separately from its eventness. Dreamings are here and now as much as they are then and before. Dreamings are neither nostalgic nor predictable. They are concern for the present-passing. Reembodied through paint, the Dreamings make the not-yet felt, asking, always, to live again, to be lived again. Once more. The repetition of the act is its infinite difference. The painting of the dots, one at a time, for hours on end, is a differential living-with that continuously reinvents with the stories that belong to a history of time-on-earth that exceeds the very notion of stable territory, calling forth worlds that extend far beyond what geography can map.

The intimacy of relation is felt in the reliving of the Dream, told as a life-giving story that intensifies contact between lineage, land, movement. In the paintings, this intimacy is experienced in the pulsations of the dots, in the rhythms of the layered surfaces at play, of intensities interweaving. These paintings ask us to move (move away! come closer! look again!), figuring movement such that what is felt is not the representation of a story but the act of the telling itself. This

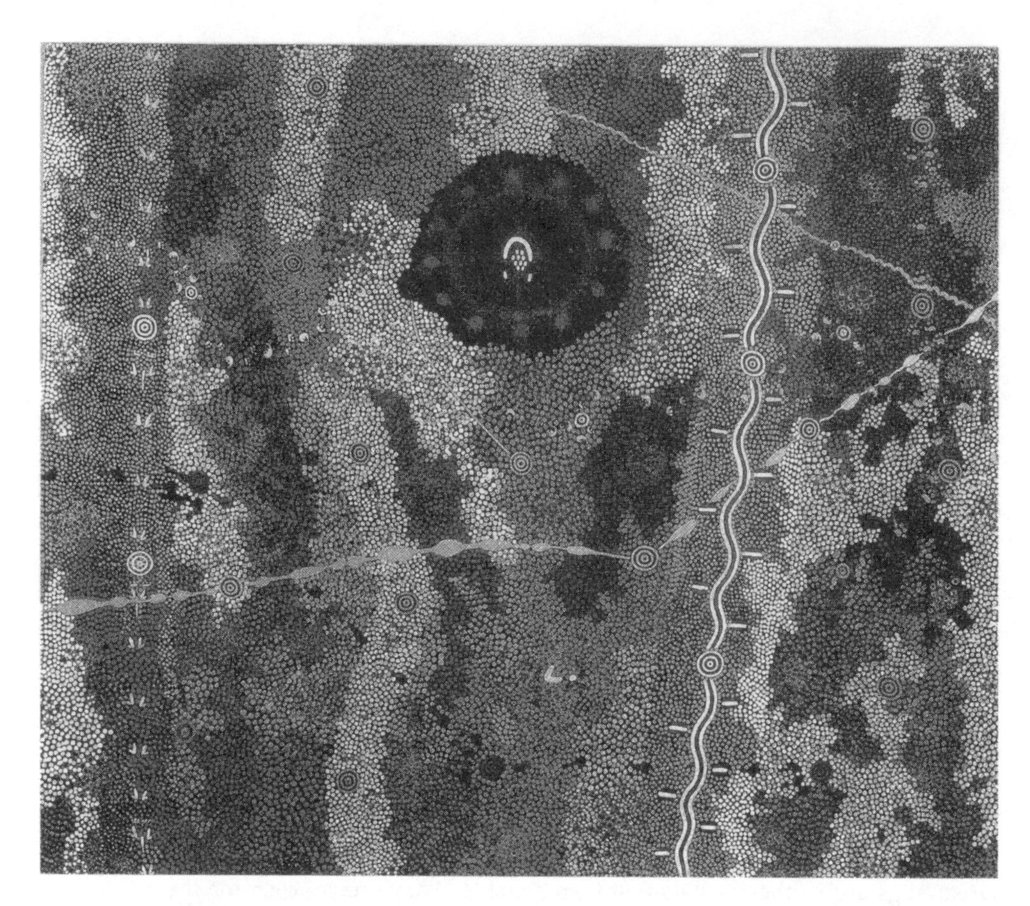

Figure 7.4
Clifford Possum Tjapaltjarri, *Mt. Denison Country*, 1978, Aboriginal Artists Agency, North Sydney, Australia.

telling creates conjunctions *and* disjunctions, insisting, as Kngwarreye is famous for saying, on "a whole lot."

Of Maps and Dots

Paintings of Dreamings call forth a directly perceived relation with their own materiality and with the thereness of the land. They map not a place but a diagram out of which a taking-form emerges. To speak of maps is always to return, in some sense, to the evocative work of Clifford Possum Tjapaltjarri. Clifford Possum's art is revered for its precision and breadth. Possum was one of the more experienced artists among those who painted in the early years of the Papunya Tula movement. Clifford Possum's map series was created between 1976 and 1979.[95] These "maps" draw out the challenging reorganization of space-time the Dreaming makes possible even while ostensibly doing so within the vocabulary of a Westernized concept of a map. In these early acrylic paintings, Clifford Possum makes felt both his relation to the land and the interrelatedness of the Dreamings for which he is custodian. In the Central Desert, a particular individual is identified not only with a network of trails, animals, food, and landmarks passed down through patrilineal descent, but also with myriad interrelated components that keep all of these categories open. A person's birthplace, where their parents or grandparents were born or initiated, extended residence networks, all of these factors influence the positioning of the individual with/in his or her Dreamings. To think of Dreamings as representing discrete spaces or particular laws is both to underestimate the ways in which Dreamings challenge linear space-time and to forget the relational aspect of ownership within Aboriginal culture. The Dreamings no more belong to the land than they do to the people. The people and the Dreaming are coextensive: they are ontogenetic networks of reciprocal exchange. A Dreaming is not an entity, not a place. It is a movement, a song and a dance, a practice of mark-making that does not represent a space-time but creates it, again and again.[96]

To assume a regular passage from past to present to future is to be imprisoned within Cartesian coordinates that have little to do with Central Desert culture. For Aborigines of the Central Desert, the past is activated in the present-passing, not passively remembered. Culture and politics in the Central Desert are there for the (re)making, challenged and expressed by an opening to certain stories of creation that intertwine in complex and infinite ways the present and the past, the human and the animal, space and time. The collective memory of the

Figure 7.5
Clifford Possum Tjapaltjarri, *Yuutjutiyungu*, 1979, Aboriginal Artists Agency, North Sydney, Australia.

future-past is passed on from generation to generation through sand paintings, dances, and songs. The Aboriginals today are not reliving their past. They are recreating their future, making use of a topological structure in which time is embedded in shifting space, and space becomes time passing.

The itineraries of the Dreaming must be seen not as a plane that can be adequately captured on a two-dimensional surface, but as functioning in many dimensions at once. As Clifford Possum paints them, the Dreamings are like knots where the actual meets the virtual in a cycle of continuous regeneration. The itineraries of the Dreaming are rule-bound but not fixed: these knots of experience are always shape-shifting. Space-time is at the heart of this complex art, as are conceptual slidings, performative experience, rituals of appearance and disappearance. This space-time is not haphazard: Dreamings must be performed lest they disappear into disuse, their songs forgotten or unsung.[97]

The country for which Clifford Possum is response-able forms a wide arc with a radius of some 100 km centered approximately 200 km northwest of Alice Springs. It stretches from Waltunpunyu, west of Central Mount Wedge in the south, up through Napperby and Mount Allan stations, northwest as far as the blue hill of Wakulpa just north of Yuendumu, and northeast across Mount Denison and Conisten Stations (Johnson 2003, 21). From the perspective of a Cartesian geography, this is Anmatyerre country. Topologically, Anmatyerre country is more complex.[98]

The teachings that allow us to conceive of landscapes as perspectival entities operational *in* space-time are in the main Euclidean. In Euclidean geometry, we know one space from another not primarily by the ways in which our bodies *create* that space but by the ways in which we *inhabit* or *enter* it. Space becomes a container for experience. By privileging inhabitation (where space always preexists experience), Euclidean geometry enables a rendering-abstract of space, abstract in the sense that it is empty before the arrival of content to fill it. Because of this abstraction of space, what is measured in Euclidean geometry is considered concrete: space is abstract, bodies and landscapes are concrete. Body and space are not one, co-determining: they are always two, *1 + 1*, body + space. It is due to this linear grammar of geometry that the colonizer is able to assert that seemingly empty space is uninhabited.

Topological space-time refutes the dichotomy between the abstract and the concrete. Topological space-time is not *1 + 1* but *n + 1*, always more-than. The Dreaming is an evocation of such a topological space-time of experience. It situates land, body, space, time, experience all in one structural node, an elastic point that fields the perpetual movement of time. Topological rendering relationally connects nature and existence, insisting that no single element be a permanent support for changing relations. In this relational network of experience, innovation is at stake even while the traditions of the past carry weight in the present. Innovation does not mean the erasure of the past. It means creating a foundation for the shifting relations of past and future in the present passing. Through the Dreaming, a multiplicity of worldings emerges. At the creation of each new experience, the many become one and are increased by one.[99]

Topology refers to a continuity of transformation that alters the figure, bringing to the fore not the coordinates of form but the experience of it. Topologies suggest that the space of the body extends beyond Euclidean coordinates to an embodiment of folding space-times of experience: pure plastic rhythm. As Massumi asks, "What if the body is inseparable from dimensions of lived abstractness that cannot be conceptualized in other than topological terms?" (2002, 177). To think topologically is to think beyond preexistent coordinates, be they for a body, a territory, a landscape, a law.

Dreamings break down the dichotomy between the abstract and the concrete. In the Dreaming, concrete and abstract overlap. The Dreaming does not function wholly abstractly or wholly concretely. It moves through their interval, giving no more credence to the now of flesh than to the virtuality of spiritual evocations of the landscape. This continuity of the actual and the virtual creates a law of alliance that is neither concrete nor abstract. This law of alliance rests on an implicit understanding that space-time is as spiritual as it is physical, as topological as it is geographic. The landscape moves, and with it, the Dreamings shift and bodies metamorphose.

A map of the landscape that relies on x/y coordinates asks us to pre-space-time ourselves within it. Turn your body this way, it suggests, face this direction. To read a Cartesian map is to ask a preformed body-concept to conform to its gridding. Topological space-time works otherwise. This is why Clifford Possum did not always render the Dreamings in a "geographically accurate" way. To even posit a concept such as the "geographically accurate," we must already have had the experience of the x/y grids of the mapping of Euclidean space that takes for granted that our journeys begin and end in directions that can be recomposed in space and time. It supposes that a body never shape-shifts, that it always sees from the same perspective and within the same field of potential relations.

Clifford Possum's maps do not ask to be read in this way. Never overly concerned with the time and space of representation, Clifford Possum painted his great map series by moving the canvas around him. Through the act of painting, the land shifted, and with this shift so did its relations to space-times of experience. Instead of strictly linking locations in gridded geometrical space, the canvas's painted surface turns its attention to the Dreaming's intensive movement. This immobile voyage moves toward experience rather than location: Clifford Possum takes his bearings not with a concept of due north but with the living relation that is the Dreaming.

What is at stake in Clifford Possum's maps is not the omnipresent observer's bird's eye view of the landscape operating according to preestablished coordinates of space-time, but the relation between aspects of a Dreaming from the standpoint of a morphogenetic body. Like a tracker who continuously updates his or her bearings and alignment in space with each change of direction in the chase, Clifford Possum does not create an archival representation of land. He creates

Figure 7.6
Clifford Possum Tjapaltjarri, *Warlugulong*, 1976, Aboriginal Artists Agency, North Sydney, Australia.

land/his Dreaming in relation to a communal painting becoming-body. He does not *represent* the Dreaming but *indexes* its intensive passage from the virtual to the actual.[100]

The Western tradition of landscape art has taught us to read paintings (and most perspectival visual phenomena) as maps. Perspective is not innate, however: it is taught. Recent research, in fact, suggests that humans orient more by the shape of the space than by its visual cues. This suggests that we orient rhythmically, responding to the movements of topological twistings and turnings.[101] This way of fielding space foregrounds the proprioceptive sense, inverting the relation of position to movement. When movement is no longer indexed to position (when mapping becomes an event), position itself becomes mobile. This is the case with Clifford Possum's maps. Whether or not they are all spatially "correct" in relation to pregiven landmarks is not the issue. What matters is not the position—not where the territories lie as such—but what they are capable of in relation to the emergent bodies the Dreamings make possible.

A fissure emerges between cognitive mapping and orientation. What Clifford Possum is trying to do with his great maps is to orient the Dreamings in relation not to a void but to a becoming-body of the future-past. To orient is to actively engage in the process of mapping. It is to make maps even as we read them. This has for thousands of years been the practice of the Aboriginals of the desert, a practice that has taken the form, among others, of drawing in the sand. These traces—the shapes in the sand—were used to teach people about time and space as they intersect. To draw a circle could mean many things: a campfire, a waterhole. What is important—and how their "meanings" are read—depends on the direct perception of relation as it takes form. What such mappings teach is to locate an intensity of reaching-toward, not an entity.

What is calculated in the mapping is experience + ability. If you ask Clifford Possum about distance, he will speak in terms of walking days, or car hours. How do I get there? The "how" of directionality creates a permutation such that space-time shapes itself around continuous shiftings. The ground trembles. The desert is not one space: it is many overlapping space-times of experience that Aboriginals call Dreamings. These Dreamings can be drawn into maps, but such maps will never lead us anywhere if we expect them to do the walking for us.

Landing Sights

Clifford Possum has described his map series as land titles. The maps followed in the wake of important protests claiming Aboriginal rights to land at a time when outstations were not yet the norm, and Aborigines of different tribes were forced to live together in imposed centers. As a political statement, his maps could be seen to perform a kind of active reading of the land, using the Dreamings (as would often be done subsequently to challenge the destruction of land by mining and road building) as a way to position himself and his people within the land rights movement. But to understand this as a straight-forward reclaiming would be misleading, because it would imply that the land as such was what was at stake. Clifford Possum was not delineating landmarks on a cognitive grid. He does not own the land, nor would he claim to. What he owns is a singular relation to the land. Aboriginal understanding of land must by extension alter what is usually meant by land titles. It is not the space itself that the Aborigines are calling for through their art but the topologies of space-time the land incites in relation to Dreamings of which they remain an active part.

Figure 7.7
Clifford Possum Tjapaltjarri, *Kerrinyarra*, 1977, Aboriginal Artists Agency, North Sydney, Australia.

Land rights as painted by Clifford Possum are dimensions of experience. The folds of this experience are made-up of the rituals that call forth the Dreamings as events. Clifford Possum's paintings are alive in their multi-dimensionality, not only as examples of "abstract" art that has "content" but as a rethinking of abstractness itself.

The space-times of experience created through Clifford Possum's map paintings can be thought as a topological hyperspace of transformation. They create relays that are not simply geographic but also experiential, proprioceptive, where space and time fold into one another.[102] Space here is performed, folding into durations that become part of the materiality of the painterly event. Be it the land "itself" or acrylic, the point of the Dreaming is that it is not a location or a representation. It cannot "exist" in a Euclidean space-time, but must always move, resituating itself in relays that are changeable, depending on seasons and tribal conjunctions.[103]

Although most topologies are non-Euclidean, topologies are not necessarily non-Euclidean. The effort here is not to create a dichotomy that would suggest that there are specific experiential states to which the Central Desert Aborigines have direct access, as opposed to the spiritually impoverished urban dweller who can only think in terms of Euclidean coordinates. The point is rather that experiential space is topological and gets regridded within Cartesian coordinates, in part because such geometric grammars seem easier to capture. To think topologically is to think dynamically: it is to situate the movement of thought at its transformational vector, deforming it into its potential. When we rerender the form static, when we stop the process, we are shortchanging the experience.

Within topological transformation, an infinite number of static structures can emerge. This might begin to explain the complexity of Aboriginal life today. To suggest that Aboriginals live exclusively in transformation would be as senseless as to say that all urban dwellers are only sustained by Cartesian maps. The potential of experiential space is everywhere present. The question is how we map it, how we live it, how it transforms us. The transformation of a topological figure into a static instance creates an object. This object—be it a doughnut or a coffee cup, both of which belong to the same topological figure—stands for itself. What is interesting about it is not necessarily its shape but its process: the fact that its ontology is one of continuous deformation. To create an object is one thing—to create a relationscape another.

Beyond Figuration: Virtual Maps

Relationscapes are a way of conceptualizing the Dreaming. Consider the work of Emily Kngwarreye, Dorothy Napangardi, and Kathleen Petyarre. Kngwarreye's work in particular propels a sensing-across that projects the viewer into a velocity of experience that far exceeds the breadth of the painted surface. Born and raised in Alhalkere, a country that extends northwest of the Utopia boundary onto Mount Skinner Station, Kngwarreye's art is known for its abstraction and its resistance to the specificity of content.[104] Kngwarreye started painting when she was nearly eighty years old. At Utopia, the main focus had been batik, a practice in which Kngwarreye had been an adept for at least ten years before taking up acrylic paints.[105]

Almost immediately after beginning to paint, Kngwarreye's paintings were cast among the great works of the twentieth century, lauded as some of the most important landscape art ever produced. Margo Neale writes: "Kngwarreye was arguably Australia's greatest painter of the 'landscape.' No artist has painted the country the way she has, inflecting it with her personal vision and innovative style. . . . Hers is not a view of the law, but rather an experience of it. She rescales the landscape to a cosmic dimension—more akin to the holistic landscape of the Aboriginal mind" (1998, 31).

To speak of Kngwarreye's work in this way only begins to get at the richness of the experience vividly and brilliantly created through her work. What is at stake for Kngwarreye shifts far beyond representation, beyond the figural toward an abstraction that embraces the passage of the actual into the virtual, an abstraction that radically recasts the figure in an attempt to undermine the idea that Dreamings *contain* experience. Kngwarreye painted with and across Dreamings, never content to give in to the idea that they should represent anything beyond experience in the making. A whole lot.

In Kngwarreye's paintings, the paint moves at great speed beyond the edges of the canvas in an exploration not of the beyond itself but of the here and now, a present that is always more than what we can actually perceive.[106] Her art runs, breathless, exhausting our attempt to catch up with it.[107] This is at the heart of the works of Kngwarreye: the experience of sensation as that which moves beyond the landmark, beyond the location or the object of study, toward a direction that is always becoming toward a rhizomatic network shape-shifting from lines to dots, from shade to shade in a living relationscape.

Two series stand out for me—though it might be possible to speak of Kngwarreye's whole oeuvre as a giant, modulating, dancing series—because of the activity of relation felt across the planes of intensity that take the form of conceptually connected panels. The first of this series is entitled *Utopia Panels.* It was made in 1996 and comprises six panels of black horizontal lines on a white background.[108] What is eerie about this series is the fact that although the black paint is applied to a white surface, the black and white interweave such that the white "background" folds forward into the black lines, thus foregrounding its backgrounding. Background here takes a more Whiteheadian meaning, referring not to a predetermined state but to an activity of interrelation that makes felt the virtually emergent. A virtually emergent state is one that has not yet appeared as such, yet holds within itself the potential for transformation. This potential is entirely relational: a background is a nexus of past actual occasions poised to be reactivated into appearance. Whitehead explains this incipient pastness through the concept of non-sensuous perception. He writes: "We can

Figure 7.8
Emily Kngwarreye, *Utopia Panels*, 3 of 18, 1996, Artists Rights Society, New York, NY.

Figure 7.9
Emily Kngwarreye, *Untitled*, 1995, Artists Rights Society, New York, NY.

Figure 7.10
Emily Kngwarreye, *Utopia Panels*, 4 of 18, 1996b, Artists Rights Society, New York, NY.

discern no clean-cut sense-perception wholly concerned with present fact. . . . The evidence on which these interpretations are based is entirely drawn from the vast background and foreground of non-sensuous perception with which sense-perception is fused, and without which it can never be" (Whitehead 1933, 181). A foregrounding of the non-sensuous evokes the has-been of the not-quite-yet. This prehension of pastness is a direct perception of a relation that is barely actual. In *Utopia Panels*, the becoming-white of the black lines evokes the perishing of the discreteness of past and present, white and black. "The present moment is constituted by the influx of the other into that self-identity which is the continued life of the immediate past within the immediacy of the present" (Whitehead 1933, 181).

Blackness transduces into whiteness such that what emerges is not simply the line but surfaces entwining, creating a complex layered resonant field of lines and depths. If non-sensuous perception is "the immediate past . . . surviving to be again lived through in the present" (Whitehead 1933, 182), what is perceived here is not the line per se but its activity—its worlding—via the metastability created by both the survival and the perishing of whiteness and blackness. But there's more to it. These are not simply straight lines. The lines breathe, dancing not only their duration but the perishing of their process. Each line comes to a halt, sometimes halfway across an individual canvas, sometimes across two canvases. These lines are occasions of experience that create their own patterns within the vaster event that is the complete series. Lines dance into one another such that the movement of the paintbrush, moving across the canvases, can almost be felt. There is a sense of effort here, but with it comes also a sense of speed. Driven intensity, absolute movement. There is no time to return to the line: the line must draw the movement. The gesture itself must become line. One pass with the paint, and that's all. Move the canvas. The result: a vastness of localized movement. A movement-across that is at once microscopic and macroscopic. A line of flight invested in the microperceptions alive in the activity of relation that populates the metastable in-betweenness of the black and white. A folding-in of foreground and background.

A second series that stands out is called *Untitled.* It also comprises six panels, and is made one year earlier, in 1995. The activity of paint is similar here, drawing the background into the foreground, creating a direct perception of the activity of relation felt through the heavy, impatient line. As with *Utopia Panels*, there is a sense of paint exhausting itself (and the canvas) by the end of the series—as though Kngwarreye's brushstrokes used all the paint the brush could hold, in one infinite gesture. In this series, the colors range from white to red to yellow, creating a pink-orange-brown-blue-greenness emergent in the mixing of the paint. Again, the lines are danced, materialized from the range accessible from shoulder to hand in a single movement that never dissociates the shoulder from the body: each line moves a body.

The first of the six canvases of *Untitled* (1995) backgrounds the yellow, creating an almost uniform surface of whitish-pink strokes across, up, and down. These strokes are fierce but relatively constrained, short in length as though staccato, marking the surface without giving in to it. This panel bleeds yellow into the next canvas. The second panel—in shades of white on a brownish

Figure 7.11
Emily Kngwarreye, *Untitled*, 4 of 6, 1995b, Artists Rights Society, New York, NY.

yellow-green—is less controlled, mad with layering, a mix of colors that seep into the background, creating a brownish-yellow-green. The lines here are mostly whitish, continuous with the first canvas, but more complex due to the thickness of shades out of which the lines emerge, the background coloring caused, probably, by paint mixing before it dries. This is an impatient canvas, lines of differing widths no longer simply moving across and down but spiraling as well. Unlike the first panel, which seems to be what it proposes, the second panel is disruptive, continuous with the first, and yet disjunctive, thus forcing the body to keep moving toward the next panel.

Here and throughout the rest of the canvases, the white of the nonpainted canvas shows through, creating an inner connection between these divergent but connected pieces. The third panel's lines are again pinkish and the composition more staid, though now the unpainted space is clearly present on three sides, creating a sense of an inner diagram functioning through a layering of backgrounds and foregrounds, as though the white lines and the white background resonated together. This whiteness of the canvas showing through is on all the subsequent panels, though only on the inner top and bottom corners of the last one.

The fourth panel is violent in its explosion of energy. The whole body—*a whole lot*—feels emergent here, animating the painting's diagram, culminating in the last canvas. Red against white against the brownish-green mix of background-becoming-foreground, the lines are wild, creating incipient topological forms on a surface that resists flatness. The fifth panel seems again more composed—more restful, the lines continuous up, down, and across, mostly white with a bit of red creating a sense of an emergent pink, a drawing across of shade that moves toward affective tone rather than simply color, for pink seems anathema to the ferocity of these active lines. In the last panel, the paint begins to run out, as though we were left with the dregs of the effort that constitutes the event of the series.

But there is also a new component, emergent in the bottom left corner of the fifth panel, a mysterious slate blue, strangely discontinuous with most of the already apparent shades, yet co-constitutive of them. This blue seems to forecast the concrescence of the series, holding the event to itself even while it proposes its continuity elsewhere. Bringing futurity into the mix, the sixth panel seems to virtually contain all the other canvases, holding the series together even while exhausting it, the paintbrush squeezing out its last drops of color. In Whiteheadian terms, the subjective form has coalesced (concresced). The last panel is the event that composes the series even as it marks the beginning of its perishing. The hands say it all: white hands multiplied in the right bottom corner, letting the series go. There is no holding on to an event that is already passing. Having reached its culmination, the series makes use of the frenzied crescendo of this diagrammatic finale to foreground the active disjunction out of which a re-virtualization of potential is born—felt, particularly, in the blue-grey island—that marks the opening for the next actual occasion to begin to take form. The painting begins and ends in one and the same (multiplicitous) gesture.

This is an energetic finale. Energetic is the word for these dancing lines, but an energy of composition, not transcendence. These paintings are of the world, in the world, and for the world. As with the first series—*Utopia Panels* (1996)—the world cannot be thought outside the eventness of the work. Kngwarreye's is an activity of worlding where "the world within experience is identical with the world beyond experience, the occasion of experience is within the world, and the world is within the occasion" (Whitehead 1933, 228).

Kngwarreye creates an artistic plane of composition that engages the plane of immanence. Her work is of potential, of sensations that are always at once percepts and affects. In *What Is Philosophy*, Deleuze and Guattari explain: percepts are not perceptions, and affects are not affections (feelings). Percepts are "independent of a state of those who undergo them" and affects do not arise from subjects but pass through them (Deleuze and Guattari 1994, 169). Affects are becomings-other of sensation. Kngwarreye's art moves the body through the interpellation of increasingly complex sensations that are connected not to one final event but to the perpetuation of events alive in the "whole." Compositions of forces are alive in her work, creating sensations as reachings-toward that do not capture the Dreamings but set them in motion, rendering the imperceptible perceptible and the perceptible imperceptible. Her paintings do not call forth the songs of the Dreamings, they dance them: "The refrain in its entirety is the being of sensation" (Deleuze and Guattari 1994, 184).

Kngwarreye's works are not simply visual events. They are physically overwhelming experiences that capture the passing of the material substrate into sensation. Sensation is not projected: movement is felt as the canvas becomes a point of departure in a vast network of alliances of which the human body is but one aspect. Metamorphoses of forces, exfoliations of experiences, these are what is at stake in Kngwarreye's "whole lot." The "whole lot" is not a subject. It is the plane of immanence, the combinations of speeds, of affects and percepts in which "the One expresses in a single and same sense all of the multiple, [where]

Being expresses in a single and same sense all that differs" (Deleuze and Guattari 1987, 254). Kngwarreye's paintings are topological hyperspaces, absolute surfaces where all nodal points are virtually copresent. They are transspatial, transmedia events where distances (of thought, of movement) defy the limits of physical space-time.

To look at the desert paintings produced in the era of acrylic dot painting is to have a sense of *survol*, of seeing the landscape from above. These paintings reflect not a passive observation of a landscape below but a way of life where above and below fold into one-another. To see the landscape through them is to experience it, to live it, engaging all surface points at the same time, virtually, actually. It is, as Raymond Ruyer might suggest, to engage in infinite *survol* across the landscape's own absolute surface. To look is to become-with the landscape, to move from within as much as from above, experiencing the Dreaming not as an outsider to the everyday but through the vista of a metamorphosis that refuses to privilege the above or the below, the close or the far. As Barbara Glowczewski writes: "[Aboriginal] cosmology defines itself as a movement of coming and going between Kankarlu (the above) which refers to the present and everything which constitutes the terrestrial and celestial environments, and Kanunju, the 'below,' which refers to the past, to the underground, to the interstellar, and everything that can happen" (1989, 213). The manifest and the latent, the finite and the infinite, the actual and the virtual: these are the concerns of Aboriginal cosmology.

Kngwarreye's paintings are sensing concepts, absolute surfaces or volumes that "have no other object than the inseparability of distinct variations" (Deleuze and Guattari 1994, 21). The Dreaming is a concept of the most extraordinary kind, a concept that speaks not of unity but of wholeness, that lives the virtuality of its concreteness transspatially in a dimension of space-time that always remains to be invented. Kngwarreye's genius is her ability to convey this through paint. Her paintings emote vibrations that are rhythms, themselves singing the songs of space-time. To create these songs, what Kngwarreye seeks—in continuity with painters such as Clifford Possum—is the annihilation of the figural. She does tell stories, but these stories rely on synesthetic experience, on a coming together of elements that are in infinite patterns of reachings-toward space-times of experience.

It is in large part the figurative that has sustained the appropriation of the landscape for the colonizing gaze. What would it mean to wrest the figure from the figurative? In Kngwarreye's work, the figure is the movement of becoming

Figure 7.12
Emily Kngwarreye, *Anooralya*, 1995, Artists Rights Society, New York, NY.

itself.[109] Her paintings are topological deformations that make sensible the untouchable. The bodies at hand—the root systems, the animals—extend beyond their coordinates in a Euclidean space-time, immanent to the space-time of creation. Kngwarreye creates, not by imposing form onto the canvas or by representing space, but by engaging the running as it runs.

Dancing the Dream

Deleuze speaks of marks made accidentally. These accidental marks are free—free of the medium, free of the context of their representation. They are not unconscious but hyperconscious. They are marks out of which new concepts are born. To watch Kngwarreye paint is to watch a woman dancing, her whole body engaged in the act, the plane of composition emerging directly from her shoulder along the elbow, wrist held firmly, both hands involved.[110] She was not a writing woman: she was a dancing woman, her wrists taut with the activity of reaching-toward and moving-with. Her paintings reflect this force of movement-with through the wholeness of the emergent line or dot, through the becoming-form of the body-land-canvas.

Kngwarreye paints the reaching-toward out of which dancing dreams are composed. This reaching-toward is an almost-touch: it touches the not-yet through which futurity will emerge. Painting the untouchable is to preaccelerate the urgency of the taking-form these extraordinary paintings propose. This suggests a noncoincidence always present in the act of mark-making, a rhythmic disjunction that recalls the latency or the virtual in any actualization. To actualize in this sense is to make-present both the future and the past. Painting is creation.[111] Kngwarreye's art is not unconscious. What she paints is absolutely real, eventful, its untouchability always an incitation to touch.

It is the rhythm of the land I see in Kngwarreye's relationscapes, a rhythm that refuses to subjugate the image to the text, the dance to the music. The rhythm is all around, it is the "whole lot": the weather, the seasons, the births and deaths, the rituals and performances, the body painting and batiks. These rhythms are sensations of the boldest kind, sensations that alter the very core of what it is to sense. There is no inside/outside to the sensations: they are as much of the body as of the land, extending synesthetically beyond all comprehension of three-dimensional space-time, leading us not toward a dimension as such but toward a topological hyperspace of relationscapes, to an immanent transcendence that is profoundly of the land, of the here and now.

Figure 7.13
Emily Kngwarreye, *Merne Kame*, 1995, Artists Rights Society, New York, NY.

Experiential work defies description. As lines become planes become topologies, the singular mark synesthetically transforms the whole. The colors reflect not only off one another but also within the shades they help create. These shades are events: Dreamings in the making.

Topological geographies create new art histories. Red against yellow, black against brown, dots, lines, circles, footprints, all of these gestures toward the Dreaming extend themselves beyond a body or a canvas, creating movements of thought. These movements of thought provoke response-ability: *we cannot but move*. We cannot but sense the shades of difference that create the activity of the land. We cannot but respond relationally. We cannot participate and then refuse the immanence of the "whole" these paintings generate.

This is the power of contemporary Aboriginal art. It incites cross-cultural transformation at an artistic as well as a political level, asking us to rethink the map, the landmark we presumed we could locate, the direction we thought we knew how to follow. In the end, we remain foreign yet politically—relationally—charged. A qualitative change has occurred shifting us from the realm of the passive observer toward the realm of the political inventor: the topological hyperspace we encounter through Aboriginal art has qualitatively altered our capacity to relate on shifting ground.

Relationscapes abound. They are not strictly relegated to the Aborigines and their experience of the Dreaming. Kngwarreye was not the first to annihilate figuration. What art such as that of Kngwarreye, Napangardi, Petyarre, or Possum does is create a movement of thought, a movement that is *marayin*, at once painting, song, dance, sacred object, and power word. Through their work, we move toward a topological hyperspace of experience, asking once again how emptiness is configured, how topologies extend our worlds, rhythmically (de) forming them, and how maps that sense-across create durations that eventfully alter how experience can unfold.

8 Constituting Facts: Dorothy Napangardi Dances the Dreaming

I should believe only in a God who understood how to dance.
—Friedrich Nietzsche, *Thus Spoke Zarathustra*

Dorothy Napangardi's *Salt on Mina Mina* (2001) measures 244 x 168 cm. Stately, *Salt on Mina Mina* (2001) moves with an intensity of quietude across a tall, vertical rectangle. The maze of dotted pathways at first evokes a grid. Lines of force make forays into conjunctive patterns only to deviate at the very moment of encounter. As with each of Napangardi's evocations of the salt lines at Mina Mina, the dotted lines ultimately defy the grid, finding passageways more or less straight across the teeming array of activity, forming intensive zones on the canvas where a dance of meeting-points creates a background for the almost-meeting of the dotted lines in the foreground. The backgrounded lines of the grid make way for the intensive zones of the foregrounded force-field that ultimately make the work resonate. These are zones of intensive magnitude where a reaching-toward alters the composition of the work-as-grid. Transductions from path to force, these zones of encounter are intensities in the making.

Salt on Mina Mina dances. It dances its trajectory, its story, it future-past passage into the present. Like all evocations of Dreamings (Jukurrpa), this painting refracts a sacred story. Napangardi's work around Mina Mina tells the story of digging sticks, of women dancing, of a meeting place for spirit ancestors both human and animal. It is the story of a rhythmic pounding of the earth with digging-sticks emerging from the ground like moving trees. It is the story of

Figure 8.1
Dorothy Napangardi, *Salt on Mina Mina*, 2001, Artists Rights Society, New York, NY.

ancestral women dancing the digging-sticks' formation across the curved root systems of the yams and other ground vegetables. It is the story of dust rising in the wake of long flowing lines of earth dancing, of women moving through, weaving in, flying above. It is the story of a snake billowing up into the sky on a magic carpet of dust, almost unnoticed by the dancing women. It is the story told around a snake ancestor—Walyankarna—who rests today at Yaturlu Yaturlu (The Granites).

Napangardi is a custodian of the story of the ancestral women with the digging sticks. Her telling of the story keeps it alive as it keeps her Dreaming: the Dreaming fashions her even as she recreates its eventful momentum in the future-past. Dreamings meander, alive with elements of futurity even as they continue to lay down the Law for generations to come. Like all stories, they are told again and again, taking form in their journey from one iteration to another, inviting the past into a present of its own making. This does not make them any less factual: Dreamings constitute facts even as they express the force of change.

Salt on Mina Mina reverberates with the movement of digging sticks dancing. It is one iteration of a story Dorothy Napangardi will tell many times in the years to come. In this painting, the pathways are multiple, their meeting points infinite. Up and down and across, the dotted lines transverse the cloth, populating the canvas with a thousand potential convergences. And yet despite the majestic quietude of the work, it will not sit still long enough to allow us to determine exactly where the encounter takes place.

Stephen Page describes Aboriginal dancing as "foot to earth" (qtd. in Mundine 2002, 68). Dancing low to the ground, the movement concentrated in the knees, it is as though the earth itself were moving the body. *Salt on Mina Mina* dances the earth moving. It does not represent women dancing: it dances their digging, moving-with the trajectory of their passing. These are not dots left behind: they are dots in the making. We feel the force of their taking-form. This is why we can't stop looking, our eyes roving over the work, incapable of finding a resting-point.

Resonant grids are rare. Usually, grids focus the eye, calling us to attention. The grid keeps a convergence between inside and outside, ensuring a containment of the bounds of its in-formation. If a force is felt, it is felt as the outside looking in, a composition of a fixed form, not a recomposing-in-movement. Napangardi's work undoes the grid, exposing its apparent stability to its own process of unravelling. Making a topology out of a Euclidean geometry, her work propels deformations that pull the whole body into their movement. *Salt on Mina Mina*'s affective tonality is one of conjunctive dissonance, a felt rhythm that invents itself in the watching. Watching/feeling Napangardi's work is like dancing the ancestral women's dance.

Salt on Mina Mina has calm corners, each of them lined with dots of approximately the same consistency. The frame is quiet, as is the intensive middle, a whiteness of dots vibrating. It is what happens in the toward of the dots' movements that is forceful, not their placing on the canvas as such. This resonance can already be felt in the space between the lines around the edges of the canvas, in the incipiency of the undulating lines moving toward the center. The incipiency felt here as the force of movement taking form is created by the intervals between the dots that foreground the sonorous beat of the background becoming foreground. What we see are not actually lines but the spaces between the dots, in-filled with intensity as movement pushes to the fore. The line becomes an intensity of vibratory movement—an actual image of an incipiency. The line quivers with movement, still and active at once. We feel movement's intensity, not its displacement.

The dotted lines in *Salt on Mina Mina* would not vibrate were it not for the gridding that holds together the painting's background. The incipient force of the work is felt through the contrast between the white dots and the black background, and between the gridded lines and the not quite meeting of the lines in the foreground. One area of the canvas makes this particularly apparent: toward the center on the right-hand side, a set of dotted lines squiggle, momentarily undoing the linear progression of the movement of the lines toward the white almost-square of the painting's calm middle. This curvature on a canvas otherwise composed of mostly straight lines gathers our attention to other deviations from the line, to the ways in which the lines in fact resist meeting, to the movements of curvature within each becoming-line. Through the contrast between foregrounded curvature and backgrounded grid, a movement takes form that resonates as a vibration more than as a displacement. It is as though we were moving and staying in place at the same time. This is how Djon Mundine describes Aboriginal dance: "Women move in a kind of minimalistic shuffle (not really a step) with the feet always in the sand" (2002, 68).

A shuffle that is not really a step is a quiver. It is an intensive movement that foregrounds not a displacement but a qualitative shift. A dance of the not-yet. Weight on the knees connects the dancer to the earth, giving form to a preacceleration that is in deep alliance with the earth moving. Aboriginal dancing dances the earth to listen to its story tell itself. "It's all about physical memory—to be able to tell the story by putting yourself in the movement" (Mundine 2002, 68). This is *Salt on Mina Mina*'s call: put yourself in the movement.

Digging sticks (Karlangu) are strongly associated with Warlpiri women in Aboriginal culture and are used to dig for yams, goannas, witchetty grubs, and other bush foods. They are also used in the culture for making shelter, fighting, and funeral ceremonies. Napangardi's investment in the digging sticks is twofold. On the one hand, the Dreaming for which she is custodian is intricately linked with the digging sticks. Her work depends on their integration as part of the story she tells. And yet her use of the digging sticks is singular. She also uses them as a technology of movement: she paints dots as though digging with the sticks through the earth. This usage of the digging sticks as a technique for painting sets her slightly apart from the tradition of dot-paintings that emerged in Australia around the 1970s.[112] Where many painters used the dots as quasi-representational devices (figuring campsites, waterholes, etc.), Napangardi's focus is on a technique for digging, a tool for making dots. Before she paints content, Napangardi paints technique.

To paint technique is to work with the potential of the tools to tell their own story. Instead of giving the form particular content, drawing (with) the technique allows Napangardi to create works that are evocative in their multiplicity while still returning to the *ways* of speaking, of dancing or singing, of her people. Her paintings evoke the "how" of her culture, keeping the "what" more private.

Since the late 1990s, when she started to focus on Mina Mina in her paintings, Napangardi has given most of her paintings two titles: *Salt on Mina Mina* and *Karntakurlangu Jukurrpa* (Digging-Stick-Possessing Dreaming). There are other titles such as *Rain on Mina Mina*, *Sandhills of Mina Mina*, *Women's Dreaming*, *Karlangu*, *Inland Sea*, but these seem not so much different subjects for painting as different aspects of the two main lineages. What is fascinating about this focus of hers is the way in which her work creates difference within repetition. Returning time and again to the digging sticks, to the dried up lake at Mina Mina (Ngayurru or Lake McKay), to the Women's Dreaming at this site, she creates an infinity of iterations within one larger theme, each of them a different rhythm dancing the same infinite dance.

Aboriginal culture works on nonlinear timelines. The past infects the present in its future re-activation, alive in the present not as past but as present-taking-form. Time dances into itself rich with past experience re-animated. Moving-with time, Dreamings reinvent an always-changing landscape that becomes alongside a changing culture. This is why Napangardi can continue to paint Mina Mina despite having returned only infrequently since she was brought to an outstation in her young childhood.[113] The Dreaming here becomes a technique for the remaking of moving time, enabling her to reinvent with the complex intermixing of memory, oral history, and dreams. Napangardi's art invents-with the landscape of her culture remaking itself, regardless of the contradictions of her current living situation, which is in many ways very distanced from her people's long nomadic history. This reinventing of culture through a recasting of experience-in-the-making flows similarly to Ngayurru, a lakebed at Mina Mina of hard-packed clay with criss-crossed salt-lines "like an intricate pattern of interwoven string," which undergoes a complete transformation on those rare occasions when it is filled with water, "teeming with seagulls, black swans, and kestrels" (Nungarrayi 2002, 8).

"In Mind"

"While I'm doing my paintings . . . I have my country in mind" (Napangardi 2002, 11). To have something "in mind" is different from representing it. It is to work with the event of coming-to-expression more than with a precomposed image. William James's concept of the "terminus" is useful in understanding the relationship between expression and event. For James, the terminus is "what the concept 'had in mind'" (1912, 61). The terminus in Napangardi's case is not the image of the Dreaming or its narrative per se but the force of its becoming through which its current iteration begins to take form. The *Karntakurlangu Jukurrpa*—a title she gives to a number of her works—is the terminus that gives momentum to Napangardi's paintings. Its function is not of mimesis—her work is not a mimetic transferring of the Dreaming as stable narrative—but of propensity. The Dreaming of the sticks gives the force of form to her work. Napangardi works with Mina Mina "in mind" to create a moving image of the intensive passage from force to form. Each painting is a composition in itself and stands out on its own as an iteration of this "in-mindness." It is not a representation of the place or a narrative of its history. It is an encounter with its resonance.

Whitehead talks about facts this way. Rather than situating "facts" as the truth-value of an iteration, Whitehead suggests that facts are those occasions of experience that are fully composed and yet stand for more than themselves: "Every proposition proposing a fact must, in its complete analysis, propose the general character of the universe required for that fact" (1929/1978, 11). A fact is not self-sustaining—it is a relational co-occurrence that marks the in-practice of an event's worlding.

The event of Mina Mina that Napangardi paints in *Salt on Mina Mina* (2002) is qualitatively quite different from her 2001 painting. The 2002 *Salt on Mina Mina*'s dimensions are 122 x 198 cm, and it lies horizontal. Where *Salt on Mina Mina* (2001) was composed of dotted lines that filled almost every part of the canvas, creating a foreground-background resonance, *Salt on Mina Mina* (2002) foregrounds the blackness of the background through the creation of open spaces. The black openings in the canvas are the places where the dots do not meet. This leaves us with the feeling that the dotted lines actually reach each other more frequently. Strangely, even though there is more open space on this canvas, it feels as though there is less of an intensive center. The canvas is both emptier and busier, its dotted lines cutting in their precision. This time the painting's diagram—its intensive force—feels wider, more dispersed, as though there were different rhythms coexisting within one intensive space.

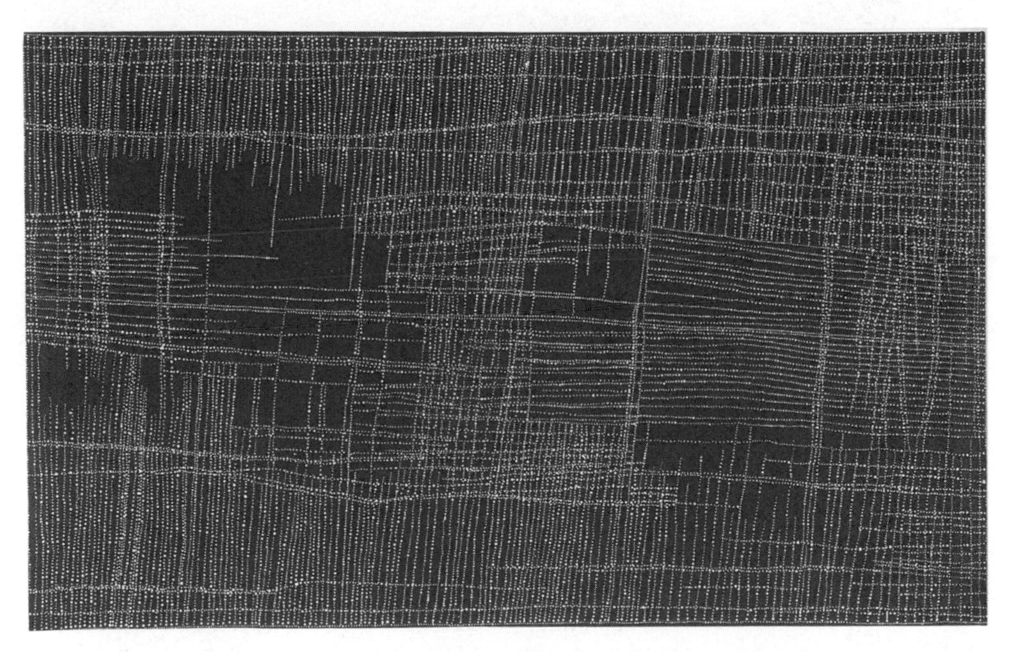

Figure 8.2
Dorothy Napangardi, *Salt on Mina Mina*, 2002, Artists Rights Society, New York, NY.

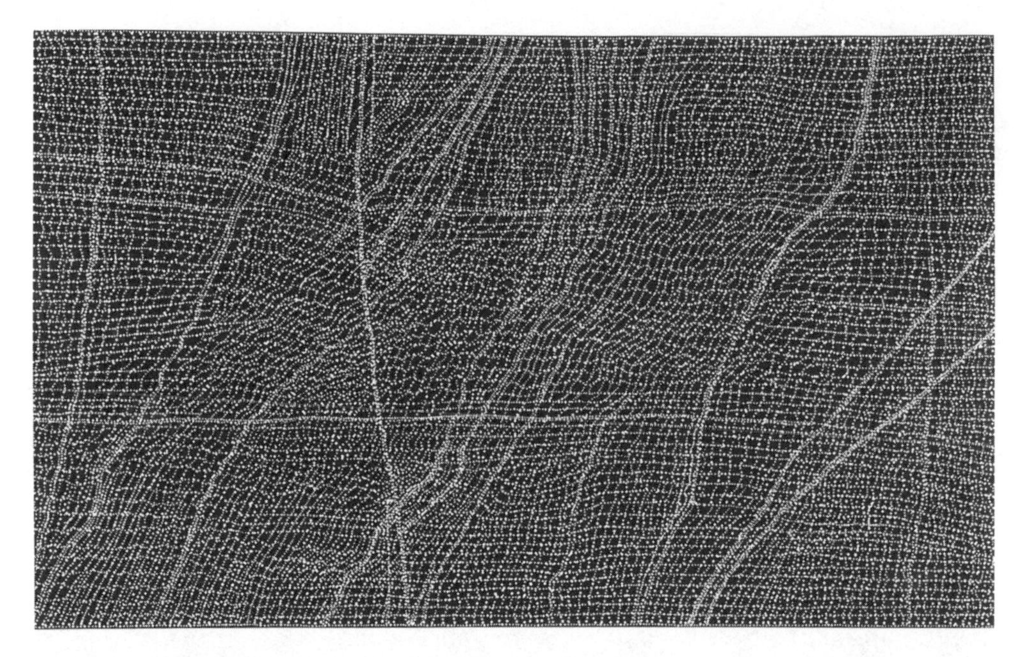

Figure 8.3
Dorothy Napangardi, *Rain at Mina Mina*, 2001, Artists Rights Society, New York, NY.

Salt on Mina Mina (2002) constitutes a fact in itself, even as it conserves deep resonances both to *Salt on Mina Mina* (2001) and to the original site and Dreaming which it had "in mind." A Dreaming is a Whiteheadian fact. It is not a form with a single iteration—it morphs across iterations that exist in time *and* compose space-times of experience. For Whitehead, each fact is more than its forms. "Form 'participates' throughout the world of facts" (1929/1978, 20). A Dreaming is a relational network of stories, dances, dreams, images. It is the fact of their eventful reiterability. This morphing force of Law is both definite and indefinite. It has parameters even while it holds within itself the potential for infinite variation. The Dreaming is a fact of present life with an intensive core that constitutes what it can do as a creative force for the future.

Rain at Mina Mina (2001) makes this potential for mutation within the Dreaming felt. In this painting, which is exactly the same size and shape as *Salt on Mina Mina* (2002), the "same" lakebed has a completely different affective tonality. Whereas *Salt on Mina Mina* (2002) is crisp and defined in its dotted lines and incipient trajectories, *Rain at Mina Mina* (2001) feels blurry, its felt-lines leaking into one another, its passages flowing to create a wide, soft intensity. These paintings, which are like mirror-images of one another, are two forms of a related fact.

What Whitehead would call their "fact of togetherness" is the nexus of the Karntakurlangu Dreaming. This nexus is populated by the various forms the iterations of the Dreaming take, from rain to salt to sand. Each painting dances the Dreaming, foregrounding an aspect of its fact. Seen this way, the "associated works" of Napangardi—the sandhills, the rain, the digging-sticks, the lakebed—find their fact of togetherness. They are divergent encounters with *aspects* of her Dreaming. *Sandhills of Mina Mina* (2002) is another of these allied iterations in the related fact of Napangardi's Dreaming. It is not a derivation, but a conjunctive force in the dyad "Salt-Lines/Karntakurlangu." In this painting—of which there are also many iterations, painted over a period from 2000 onward—Napangardi uses color on a black background, tones of red, blue, ochre with white.

Sandhills of Mina Mina (2002) measures 152 x 152 cm.[114] It is a perfect square, and yet its movement defies the strict contours of its imposed frame. Two of the corners seem to move horizontally, and two of them seem to move across, quasi-virtual paths meeting in different areas of the canvas as resonances of mixing colors. The affective tonality of the canvas is one of mutedness—it is a calm, flowing work, less jaggedly differentiated than the salt line series, and yet just as complex. Here, Napangardi composes with color, using the complementarity of the color-tones to create fields of virtual movement. As a technique in its own right, color here takes over the work of the digging sticks, creating a virtual resonance within the actual shape-shifting of the landscape. The color brings out the landscape in the work, giving consistency to a form-taking that occurs significantly where the color comes together.

In addition to the color creating a foregrounding of flowing form, the size of the dots gives the work a pulsating rhythm. Dots are of different size and consistency throughout Napangardi's work, but here, the contrast in size is felt singularly as a movement-toward, an inner vibration of a shallow relief created by the pulsation. This is a subtle relief, almost in two dimensions. What we feel is not "landscape" per se, nor "color" in its definiteness, but the very rhythm of the landscape taking form through color. We feel the affective tonality of the composition composing itself. If we abandon ourselves to perception, we see

Figure 8.4
Dorothy Napangardi, *Sandhills of Mina Mina*, 2002, Artists Rights Society, New York, NY.

not simply color but its force taking form. In the almost-color of the between, the landscape's color emerges.

Feeling the Dance

For Whitehead, facts are never built out of universals. They emerge from concrete occasions of experience. How these occasions express themselves is the fact of their existence. Napangardi paints matters of fact in flux. The flux is expressed as movement and can be felt through the seriality of her work. Seen as series, Napangardi's paintings can be said to create a Dreaming nexus. This nexus makes felt the wider complexity of the Dreaming as a continued iteration of experience-in-the-making. As part of a wider extensive continuum[115] of Aboriginal Law, Napangardi's work propels the Dreaming-as-nexus toward an iteration of its potential future form-taking. Future facts have a force of their own. Theirs is a force of becoming, a will to power. This will to power provokes feelings that alter the affective tonality of the present-passing. Painting force taking form is a painting for the future in the present. The force of Napangardi's vision is her capacity to bridge determinate matters of fact with the future mutations of expression.

Feelings are associated with facts in Whitehead's philosophy, with creativity as their conduit. The quality of expression of an artwork is its feeling. Feelings for Whitehead effect the transition of a prehension into an event. The feeling of landscape that becomes the experience of *Sandhills of Mina Mina* (2002) is a feeling of what the Dreaming had "in mind." "In mind" refers not to a stable subjectivity but to an ontogenetic in-gathering of forces that emanate from the work into the factness of the collective experience it provokes. When Napangardi says she always has her country "in mind" she is referring to a collective iteration—through Dreamings, dances, songs—that gives her in-mindness a resonance of country. The country is not "hers"—it creates her in a collective individuation that lends force to the creative gestures that are her works. This force taking form is the feeling of the work.

The Dreaming itself is a force taking form. Painting the dreaming is a regathering of forces of country for the experience of perception. Force works across strata here, from the contagion of the Dreaming as extensive continuum for Aboriginal culture as a whole to the expression of a singular instance of the force of form in the future-present experience of a painting. For Nietzsche, all things are evocations of a history of forces that struggle for iteration. As Deleuze explains: "The same object, the same phenomenon, changes sense depending on the force which appropriates it" (1983, 3). Force is appetition: hunger for expression. The appetition of an event is the insatiability of its potential. The shift from appetition to form is never a completed passage. In the work's final form, the force of its potential can still be felt. This is the work's diagram. The diagram of the work in-gathers the work's feeling. Whitehead calls the final fact of the work the *decision of emphasis*. This is how the work satisfies its becoming. This satisfaction is the present-finality of its current iteration.

Painting the Dreaming means working with the force of its potential for reiteration. An encounter with a painting such as Napangardi's *Sandhills of Mina Mina* (2002) is therefore both an event in itself associated with a time and place,[116] and an engagement with the Dreaming as extensive continuum. Participating at both levels of expression, Napangardi's paintings foreground the activity of the Dreaming's reiteration that orients the Dreaming to its ontogenetic potential. The Dreaming becomes a double iteration of multiple sense in the plurality of constellations of its form-taking. Napangardi's work activates the Dreaming's potential to create new kinds of futures in the present. Through her work, the Dreaming becomes both a technology of the future and a technique for the present, opening the present to its potential for experiential complexity. Open to the indeterminacy of experience, Dreamings such as those evoked through Napangardi's work resonate with an ontogenetic plurality of sense(s).

In creating work that remains open to an infinity of potential evocations, Napangardi's art risks that the iterations of her Dreaming be colonized, immobilized, arrested within dominant belief systems. The plurality alive in her work always risks being overtaken by the forces of encounter it invites. And yet, paraphrasing Nietzsche, Deleuze writes: "A force would not survive if it did not first of all borrow the features of the forces with which it struggles" (1983, 5). Active force always risks capture by reactive force. Such capture might result in the "translation," the "rendering" of Napangardi's work within a stabilizing narrative of identity or representation. Yet, like much Aboriginal artwork, Napangardi's art resists this risk, its complexity of iterations foregrounding the force of the Dreaming's mutations of expression rather than simply giving a narrative to the present fully formed. Perhaps this is due to the fact that Dreamings themselves have survived changing worlds (more than 50,000 years of continuous history in Australia), which suggests that they are capable of working with a coexistence of forces, bending to pressures when necessary and reemerging stronger. Their will to power, as felt in Napangardi's work, seems to be their very readiness for reemergence in a continuous dance of eternal return.

"What a will wants is to affirm its difference" (Deleuze 1983, 9). The will to power is the differential element of force. Through the will to power, force takes form. It does so by exercising its will not on a subject but on another will. The will to power of the Dreaming is the creation of novelty within the everlasting. Systems of Law that foreground the ontogenetic potential of the new, Dreamings are at once forces of the becoming-landscape (iterations of the landscape's infinite potential for renewal) and forces of creation. Dreamings *will* life and more life. For this life to take form ontogenetically, certain facts of existence must hold. As matters of fact, the Laws that are encompassed by the Dreamings impose enabling constraints on experience that open the landscape to concrete potentials. These Laws give shape to the extensive continuum that is the virtual nexus of life's force of becoming by constraining it into patterns of resonance. These patterns can take the form of songlines, of dances, of emergent formations within the landscape. They create a relationscape out of the landscape-animal-human series that does not seek to differentiate between the virtual and the real. Dreams are activities for the virtual fact of existence made concrete.

Take two more of Napangardi's canvases, this time both titled *Karntakurlangu Jukurrpa*. Both paintings were made in 2000. One of them measures 137.5 x 152.5 cm—an imperfect square—the other 130 x 239.5 cm—an elongated rectangle. *Karntakurlangu Jukurrpa* (2000a) is the more colorful of the two—with ochre as well as black and white. The two paintings are very different, and yet that they express the same matter of fact can be felt. The "how" of their expression—the force of form they make felt—is how they relate on the shared nexus of the Karntakurlangu Dreaming.

Karntakurlangu Jukurrpa (2000a) is composed of unevenly spaced squares composed of meandering dots. The effect is of geometrical shapes emerging from the two-dimensional canvas with virtual pathways between them revealing lines in the making. The edges of the canvas are whiter, which makes them recede, calling attention to the canvas's disjunctive center. As in all of Napangardi's work, the diagram is wide, yet restrained. It feels as though the force of the work is an emergent *way of looking* more than an actual taking-form. The diagram of the painting—its feeling of force taking form—is itself in movement.

In the second of this 2000 series, *Karntakurlangu Jukurrpa* (2000b), the black and white of the dots moving into lines is significantly horizontal, leading toward a center opening that is more white than black. And yet, despite

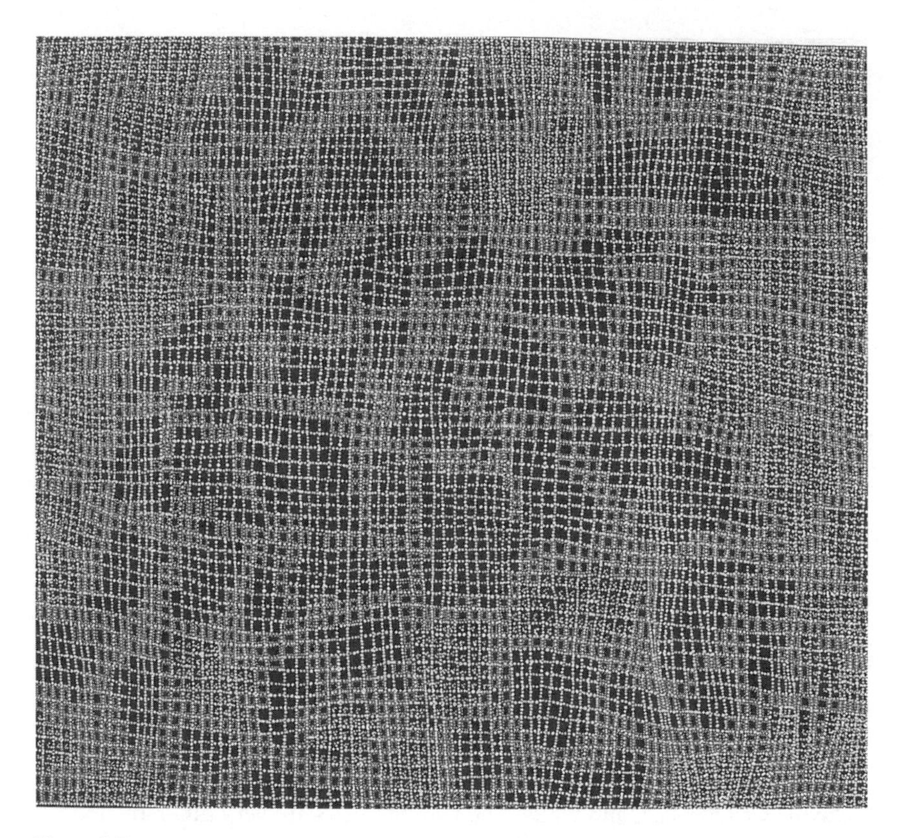

Figure 8.5
Dorothy Napangardi, *Karntakurlangu Jukurrpa*, 2000a, Artists Rights Society, New York, NY.

the overwhelming feeling of horizontality evoked by the Dreaming's diagram, closer inspection reveals that the composition is equally made up of vertical lines. The similarity to *Karntakurlangu Jukurrpa* (2000a) is the way it provokes a seeing-with of the more-than of its composition.

Karntakurlangu Jukurrpa (2000b) is held together by vertical dotted lines on its edges. These vertical lines call forth the intervals between the dots. As in all of Napangardi's works, the becoming-lines focus the movement of the painting toward its incipience, causing vision to be held up by the tonality rather than by the content of the work. We look-with, across the becoming-form of the canvas, with an intensity that pulls the becoming-image from the inside-out, propulsing the white field of the canvas's center toward the worlding it foretells. This one is a violent worlding, a movement that feels less like dancing than like a battle or a storm.

The story of Karntakurlangu tells of more than the women dancing with their digging sticks.[117] There is a continuation of the narrative told by other related Dreamings, which involves a snake ancestor called Walyankarna. The snake got its name because of the meeting place—Walyankarna—where the snake was cast into the air by the dust of the ancestral women's digging sticks. The second part of the story, as narrated by Tiger Tjapaltjarri (qtd. in Nicholls 2002, 64), reveals that the snake resumes traveling and begins to follow the women, soon becoming a snake-man.[118] Having reached them, he begins to stalk the women, spying on them dancing in long lines with their digging sticks, their movements following the cracks above the yams growing underground. In the ensuing battle between the snake-become-rapist and the ancestral women, the snake-man is killed by their digging sticks. This last portion of the story is not actually part of Napangardi's Dreaming. It is called Two Snake Dreaming and belongs to a different skin group. But perhaps its virtual presence is what we feel in

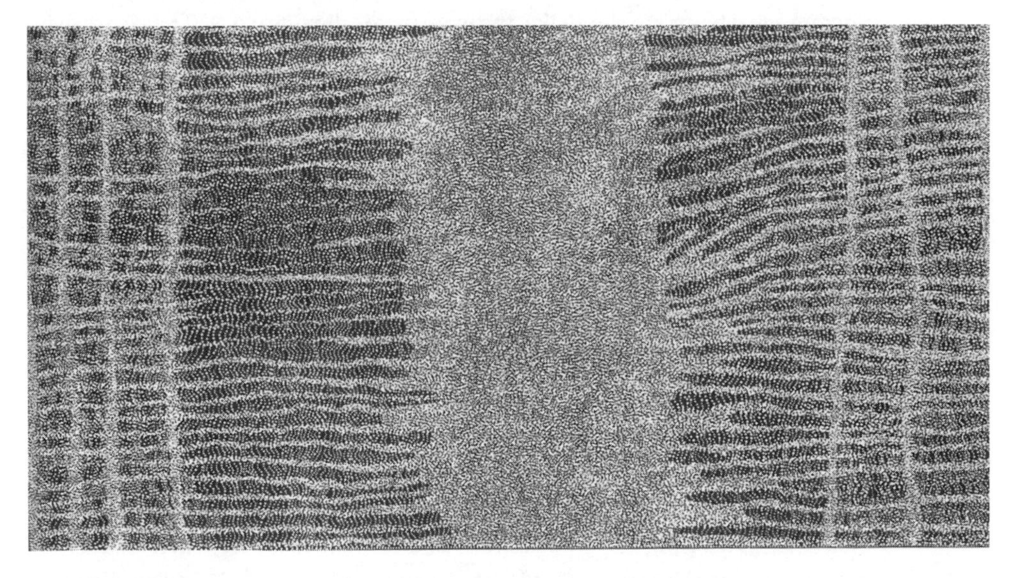

Figure 8.6
Dorothy Napangardi, *Karntakurlangu Jukurrpa*, 2000b, Artists Rights Society, New York, NY.

Napangardi's *Karntakurlangu Jukurrpa* (2000b) as the violence of a certain force of possession taking over.

Napangardi would never purposefully evoke a Dreaming not hers to tell. That strands of Dreamings emerge ontogenetically within tellings of adjacent stories emphasizes the inherent fact of relationality that is at the heart of Dreamings as a whole. In her evocation of the *Karntakurlangu Jukurrpa* (2000b), Napangardi does not tell the story of the snake's rape, and yet its presence within the larger Dreaming nexus seems to taint her Dreaming. The force of the eternal return of the Dreaming seems to be felt in *Karntakurlangu Jukurrpa* (2000b). This feeling is not a narrative that seeks to tell a missing part of a story. It is *a force for the telling* that is violent in its expression.

In Napangardi's evocation of the Karntakurlangu Dreaming in *Karntakurlangu Jukurrpa* (2000b), what is also noteworthy is the recuperative power of the violence. This is not reactive force personalized, resentfully reclaiming the past in an act of *ressentiment.*[119] It is a future-taking of the present, a reaching-toward creation. Napangardi's *Karntakurlangu Jukurrpa* (2000b) affirms the force of the Dreaming, willing it to express new manifestations of multiple sense. These manifestations are not morally inflected. They resist morality, giving equal tenure to the snake, the woman, the digging-stick. They learn-with the dynamism of the relationscape created out of their complex encounters in the future-present.

This acting of force on force that can be felt in Napangardi's work is a returning of the return, an eternal spiralling movement that makes the cycle of time felt. What is felt through this evocation of the Dreaming is time's intensive magnitude—its chthonic movement—and its infinite cycle of return. This is not incessant sameness—it is differential becoming, force acting on force to affirm difference at every turn. "Existence begins in every instant; the ball There rolls around every Here. The middle is everywhere. The path of eternity is crooked" (Nietzsche 1961, 234).

Dreamings are both actual occasion and extensive continuum, the world as it happens and the world as it envelops its happening. Law and event, experience and force of apparition, Dreamings cycle time. Their determinacy is a matter of fact, their indetermination their appetition. Force for expression makes itself felt in the Dreaming's infinite desire to take form once more. When an iteration of a particular Dreaming takes form—such as in Napangardi's *Karntakurlangu Jukurrpa* (2000c), the continuum of the Dreaming as nexus is altered. The new version of the Karntakurlangu becomes part of the fact of the Dreaming as both event and continuum. Dreaming in its totality is thus virtually present in every new actual occasion of the Dreaming. In turn, every new iteration alters the intensive magnitude of the Dreaming's extensive continuum.

This extensive-intensive relation is felt everywhere in Napangardi's work. It is a tension alive in the lines she carves into the canvas through the digging-stick dots. In *Karntakurlangu Jukurrpa* (2000c), measuring 122 x 122 cm, this tension is foregrounded. Another square painting (in its dimensions), *Karntakurlangu Jukurrpa* (2000c) evokes a complex surface of dots becoming-squares unbecoming-squares, the tone a rust color with white on a black background. This painting makes the force of the landscape's curvature felt. Along the edges, the squares are quite uniform, but as they begin to merge toward the middle, the dotted lines seem to bend. The activity of the squares' deformation is the event of the work. This intensive becoming-topological of the painting's folding surface draws the gaze to the left-of-center of the canvas, where the squares seem to recede to make space for the painting's eventual deformation. Here, the painting's becoming-form pulsates. The dynamic encounter is not between background and foreground but between curve and line, making felt a qualitative transmutation that morphs the painting from its squareness toward an intensive infinity of infolding. This diagrammatic infolding is less a shape than a feeling of force pushing into the painting's insistent deformation. The collapse of Euclidean geometry is felt as the tension of topological undoing. Force fights form, exposing the inner relations of tension in the becoming-landscape's curvature.

The extensive continuum is virtual. It has not yet been divided into space-time. The actual occasions that populate it, on the other hand, are firmly positioned in experiential space-time. That the Dreaming cooperates on both the virtual and the actual strata is emphasized by the Dreaming's adherence to a non-linear cycle of time, where what returns is not "time-as-it-was" but "time-as-it-will-become." This is a time of the future-past, a present in the making. The relationship between the forces of movement's intensive magnitude and the extensive continuum creates space-times of experience through which the return returns. This eternal return "is not the 'same' or the 'one' which comes back. . . . Return is itself the one which ought to belong to diversity and to that which differs" (Deleuze 1983, 46). Resistant to equilibrium, the relation between actual occasions and the extensive continuum incites time to become infinite not as a straight line of measured chronology but as an intensive magnitude. Time rolls into experience even as experience creates time.

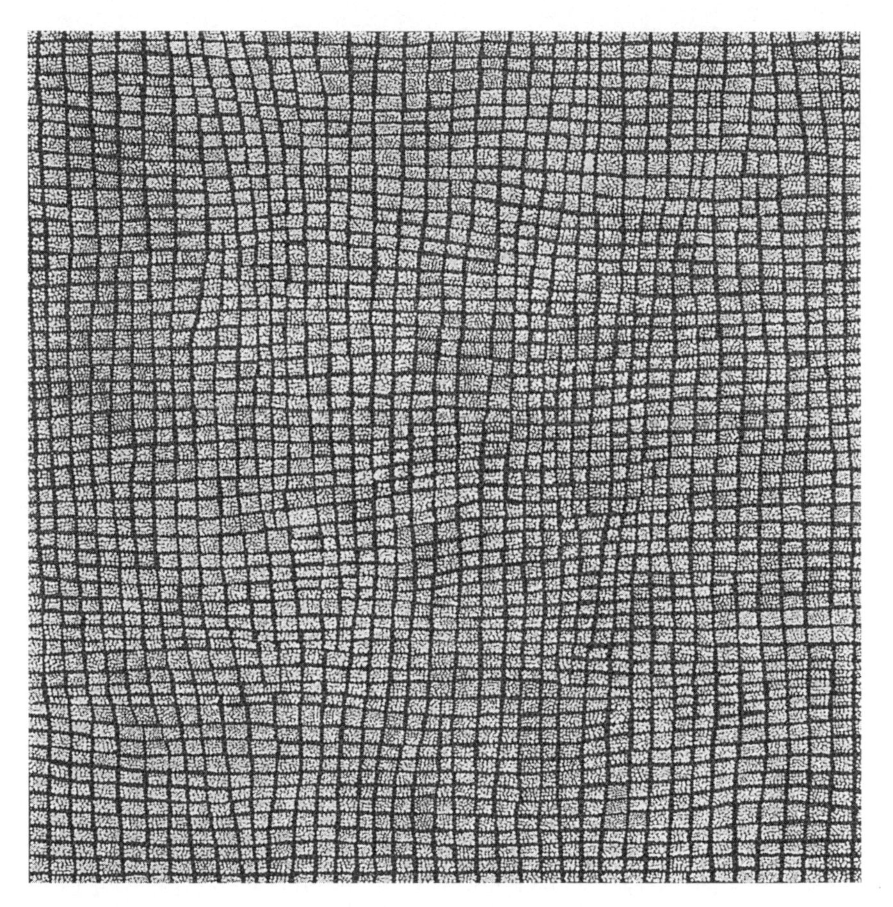

Figure 8.7
Dorothy Napangardi, *Karntakurlangu Jukurrpa*, 2000c, Artists Rights Society, New York, NY.

Drops of Perception

Napangardi's artworks are "drops of perception" (James 1996, 172). They are transitional facts that alter the vast resonance of the extensive continuum even while taking part in the actuality of the future-past taking form. There is no final state, no point of adherence where the fact becomes itself once and for all. The Dreaming's matter of fact is the potential of life to continue to become. "That the present moment is not a moment of being or of present 'in the strict sense,' that it is the passing moment, *forces* us to think of becoming, but to think of it precisely as what could not have started, and cannot finish, becoming" (Deleuze 1983, 48). The Dreaming has no ultimate identity: it is that out of which relationscapes are born. Its story is its dance of becoming.

"Now I am nimble, now I fly, now I see myself under myself, now a god dances with me" (Nietzsche 1961, 69). To paint with country "in mind" is to paint from the sky, to paint-with the world emergent. Aboriginal artists have always painted as though from above with the ground "in mind," feeling the world through its incipient movements rather than asking it to emerge fully formed. Theirs is a form of perception that activates the "drops," catching them in a collective net of creative undoing. Their art does not represent a landscape. It undoes it to redo it, feeling-with its inner movements, catching its tendencies in the passing, dancing their force. Napangardi's paintings evoke a feeling for a landscape that begins with relation, revealing its topologies alive in the here and now of future-pastness. The here and now is not a space or a time as such: it is a topological becoming on the nexus of experiential space-time.

Napangardi paints the complexity of life's contrasts, inviting the Dreaming to take form at the interstices of shades of becomings. These shades of becoming come to expression in movement throughout the work. Inventing-with the Dreaming's incessant movement, she paints its abstract concreteness, experiencing its abstraction as real, inviting the virtual to coexist with the actual force of the work-emergent. The work's appetite is felt as the force of the virtual taking form through the movement of its dance.

Napangardi creates contrasts by making the interval felt. The contrasts that populate her work are forces of vibration. They are modes of transduction between the technique—the digging sticks—and the iteration—the dots. Neither exists independently: as Whitehead points out, creativity is a social effort (1929/1978, 223). The interval would not exist without the actual dots that force it into emergence. The force of the interval can be strikingly felt in Napangardi's

Karlangu (Digging Sticks) (2001). In this black and white vertical painting, 244 x 168 cm, the black background is felt more keenly than in much of Napangardi's work,[120] inciting the white to stand out in a continual interplay of background/foreground. In the inner realm of the painting, the black opens up in oblong forms that feel like digging sticks. They take the form of digging sticks. But it is not simply their shape that gives them the resonance of the digging sticks; it is the force conveyed through the blackness pushing forward through the white. The background takes the form of the painting's title, and yet it resonates more than it represents. The contrast here is not between black and white. It is felt through the interplay of forces that evoke vibratory patterns that in turn create the movement—the force taking form—of the work. This contrast creates a rhythm that dances the taking-form of the Dreaming. We feel the digging sticks before we see them.

Once More!

The will to power of the Dreaming is the capacity to affect and be affected. "The will to power manifests itself as the sensibility of force; the differential element of forces manifests itself as their differential sensibility" (Deleuze 1983, 62–63). What is felt through the Dreaming is the force of life, asking of life that it manifest itself again: "Was that life?" asks Nietzsche. "Well then! Once more!" (1961, 178). The coming to life through the Dreaming depends on the potential of the force of life itself. And yet, as manifested in Napangardi's paintings, life and Dreaming coexist on the extensive continuum as one and the same, infinitely interwoven in an intensive movement of foreground and background. Populated and populating, the Dreaming is an embodied contrast, a determinate fact that creates the potential for indeterminacy.[121] Indeterminacy is essential as an intensive expanse for forces at play.

The event of force taking form is a definite fact with a date. In the becoming-active of force, a fight to the death has taken place between active and reactive forces. This becoming-active can never be felt as such—it can only be known in retrospect through the creation of novelty. Causing a change in nature, the becoming-active of force is a transmutation of value. "The transmuted feeling . . . is a definite physical fact whereby the final subject prehends the nexus" (Whitehead 1929/1978, 253). The becoming-active of force in Napangardi's work is the activity of pulsation we feel through her work. There is a lot at stake in this work, which so masterfully plays the forces of containment against the

Figure 8.8
Dorothy Napangardi, *Karlangu*, 2001, Artists Rights Society, New York, NY.

forces of expression. The experience of participating in the force of her work taking form gives us a feeling for the Dreaming's own will to power. This feeling for the Dreaming is experienced through the evolution of the transduction from actual occasion to nexus to extensive continuum. We feel the movement not as a given but as an active force of self-determination. This is a political act. Constituting facts involves pulling the Dreaming into experiential space-time not as a completed story but as an effect of the story's reverberate force for the present. Napangardi does not simply paint her Dreamings, she evokes the whole nexus of what a Dreaming can do through the intensive magnitude of the active force of the Dreamings' will to power.

Feeling the nexus means feeling the abstract concretely. The abstract and the concrete overlap in an eternal transvaluation of return. As Deleuze writes: "Returning is everything but everything is affirmed in a single moment" (1983, 72). This time paradox is only a paradox if we take becoming to emerge from being. The Dreaming makes no such claim. As is expressed through Napangardi's work, Dreamings are not evocations of a particular space-time. Dreamings are rhythm, contrast, vibration. Dreaming narratives are singular expressions of networks of force taking form.

Napangardi creates events for creative advance. Her work gives power: "The will to power is essentially creative and giving: it does not aspire, it does not seek, it does not desire, above all, it does not desire power. It gives" (Deleuze 1983, 85). Napangardi's paintings are plastic, variable, mobile iterations of the will to power that is the Dreaming in its infinity of variations. Hers are not general iterations: they are specific events, dated evocations, infinite reiterations of how the Dreaming's will to power can extend beyond the continuum to the everyday, toward the conjunctive disjunction of the future-past. With her paintings, Napangardi creates new feelings for thought, new images for movement.

"An intensive experience is an aesthetic fact," writes Whitehead (1929/1978, 279). Napangardi moves-with the Dreamings, dreaming their movement. She dances the dance of her people, low to the ground, movement barely seen but intensely felt, its magnitude multiply sensed. Inviting the force of movement to take hold of the image, her work propels the Dreaming toward the multiplicity of its univocity. "Once more!" it sings. Here, where the many become one and are increased by one, Napangardi dances.

Interlude: Cornering a Beginning

The camera pans through a multitude of windows. It is raining. The rain lends an opacity to the surface of the windows as though coming from within. We perceive a space within a space within a space. We watch as a woman circles, sounding a movement that seems to precede her, the camera catching her from the front, from above, leaving her behind the windows, passing toward another room. Rain, a movement inside, above, dark, shades of blue-black. *Rosas danst Rosas*, the film that was shot thirteen years after the first performance of its danced choreography, is more than a film of a dance. It is a seeing-with of dance participating with the moving screen. It is the filming of sites landing, sites that are less place-formations than affective tonalities in the passage from movement to its taking form.

This first long scene that begins with the rain, with the camera moving through a space that seems to be an endless labyrinth of windows, is a scene heavy with the languor of a relation forming between bodies, ground, and partitioned space. The presence of the camera is felt as though it were another body forcefully moving us to watch, constraining us to see not only a location or a dance but the tensile rhythm of groundedness itself. The camera works with this ground, pulling the dance into its weighted lethargy, into a vibratile exhaustion that is not a mimesis of grounded bodies but emphasizes the ground's very resonance as a dancing medium.

The ground is a landing site for the camera in *Rosas danst Rosas*. It is not a land-ing site in the sense that landing implies a grounding. It is a landing site

Rosas danst Rosas (courtesy Rosas danst Rosas, dir.), © Thierry De Mey.

in the sense that ground makes the quality of the dance felt. That ground is a landing site for *Rosas danst Rosas* means that the ground is far more than the concrete surface that holds the building upright. It is also, and more importantly, that which makes the difference in the dance, and that which the camera fields in its practice of watching-feeling. What we feel when we watch *Rosas danst Rosas* is the heaviness of bodies dropping, the crispness of their movements folding back into and away from the finiteness of the ground's unrelenting surface.

The falling sequence shown here is what first captures this quality of ground. This image of falling repeats twice in quick succession. In this series of images

Rosas danst Rosas (courtesy Rosas danst Rosas, dir.), © Thierry De Mey.

of falling, the camera becomes the protagonist of the action. The camera directs us. It provides the rhythms of the movements unfolding. This is emphasized again in a memorable sequence that follows: the four women lying down on their stomachs rise and fall, their upper torsos leading the movement. The camera works with the tensile activity of the dancers' minimal gestures, moving now to one side as though filming four bodies in one, moving again as one body rolls, the breath in contra-rhythm with the bodies folding. As quickly as they fell, now the bodies pause, holding their form as the camera waits with them, suspending our attention in tandem with the suspended bodies. Our watching merges with the weight of the women's heads moving slowly in an almost-reaching of the ground's surface. The wait is almost unbearable, the camera heavy in its quietude. And then the dancers move again, their past suspension underscored by the camera's focus on their backs arching, their heads still heavy but held.

What comes next is magical: the image snaps into a quickness, a wispy lightness as the women's weight shifts onto the tips of their fingers. This is how the image unfolds: the infinitely heavy upper bodies are held by the women's arms through a close-up accentuating the weight on a woman's tensed wrist. We feel the weight of the waiting physically as we watch. When the dancers suddenly lift palm to fingernails, the affective tone lifts perceptibly. We feel an intake of breath, as much our own as theirs, as we watch the bodies morph into weightlessness. The camera is not there only for the recording; it feels-with the bodies' shifting tonalities.

These shifting affective tonalities are landing sites. They are what Arakawa and Gins call a "depositing of sited awareness" (2002, 7). The camera focuses these sites into an in-gathering that captures them as transitory thought-feelings. We feel the shift from dances in the making to haptic experiments in the viewing.

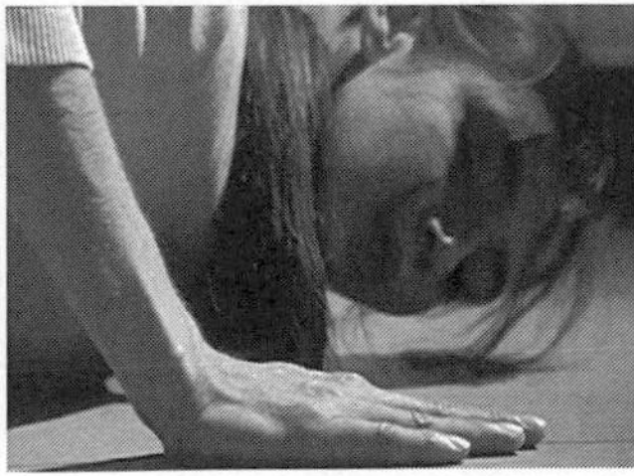

Rosas danst Rosas (courtesy Rosas danst Rosas, dir.), © Thierry De Mey.

These landing sites are not stable places, not geographical categories. They are not where the choreography begins and ends. They are what the focal points of the techniques of the dancing choreography open up.

A choreographed encounter is never wholly what it seems. You can't really choreograph movement. Movement slips through the grid, it micromoves into morphings not only unforeseeable but even unseeable, microperceptions more virtual than actual. I can train you to move-toward a sense of space, toward a quality of speed, of extension. I can offer you openings for the creations of experiential space-times. But I can't choreograph your landing sites.

This is because we are constantly in a process of fielding our surroundings, which also field us. How we think-feel a space-time of experience alters where and how we can experience it. This fielding is how Arakawa and Gins define a landing site. A landing site is an activity that is as expressive as it is organizational, a landing not so much into a place as a "dancing into attendance" (Arakawa and Gins 2002, 7).

There is never just one landing site. Landing sites fold into one another, creating infoldings of perception in the making. In the first sequence of *Rosas danst Rosas*, there is an infinity of potential landing sites interconnecting, perceived with the incipient movements of the dancers dancing. "Landing sites dissolve into each other, or abut, or overlap, or nest within one another" (Arakawa and Gins 2002, 8). But there is a tonality of landing that stands out for the viewer: it is the invitation to watch-feel the movement as the camera catches it in its formation. This activity of catching the movement directs our watching, giving it a consistency that moves the intensity of the dance into our perceptual field. We catch that intensity and feel its tonality in each of the movements of the camera. It's as though we were watching the camera move the dancers as it moves us.

Landing sites choose us, creating an associated milieu that worlds the body-environment. "The events are decision-like but far from . . . decisions" (Arakawa and Gins 2002, 9). Decision is used here in a Whiteheadian sense as the becoming-actual of a virtual potential. For Whitehead decision is what gives the event form, and by consequence, creates an individuation. The decision of the landing site is its focusing into experience. We land into the focus of an awareness that becomes us. "Actuality is the decision amid potentiality" (Whitehead 1929/1978, 42). The decision is the separating-off, the honing in that makes a particular tonality take form. A decision creates the potential for consciousness, not the other way around. A decision is like a "hook onto the environment to gain traction on it" (Arakawa and Gins 2002, 8).

Landing sites flock experience into a univocity. They are singular and multiple at once. In the scene with the heads slowly moving to the floor, the landing site is both a certain quality of hardness as well as a grounding of weightlessness. The siting of ground is also a landing into thin air—"even a mere intimation of a singling-out equals having landed on and sited" (Arakawa and Gins 2002, 10–11).

Looking with Thierry de Mey's looking with Anne Teresa de Keersmaeker's *Rosas dancing with Rosas* is a nesting within nests of potential landing sites. The camera directs with de Keersmaeker's choreographic directives, moving-with the bodies dancing. To choreograph becomes a double movement, a dancing-with the dancers dancing for the camera. The rhythmic intensity of the film depends on this double-movement that seeks not to order the movements as preliminary to the event, but to move-with their movement moving. The camera defines landing sites for perception, giving us hooks for our own process of landing.

Arakawa and Gins outline three categories of landing sites: some are "perceptual," some are "dimensionalizing," and some are "imaging." The perceptual landing sites work as a foregrounding of a conscious perception from the murkiness of experience as a whole. The dimensionalizing landing sites give the foreground a sense of measure, a traction. The imaging landing sites field widely, working-through a haze of microperceptions in the folding. To look-with movement moving is to experience this third kind of landing. Imaging landing sites are active at the level of the as-yet unprocessed, at the cusp of what James calls *pure experience*.

Like a looking-into thin air, imaging landing sites have a quality of daydreaming. They are perceptions at the level of presentational immediacy, where what we perceive is the experiential qualities of perception in the making. The film of *Rosas danst Rosas* experiments with perception dancing, capturing both the specificity of the measure of choreography landing and the haze of its microperceptual imaging. We become sited in the fielding of the quasi chaos of microperceptions, an experience that leaves us out of breath, our muscles tense with the twitching of kinaesthetic empathy. We move with the intensive magnitude of the micromovements moving.

"Nothing happens without kinaesthetic instigation, corporeal proddings" (Arakawa and Gins 2002, 11). Watching *Rosas danst Rosas* is a moving-with that animates our capacity for landing. This does not happen solely through the visuals. The experience of watching-with *Rosas danst Rosas* is profoundly audiovisual, the sound of the score and of the breathing altering the rhythms of our perception. We feel the rhythm as it lands us.

It's not that we're trying to land. "A looming non-focused-upon area . . . gets continually supplied, or roughed in, or approximated, by imaging landing sites" (Arakawa and Gins 2002, 12). The landing sites are there for the experiencing. They virtually co-constitute experience as it forms. As bodies recombine with them, the experience becomes "generalized." This means it becomes tainted with a quality, a feeling. Its affective tone resonates. It lands us. Suddenly we are no longer simply watching four bodies moving. We are feeling movement moving. We are moving-with our watching. Fielding the finding-form of microperceptibility, we move-with the movement even as we are moved by it.

This moving-with is what Arakawa and Gins call a *quasi-registering*. It gives rise to an affective tonality rather than a particular emotion. The affect predominates, not the culmination of its place-taking. Imaging landing sites are shape-shifters. They give affective resonance to the relation between experience and feeling. Morphing, they give force to the taking-form of the experience.

Landing sites corner beginnings. The ambient wholeness of the world at large is impossible to take in. It doesn't exist without a simplification, a prehension of an aspect of its potential to take form. Landing sites are how that pulling out of the nexus body-world fields an experience. "The more ambiguous the surroundings, the greater the number of imaging landing sites . . . needed for making determinations and giving things shape" (Arakawa and Gins 2002, 17). Imaging landing sites are virtual events in the making. They foreground the kinaesthetic flickering that propels the taking form of an event. In *Rosas danst Rosas*, the push-pull of the watching-dancing is felt as a tensile relation, an active becoming-with of the event forming. The landing sites of this event in formation give its tonality shape. Landing sites are "event markers in and of the event-fabric that is organism-person-environment" (Arakawa and Gins 2002, 22). Landing sites corner experience in the making.

Conclusion: Propositions for Thought in Motion

Thought in Motion

Amanda Baggs's video *In My Language* (2007) opens to a woman swaying, her back to the camera.[122] In a long shot, we watch her hands flittering, her body moving back and forth to the sound of three repeated tones. This dance of movement-sound prepares the way for the creation of a complex emergent environment that comes to life through the conjunction of objects, sound, and gesture.

For four minutes, we become transfixed by the movements of Baggs's hands, always in rhythm with a slightly modulated tonal singing. What begins as a voice becomes singing hands that roam through the space, creating the atmosphere in their passing. Flighty, these hands explore the movement of a string against metal—a rasping sound—shifting then from the string to the infinity of textures that populate the room: from string to surface to computer bag, the hands play the space. This playing transforms the space into an ambient musical instrument that moves in a dance of rhythmical becomings, Baggs's object-instruments participating in a becoming-environmental of sound, her voice always in tandem with the becoming-textural of space. Object-voice sonorities are created in tandem with the discovery of the environment's layers of experiential potential. As an accompaniment to Baggs's slow dance of feeling, we experience the space-time of the becoming-environment's dense affective tone. The shots are long and languid, their slowness rich with the eventfulness of sensation-in-the-making.

There is a shift in tone. The camera once again filming from behind her, we observe a quieter sound: paper flittering against the framed vista of the yard outside. The almost-sound of the paper moving is felt as a change in atmosphere. Then, sped up through the flittering gesture of her wrist, Baggs's voice modulates, hitting a demi-tone. We are moving again to the rhythm of the earlier section as we watch the spiral of the paper shape-shift into Baggs's twirling motion around the knobs of a dresser. From object-sound-creation (the flittering paper) to gesture-object-movement (twirling around the knob), her tonal voice-sound resonant throughout, this section of Baggs's video makes experiential musicality felt as a sound-moving-with and a moving-with-sound. This creates an amodal relay that distributes sound throughout the sensing body in movement as both the effect of movement and the instigator of experiential space-time. We experience this sound-movement tonally, affectively, through a rhythmic reinvention of the environment's sensory dimensions.

Baggs approaches not objects as such but their relational potential. No object is taken simply for what it seems to be, nor does it seem separate from her own becoming-body: each object seems to modulate the resonance of her voice, expressing its own becoming-movement in tandem with the environment moving.

The second part of *In My Language*, entitled "My Translation," is not a simple recasting of Baggs's world through language. "My Translation" is a transduction of the first part: it brings the plane of feeling onto the plane of articulation, calling forth the more-than of language's expressibility.

Throughout "My Translation," as Baggs attempts to articulate her complex multisensory environment through words, she continues to create relational encounters that render the linguistic space more intricate than words can connote. She speaks, but she also rocks, smells, touches, tastes, observes, feeling-with the environment. The experience of watching her articulating space-times of experience suggests that there is something about the eventness of Baggs's responsive environment that we'll never know, because to know it is to feel it. Communication through words will always fall short. Yet there is no question that articulation through language *is* capable of conveying a certain complexity, bridging the worlds of sensory eventness with the affective tonality of language in the making such that a dialogue between these co-arising worlds can begin. In "My Translation," Baggs begins to show us how to articulate felt thought.

Baggs's finger plays in the stream of running water. She speaks—her speech delivered by a voice synthesizer: "In this part of the video, the water doesn't symbolize anything. I am just interacting with the water as the water interacts with me." Language does not replace the sensual exploration of the relational environment: it moves with it, becoming one more technique for composition. For Baggs, communication through words remains inadequate to the singular experiences of sensation the world calls forth. Words are an extra component of the experience of articulation, not its final form. Words, Baggs suggests, cannot fully express experience's complexity. Her "translation" must therefore evoke more than the manifestation of words. It must transduce the event of language's becoming-with sensation. Language must be called forth as a layering-with of the affective tonality of expression.

Baggs creates relational nexuses that expose the world at the incipience of its sensory becoming. This sensory becoming is a form of thought. Articulation of that thought implies restricting the complexity of thoughts' prearticulation to a content-based structure of expression. Baggs resists this simplification, opting not *against* words but *for* relational complexity. Baggs explains:

> Far from being purposeless, the way that I move is an ongoing response to what is around me. Ironically, the way that I move when responding to everything around me is described as "being in a world of my own," whereas if I interact with a much more limited set of responses and only react to a much more limited part of my surroundings people claim that I am "opening up to true interaction with the world."

In My Language elaborates the sensory experience of thought's immanent prearticulation. It feels the world, thinking with it, rather than simply speaking *of* it. "But my language is not about designing words or even visual symbols for people to interpret. It is about being in a constant conversation with every aspect of my environment, reacting physically to all parts of my surroundings."

Baggs articulates felt thought. To articulate thinking-feeling is to activate the conceptual at work in the prearticulation of the experiential. To bring concepts to life rather than simply the contours of things is the first step in expressing the force of a relational environment. Bringing potential relations into actual experience, as Baggs notes, is "a way of thinking in its own right." Thought is more than a form-taking of words. It is an incipience that proposes articulation through sensation. Thought is a proposition for feeling-in-motion. It is experience's complex instigator, a force that operates at the relational cusp of becoming-events.

Amanda writes: "A lot of the way I naturally communicate is just through direct response to what is around me in a very physical sort of way. It's dealing with patterns and colors rather than with symbolic words." Prearticulation is a proposition for thought in motion.

Prearticulation

Thought prehends prearticulations from the complex nexus that is the world in motion. Prearticulation is the preacceleration of language: it is where language's affective tonality comes to expression. The world in motion is made up of planes of experience. The passage from the plane of sensation to the plane of articulation, a movement toward the actual from the virtual stratum, depends on thought's capacity to extract from the virtual quasi chaos of experience's potential unfolding. This extraction is a kind of editing of the nexus.

Bridging a vocabulary of movement with one of language requires concepts for thinking affective resonance within linguistic enunciation. Here, Andrei Tarkovsky's concept of editing might be useful. For Tarkovsky, editing is immanent to the flow of audio-images that make up the film as captured on camera. Editing is not something you impose onto the work: it is a prehension of the rhythms already virtually present in the work. Editing foregrounds the backgrounded rhythm of the work. In Baggs's video, editing functions not as the after-effect of language's imposed structure on her musical environment. Editing from within is the way language speaks through her tonal dance, the way its prearticulations can already be felt in the intervals out of which thought is provoked.

Language and thought are often situated at two extremes of a process of enunciation. For Baggs, the sensory experience of worlding does not imply a lack of language: enunciation is simply one aspect of language's tangible expressivity. Other forms of languages-in-the-making exist. These can be felt in the emergence of concepts for thought in motion articulated throughout *In My Language*. For Baggs, concepts are connected to feeling—the sensing of a texture is as important as the reading of words. These languages are not "less than" spoken words—they are the more-than of language's expressibility. Spoken words are the selected extraction from the nexus of experience that converge into appearance.

The plane of composition through which articulation eventually emerges is populated by the thought of the work, its inner rhythm. Deleuze and Guattari call this inner rhythm a “block of sensation.” “We paint, sculpt, compose, and write with sensations” (1994, 166). Blocks of sensation are forces that compose thought’s durational attitude. To edit from within is to compose with the more-than of language’s *actual* articulation. It is to work with language’s prearticulated virtual force, directing enunciation such that its virtual effects are felt within actual expression.

Editing from within seeks to create space-time, not simply reproduce it. “Rhythm is determined not by the length of the edited pieces, but by the pressure of the time that runs through them” (Tarkovsky 1987, 117). Editing from within is rhythmic editing that foregrounds the time-pressure inherent in experience. Time-pressure is a block of sensation. It is the force of a transformation that brings prearticulation’s virtual potential to life.

Diagrams

Thought in motion intensifies patterns of force, some edited in as concepts in the making, some left by the wayside for future thinkings. Francis Bacon refers to patterns of force as diagrams. Diagrams cannot be defined as such; they are felt only in their effects. They virtually resonate, recomposing sensation, collecting the intensity of rhythm and propelling it toward a becoming-work of the work. Bacon speaks of diagrams as “orders of sensation,” “levels of feeling,” each of them conceived as different orders of a singular block of sensation.

The diagram of *In My Language* is felt as the intensity of relation activated through the conjunctive series object-sound-gesture. This series territorializes the musical environment Baggs co-constitutes. Think the diagram as territory beyond representation. Representation solidifies the imaginary of preexistent worlds and asks thought to fit within their borders. Diagrams resist borders, activating tendencies of becoming-form and incipient conjunction. Think the diagram as a landing site you cannot quite define, a site that fields you more than you see it, a focal point through which the work organizes itself in a refrain of infinite unfolding. Diagrams create intensive networks that make thought resonate.

Diagrams are prearticulations of thought in motion. They foreground the work’s elastic points, its tendencies. Like biograms, which express the virtual node through which a body becomes, they are nodal points around which the future of thought’s exfoliation circulates. They make the elasticity of the almost felt, exfoliating the work’s potential across its shifting surface. Diagrams move thought, inviting the conceptual escape of "the action of invisible forces on the body" (Deleuze 2003, 36). Diagrams rhythmically call forth the relation thought-expression.

Diagrams give value to thought in the making. Valuation orients thought, proposing it as a concept for future thinking. It is integral to the process of an actual occasion taking form, but is felt as such only in the event's final satisfaction. With this satisfaction comes an inclination toward determinate expression. The process of valuation self-selects tendencially, leading the event toward certain areas of potential on the thought-world nexus. Each valuation adds a singular resonance to the nexus and becomes a potential for other actual occasions to take form, inflecting novelty into the world.

Nietzsche implores, "Value! Don't evaluate!" He proposes we conceive of value as a differential vector in the process of creation. Valuing is a form of prearticulation tantamount to the incipient process of movement's preacceleration taking form. It underscores the force of expression. In language, valuation is how words are culled from the nexus, their enunciation always coupled with their force of expression. Foregrounding valuation within language emphasizes the amodal relays that make words felt. Words: valuations that move between complex relays from gesture to sound, from vision to touch. Valuing the incipient quality of expression is to feel language's impulse, to express the taking form of thought moving. Valuation is an immanent process that situates expression's final form in a relational attitude toward the world where language dances thought's becoming-form.

Amanda Baggs's orchestral expression of the series object-sound-gesture is strangely reminiscent of Lygia Clark's relational objects.[123] Clark's relational objects create worlds: this is how their value is felt. These objects—plastic bags filled with breath, nets with stones in them—are of little artistic value in and of themselves. The value of Clark's relational objects is not expressed in their capacity to stand alone as objects. It is felt in the emergent qualities their coupling with bodies in relation brings forth. Their value lies in how the forces of potential express themselves in their relational movement toward the world. As with the "how" of the gesture-object-sound composition of Baggs's emergent musical environment, Clark's relational objects produce events in the making that are defined by the constraints of their pairings. These constraints are the limits borne out of the environment that incite the ways in which complex series can conjunctively take form.

For Baggs, enabling constraints constitute finding sound machines that resonate within the space, creating with these sounds in tandem with the rhythm of her movements and the tonal symphony of her voice, and finding modes of expression from the limited environment in which she works that evoke the complexities inherent in the merging of the planes of composition and articulation. Another enabling constraint might be how to create conditions for video capture that motivate the experiential creation of space-times of experience. For Clark, an enabling constraint would be how an object or a series of objects can make felt a conjunctive body relation that functions in the realm of therapeutic becoming. In both cases, objects become relational in conjunction with the ways in which the environment proposes its own constitutive limits. The immanent value of these objects is intrinsically connected to the relations they create within these conditions. It is *how* these relations take form that is key—and this is where the artistic process makes itself felt. Without a set of enabling constraints to make the work take form, Clark's objects would melt into an already overcoded environment. Their value is how the process of invention articulates the series they co-constitute through relational movement.

Value is never an evaluation. For Nietzsche, "evaluations . . . are not values but ways of being, modes of existence of those who judge and evaluate, serving as principles for the values on the basis of which they judge" (Deleuze 1983, 1). To value is to make relational potential the subject of enquiry. Value is how a conjunctive series moves the relation.

Feeling

Amanda Baggs feels the world. Watch her reading a book: she touches it, puts her face into it, listens to the pages rustling, smells it, looks at it. Becoming-bodies feel-with the world. Feeling-with is not without thought. It is a force for thought. Don't mistake feeling with emotion. Emotion is the rendering of an affect, feeling is its force. Affective tone is an environmental resonance of a feeling-in-action, a vibratile force that makes a resonant milieu felt. By feeling the book, Baggs brings the book into relation with a force of prearticulation that exceeds the book-as-object. The book becomes conjunctive, valued within a complex responsive environment. Culling the bookness from the book, Baggs makes the field of its musicality felt, its texture, its force of becoming not only as an object to be read but as a relation to be lived.

Feeling is a pulsion to think, a sensitivity that situates thought in the world: through feeling, thought's affective tonality is foregrounded. Feeling is affect bleeding into thought, activating complexities on the verge of expression. At the threshold of thought as creation, feeling provokes an aperture for that which has not yet been thought. Thought is a lure for feeling that prearticulates the virtual inflections of its incipient expression.

For Whitehead, feeling is the pulsion that transduces thoughts into becoming-concepts. On the plane of feeling, there are both determinations and appetitions. When a thought takes form, it moves from indetermination toward terminal determination. A feeling's determination is the form it takes as a concept. In spoken language, a concept is always more-than: it holds in reserve the virtual potential of thought-taking-form that words by themselves cannot quite articulate. This indetermination is the concept's appetition: its inherent potential for future invention.

Baggs invites us to participate in the complex interplay of the transversal passage between thought, concept, and articulation. Through feeling, thought begins to take form as a conceptual force. We experience textures giving way to qualities of form. We hear movement becoming sound. A tension is felt between the determination of language signifying and prearticulation's appetition. The milieu of appetition in Baggs's responsive environment is the relay created through the valuation of musical resonance that activates the conjunctive series object-sound-gesture and the prearticulation of an incipient worlding.

In "My Translation," Baggs is clear that words cannot fully convey the affective tonality of the environment that co-constitutes her, leaving us with a sense of hunger for what cannot be expressed. Yet what she does not explicitly say is that this very hunger is also part of how language expresses itself, an appetition that makes thought felt not as an add-on but in its incipient relation to the un-iterability of prearticulation. This valuing of emergence complexifies language as the post-iteration of a prefeeling. *In My Language* makes felt how language moves between planes, exposing the prearticulation of thought as well as the affectivity of expression. Feeling-with becomes a propensity both within and beyond the form-taking of words, a reaching-toward that propels novelty into the world. This novelty is not expressed solely in words, but neither are words precluded from it. The novelty is rhythm, its force of becoming felt as conjunctive in future series that might use words as relational objects.

It is not only the subject of Baggs's video that is inventive but the process itself. Baggs's video would not be as powerful were it simply a description of how her process moves through a prearticulation that makes concepts felt. The force of her video is the appetition it produces in the viewer to feel again, to think-with and know more. With more than 630,000 hits,[124] *In My Language* has clearly struck a chord beyond the initial curiosity about autism. *In My Language* evokes a feeling for articulation that moves us, literally altering our place—the place of language—in the world. It foregrounds language not as a personal enunciation but as a collective event articulated through relational series. In Baggs's video, prearticulation becomes preacceleration: the reaching-toward of expression as conceptual unfolding. We are moved to think.

One work can have many dynamic forms, many concepts, many feelings or thoughts. There is no single point of identity for a work. Baggs is not the subject of *In My Language*: prearticulation is. The work's subject is its dynamic form, its valuation, its conceptual resonance, its diagram. Holding to the subject as creative motor stabilizes the forces of becoming. Getting beyond this subjectivizing stance is the politics of *In My Language*. Holding the video to a representation of Baggs would situate her as the subject of autism. This would set her apart in a world of her own. This is exactly what *In My Language* struggles against. *In My Language* creates its own subject, making felt a force for expression that moves a particular mode of thought-feeling to its evolution as a language-in-the-making. Its subject is the force of becoming it proposes, a force for rethinking as much as a force for the experience of sensation's relays toward prearticulation. Baggs's video forces the passage from experience to expression, making felt the intrinsic value in the complex transduction between planes of prearticulation, including that of the political.

In My Language is not about one language. It is about how a language must always be invented in tandem with the force of the unknowable, its appetition for novelty kept alive. This feeling for the new proposes a taking-form of language where language becomes less a syntax than a milieu for expression.

In My Language concresces—takes final form—at the end of the first section, and then again, differently, in the second part. The first concrescence is felt as a symphony of complex inframodal relations between objects, gesture, and sound. The experiential quality of this first section of the video culminates in a resonant vibration of a relational environment that suggests that language is composed of a prearticulated worlding of concepts in the making. The second part, "My Translation," has a different rhythm, punctuated this time with words. Here, thought is experienced as a node of expression, its concrescence not the words as such, but the relay that punctuates the gestures moving-through in tandem and yet not strictly in conjunction with the words as they emerge from the computer. Baggs creates along a series of planes, her work-world finding subjective form not in a gathering-together of these planes but in a complex conjunction of their vibrant nodes.

Concrescence brings finality to an event, pulling it into its subjective form. This is not the end of eventness, only the end of that particular iteration. *In My Language* is like a resonant chamber for thought, its movement felt through an infinite expressivity of appetition for complex relation. Its concrescence gives another facet to a process that will continue to develop as new relays are invented in the watching. Thought felt is feeling in motion, a divisible indivisibility on its way to final form. Thinking feeling creates an appetite for experimentation.

Will to Power

An appetite for experimentation must always be connected to concrescence. A completely open system gives nothing but more openness (closure). Feeling is power's "compulsion of composition" (Whitehead 1929/1978, 119). This compulsion to compose is an aesthetic drive, a will toward sensation, a will to power. The will to power is not about individual power. The will to power activates the potential of a force to move a body to its limit. Power is a lure for feeling. Before Nietzsche called it the Will to Power, he called it the "feeling of power" (1968).

The will to power in Amanda Baggs's video is the injunction to make the world felt through the force of prearticulation. *In My Language* seeks to articulate at the limit of expression. Its will to power demands that we create concepts out of the matter-form of our environments, that we activate the virtual force of our becoming-worlds and conceive of this activation as a becoming-language, that we feel the affective quality of expression's incipient appetition. Amanda Baggs asks of the process of worlding that it include language's prearticulation, that it foreground the activity of creating concepts, that it will these concepts out of matter-form itself, that it mould the activity of process into a becoming-body of invention. She demands of expression that it value its own becoming, that it open thought and sensation beyond the actuality of what the world appears to be through words.

The will to power makes force felt. Felt force is a concept-in-waiting. There is no subject to the will to power, no outside criteria that forces. Force propulses a will toward the creation of a dynamic form, opening feeling to its activation, generating expression in its passing.

To feel power is to feel force, to be captivated by force and to capture that captivation. Will to power fields inner dynamism and moves it into actualization through a concrescence that activates new parameters for thought. It is only after the fact that the active necessity of the feeling's plane of composition—the superject[125]—takes form. This taking form is less the formation of a concrete identity than the culmination and residue of a process. To posit a subject for feeling means engaging with the creative from outside. This is an evaluative strategy, a reactive interruption of the process. Reactivity dulls force, stalling its potential for transformation.

Concepts

Concepts are one of the enabling constraints that propulse tendencies of becoming-form into aggregates of becoming-language. Concepts are aspects of a creative process already virtually active on the plane of immanence of thought. Moving beyond fixed meaning, concepts gather and articulate the intensity that transmutes the creative process from thought to expression.

A concept takes form at the threshold of expression. It cannot be defined according to categories of judgment. Judgment is a theory of coherence "concerned with a conformity of two components within one experience" (Whitehead 1929/1978, 191). The concept does not judge or evaluate the work: it *values* the work's rhythmic pressure. The concept is a gear-shift mechanism that acts on blocks of sensation, oscillating between thought and articulation. It pulsates between the actual and virtual realms. On the virtual stratum, concepts propel the becoming-event of thought: they *feel* its force. On the plane of composition, concepts articulate the dynamic form of prearticulation: they *express* the feeling of force. Concepts make multiple sense. "There is no event, no phenomenon, word, or thought which does not have multiple sense. . . . A thing has as many senses as there are forces capable of taking possession of it" (Deleuze 1993, 4).

Concepts appear as the force of expression in its incipiency. We feel a concept in the making when we are on the verge of expression but cannot yet quite articulate the passage from feeling to language. Conceptual work does not happen in already articulated language: it takes form in language's prearticulation.

Articulated concepts retain their force only when the indeterminacy of their virtual potential as feeling-thoughts is maintained and renewed.

In My Language exposes the process involved in the creation of concepts. These concepts evolve out of conjunctions between expressive nodes. The concept of sound, for instance, is felt as gesture in movement: sound stands in for the feltness of movement emergent through relational objects. We feel sound rhythmically. We find ourselves thinking sound. Sound becomes a concept for language in the making.

Not all thought transduces into a concept. Concepts are forces that take form at the junction between the emergence and expressibility of thought. Concepts move-with the force that is the virtual plurality of each incipient event. In conceptual articulation, forces work imperceptibly, and yet their virtual prearticulation can be felt. Concepts emerge in tandem with the forces' struggle for valuation within the work. The concept is an elastic point in the passage from the virtual—thought—to the actual—articulation. Concepts inflect thought toward expression. Concepts are the points of inflection that move thought toward language.

Concepts act as differentials for prearticulation. The differential produced by a concept cuts into the plane of experience, foregrounding its enunciatory potential. As a vector of transformation, the differential forces thought into the nowness of its actualization. The production of the now is the necessity—what Nietzsche calls the destiny—of language in the making. This necessity is what brings thought—via the concept—into appearance.

Terminus

Taking form always begins with the terminus. The terminus is not an end point but the energy of a beginning. The terminus kick-starts the process of articulation. There is no causal finitude here: we never know what becomes of a beginning. The directionality we have "in mind" is a relation of tension, a reaching-toward that makes us think, always more than a goal. The terminus is a force of thought toward articulation.

We often assume language's termini are words. Words are not language's termini; they are only one of the events along the way. The terminus of language is the relational folding-through of prearticulation. Language emerges not through an already-constituted thought: it merges with thought's tendency toward relation. How thought becomes relational is how language begins to take form. With prearticulation comes a feeling-with that proposes the potential of a taking form. This event in the making articulates itself in an infinity of ways, sensingly, linguistically, affectively. The terminus of language is the propensity for expression that forces an immanent conjunction into appearance. The concept proposes an actual occasion that affects experience-in-the-making by foregrounding nodes of relation that are themselves relays between different qualities of potential expressivity. Language folds in on termini, its impetus for expression always allied to the force of its prearticulation.

"Whatever terminates that chain was, because it now proves itself to be, what the concept 'had in mind'" (James 1912, 58). The terminus is not what you think you knew, not the idea you thought you had, not the way you expected to express yourself—it is a movement of thought pulled forth from the relations of tension that make up the passage from prearticulation to the concept to enunciation. Expressibility is the terminus of a thought in motion, its incipient directionality: the terminus is rarely where you thought it would be. The terminus is a relational nexus that forces thought to take form. Lodged neither in the human nor in the object, thought propels creativity as the activity of the in-between that makes relation felt, activating the "how" of the event, inciting inquiry, curiosity, play.

The terminus moves the relation bringing prearticulation to the fore. Begin with the interval and admit it into experience. Rethink what counts as art, as practice, as thought, as writing, as politics. The relation is as real as anything else—it is the associated milieu through which all else comes into contact. Relation is the incipient activating force through which the work-world nexus emerges.

For Amanda Baggs, relations are immanent. They bring forth responsive environments, activating movements of thought. Degrees of intimacy modulate the process. In Baggs's video, there is a tendencial shift between relations of sound and relations of movement. We see this in the passage from the sound-making platforms in the early sequences (such as the computer bag) to the later movement-feeling platforms (such as the knob). These platforms bring to the fore different relays for relation, emphasizing rhythm as the force that underlies the movement of sound. This thinking-in-motion is a technique. *In My Language* is, finally, a platform for experimenting with techniques of relation that move toward various forms of prearticulation and concept formation.

Techniques of relation, movements of thought, are thinkings-with as much as thinkings-about, populating the work in degrees of intimacy, moving the work's potential articulations toward future formations.

Propositions

Amanda Baggs's *In My Language* is a proposition for conceptual thought. Propositions, in Whitehead, are not rules imposed on a concept from without: they are how feeling becomes conceptual. "If by the decision of the concrescence, the proposition has been admitted into feeling, then the proposition constitutes *what* the feeling has felt" (Whitehead 1929/1978, 186). Propositions constitute a "source for the origination of feeling which is not tied down to mere datum" (Whitehead 1929/1978, 186). They are the prearticulated force of the feeling making its appearance.

For Whitehead, each occasion of experience is characterized by a flash of novelty. This flash is an appetition, a desire at work. Appetitions propel propositions. Propositions are theories in the making. "The primary function of theories is a lure for feeling, thereby providing immediacy of enjoyment and purpose" (Whitehead 1929/1978, 184).

A proposition is never a judgment. Nor is it necessarily true. It is a terminus-in-action. Focusing appetition on the transitional relation that makes thought felt, propositions cut through the event, shifting the ground. For Lygia Clark, a proposition is the capacity for any object to take relational form. "Nothing, in Clark's propositions, was ever reducible to a concrete body, empirical or organic" (Rolnik 2005, 9). Propositions move the concept into action, this movement always emergent, its creative potential never preestablished. "What I know now is that the body is more than the body" (Clark, qtd. in Rolnik 2005, 9).

Propositions are a lure for feeling. By propulsing the event toward what it can do, they effect the concrescence of an actual occasion. Assembling effects of relation across the nexus of actual occasions, propositions act as the pulling together of the stakes of language in-formation. To become articulate, in these terms, involves expressing what the feeling has felt.

Propositions never attend solely to the datum. *In My Language* is not "about" autism. It works with the emergence of a language experienced from the enabling constraints of autism, yet does much more than explicate autism's relation to language. *In My Language* proposes the creation of relational objects for thinking-in-action. It does this not only to make clear how Baggs thinks but to propose this form of expression for a rethinking of a theory of language.

Propositions cannot be relegated to a preformed body or a stand-alone object. Baggs's propositions do not tell us what an object can do. Nor do they tell us how to speak. Rather, they create enabling constraints for the opening of a relational process. Placing her objects in specific iterations of the word-world nexus—iterations called forth by the relations themselves—Baggs participates in a becoming-language that makes the passage from thought to articulation felt such that we can participate in its unfolding.

Without transduction, propositions have no force. Transduction is the unity of an event across its different phases, a processual individuation across strata that creates affinities between levels of experience. Propositions provoke transductions that alter what a particular relation can do in a given instance. Not every relational object is evocative in every instance. Each material shape-shifts into different affinities of purpose. *Dynamic osmosis*, Clark would say (Rolnik 2005).

For Baggs as for Clark, knowing the world means paying attention to its reverberations, feeling its silent forces, mixing with them, and from this fusion, reinventing the world and yourself, becoming other. From thought to concept to articulation, relational objects transduce prearticulation into the force of language's potential to speak the world.

"Being composed of a plurality of irreducible forces, the body is a multiple phenomenon" (Deleuze 1993, 40). Active and reactive forces fight for dominion in the becoming-body. The imposition onto language of a preconstituted notion of articulation threatens to make language passive. To denude language of its affective tonality is to suggest that language only makes sense through the syntax of words.

Thought is a force to contend with. Thought moves (with) language, affectively altering what language can do. Concepts foreground the capacity to be affected through language. To be affected is to go to the limit of what a thought can do. "The philosopher creates concepts that are neither eternal nor historical but untimely and not of the present . . . untimely at every epoch" (Deleuze 1993, 107). Concepts are activities of relation that take time even as they make time, animated in the process of invention that is the activity of living.

Thinking involves the microperceptions that are the virtual content of the not-yet out of which potential worlds are composed. Thinking exposes the overlappings of the actual and the virtual, their complex inadequation. Conceptual creation works at this in-between of immanence and actuality where multiplicities converge into affirmations. Creativity folds out of thought even as it proposes thought to itself. Thought is an untimely proposition.

In My Language feels untimely. It takes us out of the time of language as enunciation to the time-pressure of conceptual prearticulation. We feel the force of expression taking form even as we remain unsure of what is actually being said. Amanda Baggs asks for our participation in this becoming-environment of language taking form. As we participate in this process, we feel language as a collaborative event. We experience prearticulation and are gathered in the relationscape this tending-toward language provokes.

Relationscapes are propositions for future thinking. Amanda Baggs activates one such proposition through the notion of a constant conversation: "It is about being in a constant conversation with every aspect of my environment." A constant conversation is an untimely affair: it jumps from plane to plane, virtually participating on the plane of thought and prearticulation, becoming-actual through concept formation, finally emergent on the plane of composition of language's articulation. This infinite conversation[126] is enveloped by the terminus not of signification but of responsivity: "Far from being purposeless, the way that I move is an ongoing response to what is around me." This responsivity creates an active environment, proposing an in-gathering of forces for expression that elicit not standard responses but the novelty of conceptual innovation. "If I [don't] interact with a much more limited set of responses . . . they judge my existence, awareness, and personhood." *In My Language* proposes "a way of thinking in its own right" that is affectively resonant, conceptually complex and inventive in its articulations. It calls forth a relationscape that pairs preacceleration with prearticulation, making felt the force of movement taking form.

Notes

1. Modified translation.

2. The Sense Lab (www.senselab.ca) was conceived in 2004 and is directed by Erin Manning. It is a research-creation environment for thought in motion. The Sense Lab is now housed at the Société des Arts Technologiques (SAT) as part of the SAT-Université de Montréal research-creation project entitled Art&D.

3. The Workshop in Radical Empiricism was conceived in 2004 and is directed by Brian Massumi. In 2005, it joined the Sense Lab. All Sense Lab activities are coorganized by Erin Manning and Brian Massumi with the assistance of Sense Lab members.

4. Technologies of Lived Abstraction has also become the title of Erin Manning and Brian Massumi's coedited book series published by the MIT Press.

5. In this prelude, I have foregrounded the collaborative spirit behind Technologies of Lived Abstraction by embedding in it portions of the calls for participation, which were collectively written. For the complete texts, see the "events" rubric at www.senselab.ca.

6. For a sustained discussion of the concept of a "sensing body in movement," see Manning 2007.

7. Whitehead and committed Whiteheadians would probably find it strange to posit pastness as durational, particularly since there is no sense of duration within Whitehead's concept of extension. I think duration does figure in Whitehead's concept of extension, but only through the emergent phase when pastness shifts toward presentness. Here, what is felt is the moving-through of a microevent striving toward its completion in a time-slip of future-pastness. Pastness is pure non-sensuous extension in Whitehead, durational only when quasi-actualized through prehension. For a more sustained discussion of the

relationship between perished actual occasions and the extended continuum, see the conclusion to this book.

8. It is important to note that the prehension chair need not lead simply to an occasion of sitability. The prehension chair can just as well lead from sitability to the dread of classrooms, culminating in an actual occasion whose form is felt as imprisonment or containment.

9. "Strange Horizon" is a chapter in Massumi 2002.

10. Relational movement is the name I've given to a form of movement I've been exploring that is very influenced by Argentine tango, but also indebted to Aikido and to various methods of improvisation within contemporary dance. Relational movement grew out of Argentine tango's walking constraint. In social Argentine tango, which is fully improvised, while you never know what kind of movement will emerge, you do know that the movement will never diverge from the basic tenet of the walk: keeping one foot on the ground at all times. In the relational movement I practice, which involves face-to-face walking, I use the structure of the walk as an enabling constraint. This constraint allows the movement to remain predictably connected to a face-to-face encounter. This makes clearly felt how relation gives movement its force. Other forms of relational movement would have to design their own enabling constraints to foreground relation. A movement fully unstructured would likely not be capable of creating a sustained felt relation.

11. Proprioception is defined as the sensibility proper to the muscles and ligaments. For a more detailed engagement with proprioception, see Massumi 2002.

12. For a detailed exploration of hylomorphism, see the first chapter of Simondon 1995.

13. A phylum is defined as the division of primary rank in the classification of the animal and plant kingdoms. It is through the intermediary of assemblages that the phylum selects, qualifies, and even invents. The assemblages cut the phylum up into distinct, differentiated lineages. Simultaneously, the machinic phylum cuts across them all, taking leave of one to pick up again in another, or making them coexist. In *A Thousand Plateaus*, Deleuze and Guattari define the machinic phylum as a technological lineage. The phylum classifies machines not simply through their technicity but through their recombinations of *matter and movement*. Their definition: "Wherever we find a constellation of singularities prolongable by certain operations, which converge, and make the operations converge, upon one or several assignable traits of expression. . . . the machinic phylum is a materiality, natural or artificial, and both simultaneously; it is matter in movement, in flux, in variation, matter as a conveyor of singularities and traits of expression. . . . At the limit, there is a single phylogenetic lineage, a single machinic phylum, ideally continuous: the flow of matter-movement, the flow of matter in continuous variation, conveying singularities and traits of expression. This operative and expressive flow is as much artificial as natural: it is like the unity of human beings and Nature" (Deleuze and Guattari

1987, 409). A machinic phylum creates technical assemblages; the assemblages invent the various phyla. "A technological lineage changes significantly according to whether one draws it upon the phylum or inscribes it in the assemblages; but the two are inseparable" (Deleuze and Guattari 1987, 407).

14. For a more detailed exploration of how touch necessitates repetition, see Manning 2002.

15. The inframodal suggests that the senses are constantly in a mode of recombination, one single sense never fully responsible for a perception. The inframodal underscores the play between different levels of dominance in sense perception.

16. Deleuze and Guattari define lines of flight as potentials that resist capture. For a more detailed explanation, see Deleuze and Guattari 1987.

17. In Whiteheadian terms, the interval would be similar to an "eternal object."

18. From a 2003 interview with William Forsythe by Ozaki Tetsuya. http://www.realtokyo.co.jp/english/column/ozakiinterview.htm, 1.

19. The political is never more or less than that the body-worlds we create and that create us. The *potential* of the political must remain in the interval—preaccelerated and poised.

20. From a 2003 interview with William Forsythe by Ozaki Tetsuya. http://www.realtokyo.co.jp/english/column/ozakiinterview.htm, 2.

21. Jacques Derrida's concept of "originary technicity" (like the concept of the "posthuman") invites us to think the body as always-already prosthetic. For a detailed exploration of the concept of originary technicity, see Bennington 2000.

22. See chapter 4 for a more detailed exploration of technogenesis.

23. For more on radical empiricism, see James 1912.

24. In dance, a figure often refers to a series of steps that can be learned and repeated. Figure here conveys something quite different, associated with how shape transiently emerges from movement moving. The shape is what moves through the movement, not what the movement "arrives" at.

25. For Whitehead, the process of an actual occasion moves from prehension to subjective form to perishing, indicating that the microeventness of an occasion must always be replaced by a new occasion. The subjective form refers to the instance in an occasion where the occasion's taking-form has reached its full potential.

26. Pure experience is always associated with the ontogenetics of relation in James. He writes: "The relation itself is a part of pure experience; one if its 'terms' becomes the subject or bearer of the knowledge, the knower, the other becomes the object known" (James 1912, 4).

27. Nora Heilmann evokes Steve Paxton's small dance in one of her recent dance experiments. With Paxton's guidance, she defines the small dance as "the little movements around the skeleton that help you balance." Here, in Heilmann's words, is an exercise of Paxton's to find and work with the small dance: "Find your balance. Find your concentration. Easy breathing. Watch the small dance, the little movements around the skeleton that help you balance. Relax your coccyx. Relax your sacrum. Long inhalations. Long exhalations. Diaphragm moving down with inhalation, up with exhalation. Feel your weight on the floor. Agreeing with gravity. Organs relaxing down into the bowl of the pelvis. Bowl of the pelvis receiving the organs. Easy sternum. Easy means: observe the small dance. Feel the dome of your skull suspending upwards. Feel the length of your spine extending through your head towards the ceiling. Relax your shoulders. Feel the direction of your arms falling away from the spine. Without changing that direction, find the smallest stretch in that direction. Release. Can it be smaller? Where does it start? Where could it start? What is the smallest thing we can perceive? What is the smallest stretch? The smallest fall? The edge of movement? Relax your shoulders. Relax your arms. In the direction that your arms are hanging, without changing that direction, find the smallest stretch. Release. Feel your finger prints, beyond the fingers, pointing downwards. Feel the small dance. Adjust your mind to the continuous changes. Imagine but don't do it: imagine you are taking a step with your right foot. Imagine but don't do it: imagine you are taking a step with your right foot. With your left foot. Right, left right left, right, left. Stand. Balance. Feel the small dance" (2006).

28. The drug administered by Sacks in 1967 was L-dopa. Dopamine was found to be very effective with those suffering with Parkinson's and did prove to have startling effects on those suffering from post-encephalitis lethargica.

29. Oliver Sacks writes: "Patients lack the will to enter upon or continue any course of activity, although they might move quite well if the stimulus of command or request to move came from another person—from the outside" (1990, 9). I don't think this shows a lack of will as Sacks suggests. Movement is not simply volition—in the sense of "I want to move, or I don't want to move." Movement as outfolding is a reaching toward not only of a body, but of the very recombination of bodies and space-time. Worlding creates bodies as much as moving bodies create worlds. These are bodies always qualitatively different from the bodies of a split second before—bodies recombining, sensing toward a continual differentiation of what they know the world to be. These recombinations are not possible if movement cannot be activated. Hence an obsessive infolding that leads only to its own compulsive repetition.

30. "Inertia is a tendency of an object to resist change in its state of motion. More massive objects have more inertia; that is, they have more tendency to resist change. An elephant has a lot of inertia, for example. If it is at rest, it offers a large resistance to changes in its state of rest, and so it's difficult to move an elephant. On the other hand, a pencil has a small amount of inertia. It's easy to move a pencil from its state of rest" (www.learner.org/exhibits/parkphysics/glossary.html).

31. It is important to underline the role of habit in auto-activation. If we locate auto-activation within the register of "will," we suggest two things: (1) movement-toward happens in the actualization of a movement, not an incipiency, (2) movement-toward is a question of a conscious decision-making process. As stated in note 29, I believe neither to be the case. Auto-activation takes place in the pastness of movement moving (the register of habit) that takes movement by surprise. Our very capacity to move depends on the quality of incipiency out of which movements-toward form. Were we to think about every movement we made, we would likely be locked in nonmovement. Sack's patients lack no will. They lack the embodied relation between pastness and futurity that brings together the experience of movement with movement moving.

32. In Sacks's recent book, *Musicophilia: Tales of Music and the Brain* (2007), he returns to the question of the auto-activation of his post-encephalitic patients of the 1960s and underlines the important role music often played in their awakenings. For these patients—and indeed for many others temporarily "frozen," including those with severe Parkinson's—music plays a large role not only in creating the capacity for relation in experiential space-time but also for altering the quality of movement. Sacks talks at length of the way in which the patients' movement flows in relation to music, and how their movements tend to becomes saccadic and tense with the withdrawal of the music. This suggests that music is a key non-pharmaceutical method for awakening patients from a catatonic state *and* giving them a fluidity of movement they otherwise lack.

33. In relation to symbolic reference, Whitehead writes: "We enjoy the symbol, but we also penetrate to the meaning. The symbols do not create their meaning: the meaning, in the form of actual effective beings reacting upon us, exists for us in its own right" (1927, 56). Symbolic reference is not a preconstituted reception of the world. It is how worlding transduces experience into perception.

34. Whitehead writes: "Presentational immediacy is our immediate perception of the contemporary external world, appearing as an element constitutive of our own experience. In this appearance the world discloses itself to be a community of actual things, which are actual in the same sense as we are" (1927, 20). Presentational immediacy is intrinsically relational, in the sense that it builds out of relations with the actual world, but also nonsocial, in the sense that these relations refer directly back to the perception as such. "These qualities are thus relational between the perceiving subject and the perceived things" (Whitehead 1927, 21). Presentational immediacy's relationality is intrinsically different from the relationality of causal efficacy, where relation is that which directly gives experience form. Symbolic reference is the completion of force with form that gives nuance to constituted experience, such that the nuances of qualitative perception are directly in-mixed with the "how" of the world worlding.

35. The stories of "de-freezing" occur after Sacks administers L-dopa and the patients begin to have the experience of reaching-toward. Their "return" to their still state becomes unbearable to them when L-dopa no longer operates effectively, which causes many of them to devise systems for unfreezing themselves.

36. This explains also why, when "awakened," the patients could not situate themselves in time. This is particularly flagrant with Rose, who continues to act like a young girl in her twenties despite the fact that she is much older (in her sixties) when Sacks administers L-dopa.

37. This should not be mistaken with instinct: "The doctrine of symbolism developed [here] . . . enables us to distinguish between pure instinctive action, reflex action, and symbolically conditioned action. Pure instinctive action is that functioning of an organism which is wholly analyzable in terms of those conditions laid upon its development by the settled facts of its external environment, conditions describable without any reference to its perceptive mode of presentational immediacy. This pure instinct is the response of an organism to pure causal efficacy" (Whitehead 1927, 78).

38. The quotation continues: "This means descriptions (what we think of as co-descriptions) of movement that can exist in both its own terms (as in physical) as well as in the symbolic abstractions that are necessary in order to use these techniques of gesture modeling, simulating, learning, following etc. with the computer." deLahunta, "Co-descriptions and Collaborative Composition" (opening presentation, NIME06/IRCAM workshop Choreographic Computations, Paris, France, June 4, 2006a).

39. deLahunta, "Co-descriptions." For an exploration of a decade of dance and technology, see also Scott deLahunta, "Dance (in the Presence and Absence of) Technology," in *En movement (inaugural issue)*, ed. B. Raubert and Q. Noguero, 16–17 (Barcelona: Theatre Institute Mercat de les Flors, October 2006b).

40. This is not to suggest that sincere thought has not been given to these issues. Many very interesting and innovative software composers are currently working with dancers and choreographers to explore the potential of creative continuums between software and innovative dance. In his recent dance/new-technology work, Scott de Lahunta calls this "choreographic compositions," suggesting that the choreography of the dance is entwined in the double process of composing software and creating movement.

The exploration of new technology with dance has a history that can be traced to the 1960s with choreographer Jeanne Beaman and computer scientist Paul Le Vasseur who created computer generated choreography using an IBM 7070. This platform randomly chose a sequence of events from a list of movements. John Lansdown, an architect, similarly explored the potential of using the computer as an autonomous composer, rather than to support or augment the existing creative process. Merce Cunningham's methods are also well-known: the 3-D human figure animation software LifeForms continues to be used today in innovative work by Trisha Brown and William Forsythe. According to de Lahunta, what is new about the recent current of dance and new technologies is how systems are being built in correspondence to a choreographic creative process with an emphasis on the "shared understanding that emerges through the collaborative process. This is what we think to be both technically and creatively innovative" (deLahunta, "Co-descriptions"). This chapter does not seek to deny this important research, but to ask how such a process can or does become technogenetic.

41. For more on the machinic, see Deleuze and Guattari 1987. See also Guattari 1995.

42. For more on Artaud's concept of the Body without Organs, see Deleuze and Guattari 1987.

43. For a reading of the posthuman, see Hayles 2000.

44. Richard Beardsworth is influenced by Jacques Derrida in his usage of originary technicity. It comes up in many of Beardsworth's texts. For an example of how he uses originary technicity in his work, see http://tekhnema.free.fr/3editorial.htm.

45. There is new work in technology and dance that has evolved beyond the use of the prosthetic, and as the field develops, we will no doubt see new and inventive ways of thinking the technogenetic body. One new direction includes biotechnological art (see Yann Marussich's *Bleu Provisoire* [2001, http://www.yannmarussich.ch/?m1=2&p=7], which uses biochemical reactions as the central node of the piece).

46. For an analysis of interactivity, see Massumi and Dove 1999.

47. There is of course no telling what technology will be able to do in the future. However the relationship between bodies and technology develops, this junction will likely be most creative when each aspect of the work is opened to its technogenetic limit. However interesting technology becomes, without a lively vocabulary for the moving body, the technology will remain a tool rather than a technique for discovery.

48. For more on the ways in which actual occasions are always contemporarily independent events, see Whitehead 1933.

49. On the half-second delay of perception, see Whitehead 1933. See also Massumi 2002.

50. For a stimulating reading of active recollection in Bergsonian thought, see Deleuze 1991b.

51. Whitehead defines organisms according to their perceptual capacities, making a difference between what he calls "lower grade" and "higher grade" organisms. An example of a lower grade organism engaged in perception would be the causal relation between flower and sun that causes the flower to turn to the sun. See Whitehead, *Adventures of Ideas.*

52. The idea of breathing space is evocatively brought forward by Michael Schumacher in Christopher Salter's 2007 piece entitled *Thresholds/Schwelle*. In this piece, Schumacher recomposes space-time through the tactility of breath.

53. See the chapter of the same name in Massumi 2002.

54. Stelarc's work is evocative in relation to technogenesis. For a stimulating reading of his work, see Massumi, "The Evolutionary Alchemy of Reason," chapter 4 in Massumi 2002.

55. I am evoking the Derridean usage of the supplement here as the more-than that is always integral to an open system. For a detailed exploration of the supplement, see Derrida 1978.

56. The amodal suggests that we sense across sense modes and that sense perception occurs in its emergent phase in a between that is as much body as world. The concept of "amodal completion" is developed by Albert Michotte. See Michotte 1991.

57. Whitehead calls forth this notion of non-sensuous perception in order to sidestep the tendency to think we make sense only through sense-data. Whitehead's work challenges the theory of sensory-reception whereby an impulse "out there" is processed by a mediating brain/body function that makes sense of a preexisting world.

58. In this case, Whitehead would say that the ground is "negatively" prehended.

59. *Who's Afraid of Red, Yellow and Blue* (2007) was shown in a very large, high-ceilinged gallery space at the Museum of Contemporary Art San Diego. The work comprises three volumes, each defined by a 16 x 22 ft floor of lacquered aluminum panels (red, yellow, and blue) with an identical ceiling (suspended by cables from the gallery rafters). There are no walls to the volumes, so the viewer can look through the entire structure, walk in the narrow corridors separating the three "rooms," or perceive it from wider afield. The non-cubes of color give a sense of an open enclosure where the middle space—where your perception usually occurs, is free of objects. The result: space-time itself becomes colored. Looking into the panels reveals reflections in the panels of complimentary colors. The complementary colors appear across the panels (if you look into the yellow, the reflection of the blue panel appears as purple). Complementary colors also appear in the reflection of the gallery's clear windows, which, seen through the lacquered panels, now appear to be purple, green, and orange. The reflective panels also cause an uncanny experience of mirroring, where we see ourselves reflected both standing up (looking directly at the panel at our feet) and upside down (looking at our reflection through the reflection of the hanging panel as reflected in the floor-level panel).

In a discussion afterward with Robert Irwin, he emphasized the importance of surprise in art. He said that since he cannot mock up the space before an exhibition, how the work emerges is always an event. For Irwin, a space doe not contain art, it conditions art's process. Art creates perceptual events, and these are what Irwin is most interested in. *Who's Afraid of Red, Yellow and Blue* (2007) becomes-with the environment it proposes, opening art to its own perceptual unfolding.

60. A stable perception of "just red" is impossible. What holds our perception of "redness" is its unstable relation to other colors, green in particular. For a more detailed exploration of color see Massumi, "Brightness Confound," in Massumi 2002.

61. Marey defines the imperceptible as that which the eye can't see but is actually there.

62. I can only assume that given Marey's explicit focus on measurability and positivism, this turn to the experiential and even the artistic (which he claimed was never a focus of his research) happened despite his best intentions.

63. My work on Valéry is indebted to a wonderful piece written by Brian Massumi, entitled *The Ideal Streak,* where he situates drawing in relation to new media. This piece was presented as a keynote address at Cornell University in 2006.

64. William James defines *pure experience* as "the instant field of the present [that] is always experienced in its 'pure' state, plain unqualified actuality, a simple that, as yet undifferentiated into thing and thought, and only virtually classifiable as objective fact or as some one's opinion about fact" (1912, 69).

65. Henri Bergson defines *duration*: "This indivisible continuity of change is precisely what constitutes true duration . . . Real duration is what we have always called time, but time perceived as indivisible" (1992, 149).

66. "[This is] confirmed with the zoetrope: at one point in both the trot and the gallop, all four of the horse's legs were off the ground: 'the body of the animal is, for an instant, suspended in the air'" (Marey, qtd. in Braun 1992, 30–31).

67. "When the eye ceases to see, the ear to hear, touch to feel, or indeed when our senses give deceptive appearances, these instruments are like new senses of astonishing precision" (Marey, qtd. in Braun 1992, 40)

68. Preacceleration foregrounds virtual movement.

69. The first machine for the experimentation with gases was built by Marey in 1899 and had twelve channels. The second one (1899–1900) had twenty-one channels, and the third (in 1901) had fifty-seven channels. The more channels, the more visible the trace of the object passing through the smoke.

70. In Deleuzian terms, these would actually be time-images since they make time felt, foregrounding movement's durational force. See Deleuze 1989.

71. Deleuze uses the word *agencement* to evoke the relational aspects of collective individuation. Agencement is translated as *assemblage* for lack of a better word. While assemblage does connote the co-constitutive aspects of agencement, it does not convey its force.

72. Abstract machines are singular, yet collective. They are immediately situated within the milieu that co-constitutes them. Deleuze and Guattari write: "Abstract machines operate within concrete assemblages: they are defined by the fourth aspect of assemblages, in other words, the cutting edges of decoding and deterritorialization. They draw these cutting edges. There they make the territorial assemblage open onto something else . . . . Abstract machines consist of *unformed matters and nonformal functions*. . . . Abstract,

singular and creative, here and now, real yet nonconcrete, actual yet non-effectuated—that is why abstract machines are dated and named. . . . Not that they refer to people or to effectuating moments; on the contrary, it is the names and dates that refer to the singularities of the machines, and to what they effectuate" (1987, 510–511).

73. Marta Braun writes that "by 1882, Marey had succeeded in making the camera into a scientific instrument that rivalled his graphing instruments in its power to clearly express change over time. . . . He captured ongoing phases of movement and spread them over the photographic plate in an undulating pattern of overlapping segments. . . . Marey's last investigations into movement were done with a cinema camera, an instrument he invented (seven years before the advent of commercial motion pictures) to overcome the limitations of his photographic method" (1992, xviii).

74. To catch the seagulls in flight, Marey would have preferred to adopt a photographic technique like that used by Muybridge in his "moving" stills of horses. His preference would have been to use three chronophotographic cameras synchronically with electromagnetic releases, one of them at 15 meters to catch the flight from above. But Marey only had one camera. Forced to create a technique with limited means, Marey positioned his camera at 14 meters (attached to tall conifers) and shot the flight from above (as he would with the walk later). The soil had been covered in black velvet. Then he shot a series obliquely and one from the side, always at 50 images per second (Mannoni 2004, 29). Still, he was disappointed not to have been able to create the synchronicity he admired in Muybridge's work: "Since the insufficiency of our installation did not permit us to simultaneously gather three kinds of chronophotographies, we must not expect a perfect concordance between the three images" (Marey, qtd. in Mannoni 2004, 29).

Marey's images are thrilling in their polyrhythmicality, much more so than had they perfectly emulated Muybridge's technique that foregrounds movement's poses. Duration is felt in Marey's chronophotographic images, not synchronic cadence. In her book on Marey, Braun is very critical of the popular tendency to associate Muybridge with Marey and to assume that their work is synonymous. She underlines the fact that Muybridge's use of multiple camera systems does not convey a sense of the space traversed or of time passing. "Each photograph was made by a different camera (in tandem with the moving subject) against the same background as the one before and after it, but from a different vantage point. As a result the subject and the camera seem to move in unison and thus effectively cancel out the sense of movement; the only aspects that change are the gestures of the subject, and any sense of movement must be constructed by the viewer from these gestures, frame by frame" (Braun 1992, 237).

All of Muybridge's photographic compositions were recompositions: the assembled images were rephotographed and printed. Moreover, as Braun notes, the relationship of the images, in some 40 percent of the plates, is not what Muybridge states it to be. His photo montages were even printed with a disclaimer that warned the viewer that the perfect uniformity of time, speed, and distance was not always obtained (Braun 1992, 238)! Where Marey was creating (animated) movement for perception, Muybridge was creating (cinematic) simulations of displacement.

75. Four days after Muybridge's images appeared in *La Nature*, Marey wrote the editor (his friend and fellow aeronaut Gaston Tissandier) to ask for Muybridge's contact information. He writes: "I am filled with admiration for Mr. Muybridge's instantaneous photographs you published. . . . Could you put me in touch with the author? I would like to ask him to assist in the solution of certain physiological problems, so difficult to resolve by other methods. I was dreaming of a kind of *photographic gun*, to seize the bird in a pose or, even better, in a series of poses marking the successive phases of the movement of its wings" (Marey, qtd. in Braun 1992, 47). Muybridge responded to Marey by sending him various images (of animals and humans taken with a varying number of cameras—from twelve to thirty).

76. McLaren was also a precursor in sound, working both with electronic sound and with drawing sound. His technique of drawing music is particularly interesting. Taking the 35mm film stock, he began by drawing "a lot of little lines on the sound-track area of the 35mm film. Maybe 50–60 lines for every musical note. The number of strokes to the inch controls the pitch of the note: the more, the higher the pitch; the fewer, the lower is the pitch. The size of the stroke controls the loudness: a big stroke will go 'boom' and a smaller stroke will give a quieter sound. . . . The tone quality, which is the most difficult element to control, is made by the shape of the strokes" (McLaren, qtd. in Richard 1982, 40). With sound as with images, McLaren's purpose was not to mimic sounds as they exist in the world, but to create "new sounds which cannot be obtained by any other means. It is the creation of 'symphonies of burps and rude noises'" (qtd. in Richard 1982, 41).

77. See Gil 2006. A version of the manuscript is published in Portuguese under the title *Movimento Total: O Corpo ea Danca* (Lisbon: Relógio d´Água, 2001).

78. This is not a Heideggerian thrownness. It is a becoming-with-movement that emphasizes how a body co-arises with its worlding.

79. Despite this emphasis on series in *Olympia*, it is uncanny how composed each of the shots is on its own. To create such successful series both within and across shots, it may be necessary to live up to Riefenstahl's standards of perfection.

80. For a detailed analysis of the synesthetic biogram, see Massumi 2002.

81. This is precisely Bergson's critique of cinema, one that Deleuze turns on its head (through Bergson) in his cinema books. Deleuze shows that Bergson's theory of duration can be used to make felt the virtual movement at work in the cinematic interval. See Deleuze 1986 and 1989.

82. For a more detailed analysis of commanding form, see Langer 1953.

83. For a more detailed exploration of contemporary affective politics and the politics of preemption, see Brian Massumi, "Potential Politics and the Primacy of Preemption," *Theory & Event* 10, no. 2 (2007).

84. For an excellent discussion on concreteness and abstraction, see the introduction to Massumi 2002 entitled "Concrete Is as Concrete Doesn't."

85. Following most writing on Aboriginal art, I refer to the artists by their skin names rather than by their given names. These skin names are general appellations that refer to the complex kinship system in Aboriginal social organization. This system "determines how people relate to each other and their roles, responsibilities and obligations in relation to one another, ceremonial business and land." The "skin system [is] a method of subdividing the society into named categories which are related to one another through the kinship system" (http://www.clc.org.au/ourculture/kinship.asp).

86. Clifford Possum Tjapaltjarri, quoted in Johnson 2003, 16. Loosely translated, "To dream is never an individual affair."

87. Jukurrpa was earlier referred to as "Dream Time." It refers both to Dream (story) and to Law.

88. Many of these observations are also valid for other Aboriginal peoples. Rather than make wide claims about Aboriginals as a whole, however, my focus here is on the Aboriginals of the Central Desert and the ways in which their art practice continues to sustain the Dreaming.

89. Kirda "own" given countries and have primary economic and spiritual rights as regards these space-times. Kurdungurlu are guardians for the countries owned by the Kirda. Kurdungurlu ensure that Kirda fulfill social and ritual obligations associated with the Dreamings in their care. They also ensure that the Kirda maintain the responsibility of associated sites and access to economic resources of their country. In ceremony, Kirda and Kurdungurlu interact closely. Their roles are complimentary: when Kirda have their bodies painted for ritual purposes, Kurdungurlu grind the ochres, do the actual painting and give advice on appropriate symbols. The roles are reversed for other sites and Dreamings (Anderson and Dussart 1988, 95).

90. All of Glowczewski's work is originally in French. My translations throughout.

91. It can also happen that the birth of a child happens in a "no man's land," a zone that is not part of that clan's Dreaming itineraries. In this case, the person will create his own clan in relation to the dream of conception associated with his passage from the virtual to the actual (Glowczewski 1989, 206).

92. For the Yolngu, a single word, *marayin*, designates at once painting, songs, dances, sacred objects, and power words (Glowczewski 2004, 311).

93. To consider the Dreaming as a finished narrative is to overlook the fact that for each Dreaming site there is the potential of emergence of other associated Dreamings. Dreamings by definition are mobile, leaving traces that remain to be deciphered and performed. To perform is not an accessory of the Dreaming. It is the way the Dreaming affirms itself and is

actualized. Dreamings are sites of negotiation rather than entities. As with the sand drawings, the creation of stories demands a continual erasure. To create is to start again. A member of the Warlpiri at Lajamanu states: "Our Law is not written. It is firm, like a rock, a becoming trace, like the sea that rises, that ebbs and flows" (qtd. in Glowczewski 2004, 302).

94. For an engaging exploration of affect and sensation in Aboriginal painting, see Biddle 2007. On the relation between perception and experience in contemporary central desert Aboriginal art, she writes: "*Breast, Bodies, Canvas* argues that to encounter Central Desert art is to encounter Aboriginal Culture as lived reality. This is an encounter which, given the size, force and effects of contemporary Desert artworks, cannot be ignored. These paintings are understood to be crucial performances of otherwise endangered cultural sentiments. They evoke in the viewer sensations and sensibilities that must be *felt* as well as *thought*" (Biddle 2007, 11). These are capitalized in the quote and tend to be capitalized in Aboriginal writings.

95. These paintings are entitled *Warlugulong* (1976, with Tim Leura), *Warlugulong* (1977), *Kerrinyarra* (1977), *Mount Denison Country* (1978), and *Yuutjutiyungu* (1979).

96. Michael Jagamara Nelson states: "Without the story, the painting is nothing" (qtd. in Johnson 1997, 133). This notion of story has been quite difficult for ethnographers, curators, and consumers of Aboriginal dot painting to understand. Johnson writes: "The 'correct' ascription for a particular design element in a painting is in fact not always so readily determined—not even by the artist himself" (1997, 134). The imposition of truth misses the point of the Dreaming. The stories themselves must be told correctly, but how they are performed varies greatly. A story told by the wrong person is unauthorized, a concept far more important than the "inauthentic." Copying or standard forms of authorship are not the issue. What is at stake is working out the correct relation between the Kirda and the Kurdungurlu as well as being able to recount the stories by singing their trajectories: most paintings are sung even while they are being created. To criticize a painting on aesthetic grounds is to criticize the artist's Dreaming—the artist's very becoming.

97. Dreamings can fall into misuse due to the death of a Kirda, or they can re-manifest themselves in a dream. Dreams, shared in performative rituals with the members of a community, can re-become Dreamings this way, creating geographies that re-stratify in time, bringing to life new lines of flight.

98. Topology refers to mostly non-Euclidean geometry where figures are subjected to deformations so drastic that all their metric and projective properties are lost, creating an elliptical geometry that challenges the very notion of stable form (Courant and Robbins 1996, 235).

99. The idea of the one and the many comes from Whitehead 1929/1978, 26.

100. Jennifer Biddle also makes this point in her interesting article "Country, Skin, Canvas: The Intercorporeal Art of Kathleen Petyarre." She writes: "The potency of Petyarre's

work arises, arguably, from the very materiality of marks made in the Central and Western Desert context. It is not *what* these marks represent but *how* they are made that is determinative. To stay within the Peircean framework, these marks are not so much 'icons' (signs that look like what they represent) as they are 'indexes' (signs that remain existentially tied to what they 'represent'). Central and Western Desert marks are 'indexes' in so far as they embody original ancestral potency. This potency does not simply arise. It must be enacted by precise repetitious and regulatory operations—what might otherwise be called Law" (Biddle 2003, 64).

101. The Möbius strip is topological.

102. Brian Massumi writes: "The folding of the Euclidean and non-Euclidean into and out of each other is itself understandable only in topological terms. This hinge dimension between quantitative and qualitative space is itself a topological figure—to the second degree, since topology already figures in it. It is a topological hyperfigure. The non-Euclidean, qualitative, and dynamic is more encompassing than the Euclidean, quantitative, and static, by virtue of this double featuring" (2002, 184).

103. I am not saying the Dreamings themselves walk away. To understand the landscape of the Dreamings as topological, it must first be clear that we are not talking about points on a grid. Uluru remains Uluru. What changes is the intensive movement of the relationscape. By intensive movement I mean the relational network between Uluru-as-event and its condensation in space-time. To say that Uluru is stable is to suggest that space is there to be encountered (and left behind). The point of Aboriginal land claims is that space-time is alive.

104. As mentioned before, she refers not to particular sites or Dreamings as such. Her expression is that what she paints is a "whole lot."

105. With regards to the role batik plays in the art of painters from Utopia, see Biddle 2003. She writes that batik taught these women to "conceptualize in advance the space left over from any mark; that is, to conceptualize the trace itself first, for what is marked first with wax comes out, after the fabric is dyed, as unmarked" (2003, 67). Biddle develops an analysis of the workings of the trace based on this idea of marking, suggesting that marks are "made *in* not *on* a surface" and therefore neither secondary nor ancillary. The trace, Biddle argues, "is what reactivates ancestral presencing" (2003, 67).

106. Kngwarreye's paintings are often recognizable by the patterns she creates on the folded-over edges of the canvas.

107. The intensity of painting, of dancing the line, seems to take a toll on her health and energy. There are many instances when Kngwarreye was on the verge of stopping to paint. In line with the beliefs of her peoples, she believed it was time for the younger generation to take over. She felt that her position as a prominent money-maker *and* as an elder was at odds with some aspects of her tradition.

108. This differs from the standard practice, where dark colors are gessoed onto the canvas.

109. Gilles Deleuze argues that the figure and the figurative are not the same. For a more detailed explanation, see his work on Bacon (Deleuze 2003).

110. Videos of Kngwarreye painting give a sense of her practice of dancing-while-painting.

111. Deleuze writes: "So the act of painting is always shifting, it is constantly oscillating between a beforehand and an afterward: the hysteria of painting" (2003, 80).

112. See Barbara Glowczewski 1991a. See also, among others, Johnson 1996; Muecke, Benterrak, and Roe 1984; and Morphy 1998.

113. In "Grounded Abstraction: The work of Dorothy Napangardi," Christine Nicholls tells Dorothy Napangardi's story: until Napangardi was about seven or eight years old, the extended family traveled around the Mina Mina area, living on the bush tucker, and drinking from its soakages and claypans. The gold rushes of 1910 and 1932 had brought prospectors on to Warlpiri lands, and the beginnings of pastoral settlement in 1917 to the west brought more non-indigenous interlopers. Colonial expansion meant that the best waterholes and soakages were often expropriated to support the growth of the cattle industry. In 1957 Napangardi's family was moved to Yuendumu under pressure under the Assimilation Policy. Later, the entire family absconded back to Mina Mina. Currently, Napangardi lives in Alice Springs. See Nicholls 2002.

114. Some of the *Sandhills* paintings are as small as 30cm x 30 cm.

115. The extensive continuum is one of the key concepts in Whitehead's process philosophy. It underlies the whole world, past, present, and future. In and of itself, it has no properties. It is what gives consistency to a world in the making. "The properties of this continuum are very few and do not include the relationships of metrical geometry. An extensive continuum is a complex of entities united by the various allied relationships of whole to part, and of overlapping so as to possess common parts, and of contact, and of other relationships derived from these primary relationships" (Whitehead 1938, 62).

116. In *A Thousand Plateaus*, Deleuze and Guattari underline the fact that events are always associated to singular places and times, hence the dating of each of the plateaus.

117. This Dreaming is also called Kana-Karlangu and alternately refers to the "Digging-Stick Possessing-Dreaming" and the "Women-Belonging-Dreaming." The story is told by Punayi (Jeannie) Herbert Nungarrayi—as it was related to her, by her elders from the Kunajarrayi side, who own part of the Dreaming—in the introduction to *Dancing Up Country: The Art of Dorothy Napangardi*.

118. Nicholls tells this story in *Dancing Up Country*. See Nicholls 2002.

119. In Nietzsche's philosophy, *ressentiment* is used to describe the nostalgia for the past embodied by those Nietzsche calls "the last men." *Ressentiment* is a living in the past that denies the present its force of creative renewal.

120. While a few of Napangardi's paintings are black on white background, most of them are white on black. Nonetheless, it is often difficult to discern the black as background and to be certain that she didn't paint them the other way around. There is always a sense, in her work, of the background moving forward.

121. Whitehead defines *contrast*: "Every realized contrast has a location, which is particular with the particularity of actual entities. It is a particular complex matter of fact, realized, and, because of its reality, a standing condition in every subsequent actual world from which creative advance must originate" (1929/1978, 230).

122. http://www.youtube.com/watch?v=JnylM1hI2jc.

123. Lygia Clark is a Brazilian artist (1920–1988) associated with the Brazilian constructivist movements of the mid-twentieth century. She is thought to be one of the first proponents of performative installation work, through which she developed many techniques and processes for interaction and participation. In her mid- to late career, Clark moves away from the museum to an exploration of the relation between art and society, developing a "therapeutic" approach to installation and performance work. It is in this period that she most clearly develops her work with relational objects. At this stage, she investigates primarily how objects can motivate new qualities of relationality, creating events in the making. She refers to this "therapeutic" work as "ritual without myth" and underscores the fact that her work has no representative meaning: its purpose is simply to motivate new forms of relation. Art for Clark becomes a living experience where artist and participant can no longer be separated.

Relational objects function at the threshold between art and world, not simply bringing art to world, but creating relational intervals through which worlds are invented anew. About Clark, Rolnik writes: "To know the world is to pay attention to its corporeal reverberation, to impregnate oneself with its silent forces, to mix with them, and from this fusion, to reinvent the world and oneself, to become other. Plane of knowledge or body and landscape take form et reform through an infinite conversation" (2005, 13; my translation). For a more detailed account of Clark as an artist and researcher, see Rolnik 2005.

124. As of mid-2008, *In My Language* has been viewed 632,130 times, has received 2.632 ratings (with a value of four and a half stars), has been made a favourite 2,664 times, and has received 1,549 comments. Comments include: "Thank you for your thoughtful and enlightening video. Your multilingual abilities combined with the reach of the internet offer a unique opportunity. May we all may continue to share in the benefits" (http://www.youtube.com/watch?v=JnylM1hI2jc).

125. The superject is in continuum with Simondon's notion of individuation. Amanda Baggs would be the superject of *In My Language*. This means that in concrescing, the video proposes an individuation of Amanda Baggs. This instance of Baggs as superject does not promise a reiteration of the same Amanda Baggs in another instance. Her subjectile-position is particular to that specific concrescence. Identity-formation is always specific to a given actual occasion in Whitehead, thus mobile across events.

126. See Blanchot 1992.

Bibliography

Anderson, Christopher, and Françoise Dussart. "Dreamings in Acrylic: Contemporary Western Desert Art." In *Dreamings: The Art of Aboriginal Australia,* ed. Peter Sutton, 89–142. New York: Braziller Publishers, 1988.

Arakawa, and Gins, Madeline. *Architectural Body*. Tuscaloosa: Alabama University Press, 2002.

Artaud, Antonin. "To Have Done with the Judgment of God." In *Antonin Artaud Selected Writings*, edited by Susan Sontag, 555–574. Berkeley: University of California Press, 1976.

Attwood, Bain, and Markus, Andrew. *The Struggle for Aboriginal Rights: A Documentary History*. Sydney: Allen and Unwin, 1999.

Bardon, Geoffrey, and Bardon, James. *Papunya: A Place Made after the Story—The Beginnings of the Western Desert Painting Movement.* Melbourne: The Miegunyah Press, 2004.

Bastiancich, Aflio. *Norman McLaren: Précurseur des nouvelles images*. Montreal: Dreamland, 1997.

Beardsworth, Richard. *Derrida and the Political.* New York: Routledge, 1996.

Bell, Diane. *Ngarrindjeri Wurruwarrin: A World that Is, Was, and Will Be.* Melbourne: Spinifex Press, 1998.

Bennington, Geoffrey. *Interrupting Derrida*. New York: Routledge, 2000.

Bergson, Henri. "The Idea of Duration." In *Bergson—Key Writings*, edited by Keith Ansell Pearson, 49–80. London: Continuum, 2002.

Bergson, Henri. *The Creative Mind—An Introduction to Metaphysics*. Translated by Mabelle Anderson. New York: Citadel Press, 1992.

Bergson, Henri. *Matter and Memory*. Translated by N. M. Paul and W. S. Palmer. New York: Zone, 1990.

Bergson, Henri. "Essai sur les données immédiates de la conscience," in *Oeuvres*, ed. A. Robinet. Paris: PUF, 1959/1970.

Bergson, Henri. *La pensée et le mouvant*. Paris: PUF, 1938.

Bergson, Henri. *Time and Free Will: An Essay on the Immediate Data of Consciousness*. Translated by F. L. Pogson. London: George Allen and Unwin, 1910.

Berndt, Ronald M., and Catherine H. Berndt. *The World of the First Australians—Aboriginal Traditional Life: Past and Present*. Canberra: Aboriginal Studies Press, 1999.

Biddle, Jennifer Loureide. *Breasts, Bodies, Canvas: Central Desert Art as Experience*. Oakland: Oakland Museum of California, 2007.

Biddle, Jennifer Loureide. "Country, Skin, Canvas: The Intercorporeal Art of Kathleen Petyarre." *Australian and New Zealand Journal of Art—Indigenous Art of Australia and the South Pacific* 4, no. 1 (2003): 61–76.

Blanchot, Maurice. *The Infinite Conversation*. Translated by Susan Hanson. Minneapolis: University of Minnesota Press, 1992.

Boccioni, Umberto. "Plastic Dynamism 1913." In *Futurist Manifestos*, edited by Umbro Apollonio, 92–95. Boston: Museum of Fine Arts, 1970a.

Boccioni, Umberto. "Technical Manifesto of Futurist Sculpture 1912." In *Futurist Manifestos*, edited by Umbro Apollonio, 51–65. Boston: Museum of Fine Arts, 1970b.

Boccioni, Umberto. "Futurist Sculpture." In *Modern Artists on Art*, edited by Robert L. Herbert, 50–57. Englewood Cliffs, NJ: Prentice Hall, 1964.

Braun, Marta. *Picturing Time: The Work of Étienne-Jules Marey (1830–1904)*. Chicago: University of Chicago Press, 1992.

Brody, Anne Marie. *Contemporary Aboriginal Art: The Robert Holmes à Court Collection*. Perth: Heytesbury Holdings, 1990.

Chaloupka, George. *Journey in Time: The 50,000 Year Story of the Australian Aboriginal Rock Art of Arnhem Land*. Sydney: Reed New Holland, 1999.

Chatwin, Bruce. *The Songlines*. London: Pan Books, 1988.

Clark, Lygia. *Lygia Clark: de l'oeuvre à l'événement—Nous sommes le moule. A vous de donner le souffle.* Nantes: Musée des Beaux Arts, 2005.

Cunningham, Merce. "Choreography and the Dance." In *The Creative Experience,* edited by Stanley Rossner and Lawrence E. Abt. Reprinted in *Celant Germano,* ed. Merce Cunningham, 42–49. Milan, Italy: Edizioni Charta, 1999.

Dagognet, François. *Étienne-Jules Marey—A Passion for the Trace.* New York: Zone, 1992.

Dalcroze, Émile-Jacques. *Rhythm, Music, and Education.* Translated by Harold F. Rubinstein. New York: G. P. Putnam and Sons, 1921.

deLahunta, Scott. "Co-descriptions and Collaborative Composition." Opening presentation at Choreographic Computations (a NIME06/IRCAM workshop), Paris, France, June 4, 2006a.

deLahunta, Scott. "Dance (in the Presence and Absence of) Technology" in *En movement (inaugural issue),* ed. B. Raubert and Q. Noguero, 16–17. Barcelona: Theatre Institute Mercat de les Flors, 2006b.

deLahunta, Scott. "Open Source Choreography?" In *Code: The Language of Our Time. Katalog zur Ars Electronica 2003,* 304–310. Ostfildern-Ruit, Germany: Hatje Cantz, 2003.

deLahunta, Scott. "Software for Dancers: Coding Forms." *Performance Research* 7, no. 2 (2002): 96–102.

Deleuze, Gilles. *Francis Bacon: The Logic of Sensation.* Translated by Daniel W. Smith. Minneapolis: University of Minnesota Press, 2003.

Deleuze, Gilles. "Spinoza and the Three 'Ethics.'" In *The New Spinoza,* edited by Warren Montag and Ted Stolze, 21–34. Minneapolis: University of Minnesota Press, 1997.

Deleuze, Gilles. *Difference and Repetition.* Translated by Paul Patton. New York: Columbia University Press, 1994.

Deleuze, Gilles. *The Fold: Leibniz and the Baroque.* Translated by Tom Conley. Minneapolis: University of Minnesota Press, 1993.

Deleuze, Gilles. *Bergsonism.* Translated by Hugh Tomlinson and Barbara Habberjam. New York: Zone Books, 1991a.

Deleuze, Gilles. *The Time-Image.* Translated by Hugh Tomlinson and Robert Galeta. Minneapolis: University of Minnesota Press, 1991b.

Deleuze, Gilles. *Expressionism in Philosophy: Spinoza.* Translated by Martin Joughin. New York: Zone Books, 1990a.

Deleuze, Gilles. *The Logic of Sense.* Translated by Constantin V. Boundas. New York: Columbia University Press, 1990b.

Deleuze, Gilles. *Cinema 2—The Time-Image*. Translated by Hugh Tomlinson and Robert Galeta. Minneapolis: University of Minnesota Press, 1989.

Deleuze, Gilles. *Le Pli: Leibniz et le baroque*. Paris: Éditions de minuit, 1988a.

Deleuze, Gilles. *Spinoza: Practical Philosophy*. Translated by Robert Hurley. San Francisco: City Lights Publishers, 1988b.

Deleuze, Gilles. *Cinema 1—The Movement-Image*. Translated by Hugh Tomlinson and Robert Galeta. Minneapolis: University of Minnesota Press, 1986.

Deleuze, Gilles. *Nietzsche and Philosophy*. Translated by Hugh Thomlinson. New York: Columbia University Press, 1983.

Deleuze, Gilles, and Felix Guattari. *What Is Philosophy*. Translated by Graham Burchell and Hugh Tomlinson. London: Verso, 1994.

Deleuze, Gilles, and Felix Guattari. *A Thousand Plateaus*. Translated by Brian Massumi. Minneapolis: University of Minnesota Press, 1987.

Deleuze, Gilles, and Claire Parnet. *Dialogues*. Translated by Hugh Tomlinson and Barbara Habberjam. London: Athlone, 1987.

Derrida, Jacques. *Dissemination*. Translated by Barbara Johnson. Chicago: University of Chicago Press, 1981.

Derrida, Jacques. *Of Grammatology*. Translated by Gayatri Spivak. New York: Columbia University Press, 1978.

Didi-Huberman, Georges. "Le Mouvement de toute chose." In *Mouvements de l'air: Étienne-Jules Marey, photographe des fluides*, edited by Georges Didi-Huberman and Laurent Mannoni, 173–337. Paris: Gallimard, 2004.

Dreaming Their Way: Australian Aboriginal Women Painters. Exhibition catalog. New York: National Museum of Women in the Arts, 2006.

Emily Kame Kngwarreye—Alhalkere: Paintings from Utopia. Exhibition catalog. Melbourne: Queensland Art Gallery, 1998.

Feldenkrais, Moshe. *The Elusive Obvious*. Cupertino, CA: Meta Publications, 1981.

Flood, Josephine. *The Original Australians: Story of the Aboriginal People*. Crows Nest, Australia: Allen and Unwin, 2006.

Forsythe, William. *Improvisation Technologies: A Tool for the Analytical Dance*. Karlsruhe, Germany: ZKM, 2003.

Forsythe, William. *Programme-Chatelet*. Exhibition catalog. Paris: Chatelet Musical Theater of Paris, 1995.

Gil, José. “Le mouvement total.” Unpublished manuscript, 2006.

Gil, José. “The Dancer’s Body.” In *Shock to Thought*, edited by Brian Massumi. New York: Routledge, 2002.

Glowczewski, Barbara. *Rêves en colère avec les Aborigènes australiens*. Paris: Plon, 2004.

Glowczewski, Barbara. *Du rêve à la loi chez les Aborigènes: Mythes, rites et organisation sociale en Australie*. Paris: PUF, 1991a.

Glowczewski, Barbara, ed. *Yapa: Peintres Aborigènes de Balgo et Lajamanu*. Paris: Beaudoin Lebon, 1991b.

Glowczewski, Barbara. *Les rêveurs du désert: Aborigènes d’Australie*. Paris: Plon, 1989.

Grattan, Michelle, ed. *Reconciliation: Essays on Australian Reconciliation*. Melbourne: Black Inc., 2000.

Guattari, Felix. *Chaosmosis: An Ethico-Political Paradigm*. Translated by Paul Bains and Julian Pefanis. Indianapolis: Indiana University Press, 1995.

Hayles, Katherine. *How We Became Posthuman*. Chicago: University of Chicago Press, 2000.

Hébert, Pierre. *Corps, Langage, Technologie*. Montreal: Les 400 coups, 2006.

Hébert, Pierre. *L’ange et l’automate*. Montreal: Les 400 coups, 1999.

Heilmann, Nora. “Rupture in Space: Translocal Dance Performance Creation.” 2006. http://ruptures.wordpress.com/.

Hinton, David B. *The Films of Leni Riefenstahl*. Kent: Scarecrow Press, 2000.

Irwin, Robert. “Notes pour un modèle, 1977.” In *Double Diamond 1997–1998*, 26–35. Lyon: Musée d’Art Contemporain, 1998.

James, William. *Some Problems of Philosophy: A Beginning of an Introduction to Philosophy*. Lincoln: University of Nebraska Press, 1996.

Johnson, Vivien. *Clifford Possum Tjapaltjarri*. Adelaide: Art Gallery of South Australia, 2003.

Johnson, Vivien. *Michael Jagamara Nelson*. Sydney: Craftsman House, 1997.

Johnson, Vivien, ed. *Dreamings of the Desert*. Adelaide: Art Gallery of South Australia, 1996.

Kierkegaard, Soren. *Repetition*. Edited and translated by Howard V. Hong and Edna H. Hong. Princeton, NJ: Princeton University Press, 1983.

Kleinert, Sylvia, and Margo Neale, eds. *The Oxford Companion to Aboriginal Art and Culture*. Oxford: Oxford University Press, 2000.

Langer, Susanne. *Feeling and Form*. New York: Charles Scribner's Sons, 1953.

Lynn, Greg. *Animate Form*. Princeton, NJ: Princeton Architectural Press, 1999.

MacKenzie, Andrew. *Famous Australian Art: Albert Namatjira 1902–1959*. Brisbane: Oz Publishing Co., 1988.

Manning, Erin. *Politics of Touch: Sense, Movement, Sovereignty*. Minneapolis: University of Minnesota Press, 2007.

Manning, Erin. *Ephemeral Territories: Representing Nation, Home, and Identity in Canada*. Minneapolis: University of Minnesota Press, 2003.

Mannoni, Laurent. "Marey Aéronaute: De la méthode graphique à la soufflerie aérodynamique." In *Mouvements de l'air: Étienne-Jules Marey, photographe des fluids*, edited by Georges Didi-Huberman and Laurent Mannoni, 6–86. Paris: Gallimard, 2004.

Marey, Étienne-Jules. *Le Mouvement*. Nîmes: Editions Jacqueline Chambon, 1894/2002.

Massumi, Brian. "The Ideal Streak." Keynote presentation, Thinking the Surface: A Conference on Screens, Mobilities, Environments in the Global Age, Cornell University, October 27–28, 2006.

Massumi, Brian. *Parables for the Virtual: Affect, Movement, Sensation*. Durham, NC: Duke University Press, 2002.

Massumi, Brian, and Toni Dove. "The Interface and I: A Conversation Between Brian Massumi and Toni Dove." *Artbyte: The Magazine of Digital Art)* 1, no. 6 (1999): 30–37.

Matisse, Georges. *Les sciences physiologiques*. Paris: Payot, 1924.

McCulloch, Susan. *Contemporary Aboriginal Art: A Guide to the Rebirth of an Ancient Culture*. Honolulu: Hawaii University Press, 1991.

McLaren, Norman. *Norman McLaren—The Masters Edition*. DVD. Ottawa: National Film Board, 2006.

McWilliams, Donald. *Creative Process: Norman McLaren*. Ottawa: National Film Board, 1990.

Mei, Rosa. "Forsythe's 'Ricercar' = One Confused Room." *Flash Review: Etch a Sketch in Streamlined Indigo* 2 (2003). http://www.danceinsider.com/f2003/f1119_2.html.

Michaels, Eric. *Bad Aboriginal Art: Tradition, Media, and Technological Horizons*. Minneapolis: University of Minnesota Press, 1994.

Montag, Warren, and Ted Stolze. *The New Spinoza*. Minneapolis: University of Minnesota Press, 1997.

Morphy, Howard. *Aboriginal Art*. London: Phaidon, 1998.

Morphy, Howard, and Margo Smith Boles. *Art from the Land: Dialogues with the Kluge-Ruhe Collection of Australian Aboriginal Art*. Charlottesville: University of Virginia Press, 1999.

Muecke, Stephen. *Ancient and Modern: Time, Culture and Indigenous Philosophy*. Sydney: New South Wales Press, 2004.

Muecke, Stephen. *Textual Spaces: Aboriginality and Cultural Studies*. Sydney: New South Wales University Press, 1992.

Muecke, Stephen, Kim Benterrak, and Paddy Roe. *Reading the Country*. Fremantle, Australia: Fremantle Arts Centre Press, 1984.

Muecke, Stephen, and Adam Shoemaker. *Aboriginal Australians: First Nations of an Ancient Continent*. London: Thames and Hudson, 2004.

Mundine, Djon. "A Dance through the Desert." In *Dancing Up Country: The Art of Dorothy Napangardi*, 68–71. Sydney: Museum of Contemporary Art, 2002.

Myers, Fred R. *Painting Culture: The Making of an Aboriginal High Art*. Durham, NC: Duke University.

Mythology and Reality: Contemporary Aboriginal Desert Art from the Gabrielle Pizzi Collection. Exhibition catalog. Bulleen: Heide Museum of Modern Art, 2004.

Napangardi, Dorothy. "Statement by Dorothy Napangardi." In *Dancing Up Country: The Art of Dorothy Napangardi*, 10–11. Sydney: Museum of Contemporary Art, 2002.

Neale, Margo, ed. *Emily Kame Kngwarreye—Alhalkere: Paintings from Utopia*. Brisbane: Queensland Art Gallery, 1998.

Nicholls, Christine. "Grounded Abstraction: the Work of Dorothy Napangardi." In *Dancing Up Country: The Art of Dorothy Napangardi*, 60–67. Sydney: Museum of Contemporary Art, 2002.

Nietzsche, Friedrich. *The Will to Power*. Translated by Walter Kaufmann. New York: Vintage, 1968.

Nietzsche, Friedrich. *On the Genealogy of Morals, Ecce Homo*. Edited and translated by Walter Kaufmann. New York: Vintage, 1967.

Nietzsche, Friedrich. *Beyond Good and Evil: Prelude to a Philosophy of the Future*. Edited and translated by Walter Kaufmann. New York: Vintage, 1966.

Nietzsche, Friedrich. *Thus Spoke Zarathustra*. Edited by Walter Kaufmann. Translated by R. J. Hollingsdale. New York: Penguin, 1961.

Nungarrayi, Punayi (Jeannie) Herbert. "Introduction." In *Dancing Up Country: The Art of Dorothy Napangardi*, 6–9. Sydney: Museum of Contemporary Art, 2002.

One Sun One Moon: Aboriginal Art in Australia. Exhibition catalog. Sydney: Art Gallery of New South Wales, 2007.

Pike, Jimmy, and Pat Lowe. *Jilji: Life in the Great Sandy Desert*. Broome, Australia: Magabala Books, 1990.

Portanova, Stamatia. "The Intensity of Dance: Body, Movement, and Sensation across the Screen." *Extensions: The Online Journal of Embodied Technology* 2 (2005). http://www.wac.ucla.edu/extensionsjournal/v2/portanova.htm.

Richard, Valliere T. *Norman McLaren—Manipulator of Movement*. Toronto: Associated University Presses, 1982.

Riefenstahl, Leni. *Die Nuba Von Kau*. Berlin: Ullstein, 1991.

Riefenstahl, Leni. *Memoiren*. Munich: Taschen, 1987.

Riefenstahl, Leni. *Die Nuba: Menschen wie von einem anderen Stern*. Munich: Deutscher Taschenbuch Verlag, 1973.

Robert Irwin. Exhibition catalog. Los Angeles: Museum of Contemporary Art, 1993.

Rolnik, Suely. "Enfin qu'y a-t'il derrière la chose corporelle." In *Lygia Clark: de l'oeuvre a l'événement—Nous sommes le moule. A vous de donner le souffle*, 9. Nantes: Musée des Beaux Arts, 2005.

Sacks, Oliver. *Musicophilia: Tales of Music and the Brain*. New York: Knopf, 2007.

Sacks, Oliver. *Awakenings*. New York: Harper Perennial, 1990.

Schaub, B. H. *Riefenstahl's Olympia*. Frankfurt: Fink Verlag, 2003.

Schechter, Bruce. "Still Standing." *New Scientist* 2286 (April 14, 2001). http://www.newscientist.com/article/mg17022865.100-still-standing.html.

Simondon, Gilbert. *L'individu et sa genèse physico-biologique*. Grenoble: Jérome Millon, 1995.

Simondon, Gilbert. *Du Monde d'existence des objets techniques*. Paris: Aubier Montagne, 1969.

Tarkovsky, Andrei. *Sculpting in Time: The Great Russian Filmmaker Discusses His Art*. New York: Knopf, 1987.

Thines, George, Alan Costall, and George Butterworth, eds. *Michotte's Experimental Phenomenology of Perception*. Hillsdale, NJ: Lawrence Erlbaum, 1991.

Trimborn, Jürgen. *Riefenstahl: Eine deutsche Karriere*. Berlin: Aufbau Verlag, 2002.

Valéry, Paul. *Degas, Danse, Dessin*. Paris: Gallimard, 1938.

Walsh, Michael, and Colin Yallop, eds. *Language and Culture in Aboriginal Australia*. Canberra: Aboriginal Studies Press, 1993.

Warlukurlangu Artists. *Yuendumu Doors*. Canberra: Australian Institute of Aboriginal Studies, 1987.

Weschler, Lawrence. *Seeing is Forgetting: The Name of the Thing One Sees: A Life of Contemporary Artist Robert Irwin*. Berkeley: University of California Press, 1982.

Whitehead, Albert North. *Modes of Thought*. New York: Free Press, 1938.

Whitehead, Albert North. *Adventures of Ideas*. New York: Free Press, 1933.

Whitehead, Albert North. *Process and Reality*, edited by David Ray Griffin and Donald W. Sherburne. New York: New Press, 1929/1978.

Whitehead, Albert North. *Symbolism*. New York: Fordham University Press, 1927.

Wildmann, Daniel. *Begehrte Körper: Konstruktion und Inszenierung des 'arischen' Männerkörpers im 'Dritten Reich'*. Zurich: Königshausen & Newmann, 1998.

Yuendumu Doors. Exhibition catalog. Canberra: Australian Institute of Aboriginal Studies, 1987.

Index